THE TASK
OF DOGMATICS

PROCEEDINGS OF THE LOS ANGELES THEOLOGY CONFERENCE

This is the fifth volume in a series published by Zondervan Academic. It is the proceedings of the Los Angeles Theology Conference held under the auspices of Biola University, in January 2017. The conference is an attempt to do several things. First, it provides a regional forum in which scholars, students, and clergy can come together to discuss and reflect upon central doctrinal claims of the Christian faith. It is also an ecumenical endeavor. Bringing together theologians from a number of different schools and confessions, the LATC seeks to foster serious engagement with Scripture and tradition in a spirit of collegial dialogue (and disagreement), looking to retrieve the best of the Christian past in order to forge theology for the future. Finally, each volume in the series focuses on a central topic in dogmatic theology. It is hoped that this endeavor will continue to fructify contemporary systematic theology and foster a greater understanding of the historic Christian faith amongst the members of its different communions.

LOS ANGELES
THEOLOGY
CONFERENCE

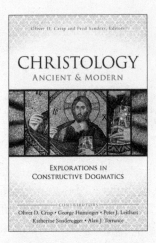

CHRISTOLOGY, ANCIENT
AND MODERN:
*Explorations in Constructive
Dogmatics, 2013*

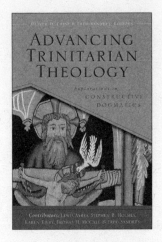

ADVANCING
TRINITARIAN THEOLOGY:
*Explorations in Constructive
Dogmatics, 2014*

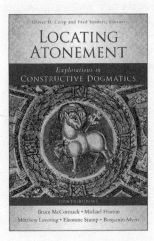

LOCATING ATONEMENT:
*Explorations in Constructive
Dogmatics, 2015*

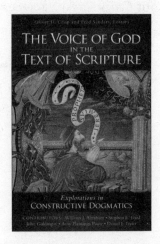

THE VOICE OF GOD IN THE
TEXT OF SCRIPTURES:
*Explorations in Constructive
Dogmatics, 2016*

THE TASK OF DOGMATICS:

Explorations in THEOLOGICAL METHOD

Oliver D. Crisp and Fred Sanders, Editors

ZONDERVAN

The Task of Dogmatics
Copyright © 2017 by Oliver D. Crisp and Fred Sanders

This title is also available as a Zondervan ebook.

Requests for information should be addressed to:
Zondervan, *3900 Sparks Dr. SE, Grand Rapids, Michigan 49546*

Library of Congress Cataloging-in-Publication Data

Names: Los Angeles Theology Conference (5th : 2017 : Biola University), author. | Crisp, Oliver, editor. | Sanders, Fred (Fred R.), editor.
Title: The task of dogmatics : explorations in theological method / Oliver D. Crisp and Fred Sanders, editors.
Description: Grand Rapids, MI : Zondervan, [2017] | Includes bibliographical references and index.
Identifiers: LCCN 2017023305 | ISBN 9780310535492 (softcover)
Subjects: LCSH: Dogma—Congresses. | Theology, Doctrinal—Congresses.
Classification: LCC BT19 .L67 2017 | DDC 230.01—dc23 LC record available at https://lccn.loc.gov/2017023305

Cover design: Matt Van Kirk
Cover photo: Kunsthistorisches Museum, Vienna, Austria/Bridgeman Images
Interior imagery: Wxs/Wikimedia Commons, CC BY-SA 3.0

Printed in the United States of America

17 18 19 20 21 22 23 24 25 26 27 /DHV/ 15 14 13 12 11 10 9 8 7 6 5 4 3 2 1

In memoriam:

The Reverend Professor John Bainbridge
Webster, DD, FRSE

CONTENTS

ACKNOWLEDGMENTS

THE EDITORS WOULD LIKE TO THANK Dr. Paul Spears as Director of the Torrey Honors Institute, and the faculty and administration of Biola University for their support for the Fifth Los Angeles Theology Conference (LATC) in January of 2017, out of which these published proceedings grew. Without the assistance of Jessamy Delling and Caleb Aguilera who oversaw much of the practical side of the event, this conference would not have run as smoothly as it did. We are grateful to them. Thanks too to Fuller Theological Seminary for its ongoing support of LATC. As with the previous volumes in this series, the editors wish to record grateful thanks to *our* editor (and colleague), Katya Covrett, for her invaluable assistance before, during, and after the conference proceedings. Thanks too to the Zondervan Team (aka "The Z Team")—Stan Gundry as editor-in-chief, Jesse Hillman, Kari Moore, and Josh Kessler.

We had hoped to have Professor John Webster as a plenary speaker at the conference. Sadly, he passed away in May 2016. John was one of the most important voices in the contemporary renewal of dogmatic theology; he will be greatly missed. The conference and this book are dedicated to his memory. "For we know in part and we prophesy in part, but when completeness comes, what is in part disappears. . . . For now we see only a reflection as in a mirror; then we shall see face to face. Now I know in part; then I shall know fully, even as I am fully known" (1 Cor 13:9–10, 12). Does the dogmatic task cease when we come face-to-face with the One to whom we are fully known? Perhaps it is only the beginning. No doubt John knows.

LIST OF CONTRIBUTORS

Michael Allen—is academic dean and John Dyer Trimble Professor of Systematic Theology, Reformed Theological Seminary, Orlando, Florida. He holds BA, MA, and PhD degrees from Wheaton College.

James M. Arcadi—is a postdoctoral fellow in the School of Theology, Fuller Theological Seminary. He graduated with a BA from Biola University, an MDiv and ThM from Gordon-Conwell Theological Seminary, and a PhD from the University of Bristol, UK.

Henri Blocher—is emeritus professor of systematic theology at Faculté Libre de Théologie Évangélique de Vaux-sur-Seine. From 2003–2008 he occupied the Gunter Knoedler Chair of Systematic Theology, Wheaton College Graduate School of Biblical and Theological Studies. He was awarded a DD (h.c.) by Gordon-Conwell Theological Seminary in 1989, and a DD (h.c.) by Westminster Theological Seminary (Philadelphia) in 2014.

Brannon Ellis—is a publisher with Lexham. He holds a BA from Ball State University, an MA from Westminster Theological Seminary in Escondido, California, and a PhD from the University of Aberdeen.

Joshua Malone—is associate professor of theology, Moody Bible Institute, Spokane, Washington. He holds a BS from Texas A&M University, a ThM from Dallas Theological Seminary, and an MTh and PhD from the University of Aberdeen.

Gavin Ortlund—is a resident fellow at the Carl F. H. Henry Center for Theological Understanding at Trinity Evangelical Divinity School in Deerfield, Illinois. He earned a BA from the University of Georgia, an MDiv from Covenant Theological Seminary, and a PhD from Fuller Theological Seminary.

Katherine Sonderegger—holds the William Meade Chair in Systematic Theology, Virginia Theological Seminary. She earned an AB from Smith College, the STM and DMin degrees from Yale University, and a PhD from Brown University.

CONTRIBUTORS

Darren Sumner—teaches at Fuller Theological Seminary. He holds a BA from Seattle Pacific University, an MA from Wheaton College Graduate School, an MDiv from Princeton Theological Seminary, and a PhD from the University of Aberdeen.

Scott R. Swain—is president of Reformed Theological Seminary, Orlando, Florida, where he also holds the James Woodrow Hassell Chair of Systematic Theology. He earned a BA from the University of North Florida, MDiv and ThM degrees from Southeastern Baptist Theological Seminary, and a PhD from Trinity Evangelical Divinity School.

Chris Tilling—is senior lecturer in New Testament Studies at St. Mellitus College, London, and a visiting lecturer in the Department of Theology and Religious Studies, King's College, London. He earned an MTheol at the University of St. Andrews, and a PhD at London School of Theology.

Kevin J. Vanhoozer—is research professor of systematic theology at Trinity Evangelical Divinity School. He holds a BA from Westmont College, an MDiv from Westminster Theological Seminary, and a PhD from Cambridge University.

Sameer Yadav—is assistant professor of theology at Westmont College. He graduated with a BA from Boise State University, an STM from Yale Divinity School, and a ThD from Duke University.

ABBREVIATIONS

ANF   Ante-Nicene Fathers
CD   *Church Dogmatics*, by Karl Barth (ed. Bromiley and Torrance)
CCEL   Christian Classics Ethereal Library
CCT   Challenges in Contemporary Theology
CSEL   Corpus Scriptorum Ecclesiasticorum Latinorum
Inst.   *Institutes of the Christian Religion*, by John Calvin (ed. McNeill,
            trans. Battles)
IJST   *International Journal of Systematic Theology*
Mod. Theo. *Modern Theology*
NPNF   Nicene and Post-Nicene Fathers, series 1 (NPNF[1]) and 2
            (NPNF[2])
OECS   Oxford Early Christian Studies
PPS   Popular Patristics Series
SJT   *Scottish Journal of Theology*
ST   *Summa Theologiae*, by Thomas Aquinas (trans. Fathers of the
            English Dominican Province)
WTJ   *Westminster Theological Journal*

INTRODUCTION

WHERE TO BEGIN? This question is not just a concern for writers of fiction. It is also a problem for the theologian. It is, in fact, a question about theological method. *Where* one begins theologically is often as important in shaping the end product as *how* one proceeds theologically. We might say that where you start and how you get to your goal are two fundamental issues in theological method. It is like preparing to set out on a journey. Before embarking upon the trip, one must consider where it will begin and where it will end, as well as how to go about getting from the beginning to the end—whether on foot, on horseback, by car, or by means of some other mode of transport. In some ways, this is similar to the task of dogmatics, which is itself an intellectual journey where the great themes of the gospel are set out and arranged to highlight certain key ideas, or focus attention on certain topics. In this way, how dogmatics is organized, including the particular ordering and privileging of certain themes and notions, is as much a part of the methodological task as the place where one starts.

In casual usage, the two terms "dogmatics" and "systematic theology" are often treated synonymously, to indicate what working theologians produce. But the two terms carry differing connotations worth attending to. These may be picked out by noting the root terms "system" and "dogma." Systematic theology tends to be the broader term, including all sorts of discussions of theological topics, even those details that have not been the subject of official ecclesial teaching. The idea of system may sometimes include the notion that there is a central, coherent principle that generates the theological statements, but it always includes the idea of an integrated whole in which the interconnection of the parts is explicated. Dogmatics is a subfield, being the section of systematic theology that is relevant to church dogma. It theologizes about the subject matter of official, public declarations of responsible church authorities in Christian history. In doing so, it explicitly locates the dogmatician within the church, reckoning with the confessional significance of dogma. It seems more natural to us to speak of an individual theologian's systematic theology, but it sounds odd to speak of an individual theologian's dogmatics. In the middle of the twentieth century, it made sense that Paul Tillich entitled his magnum opus, with its philosophical preoccupations and its concern for answering secular questioners, his *Systematic Theology*. Likewise, the most apt name for Karl Barth's multivolume theological work in service of Christian proclamation was the *Church Dogmatics*. The terms are not fixed, and variations in usage exist, but the distinction is evident if we imagine Tillich writing a *Dogmatics* or Barth writing a *Systematic Theology*. It wouldn't be right.

Often theologians distinguish between formal and material (or substantive) considerations in dogmatics. On the one hand, a formal consideration has to do with how a thing is conceived and organized. To return to our previous example, the formal qualities of the journey include the places where it begins and ends, and the mode of transport taken. On the other hand, the substance of the journey is the sequence of events that comprise the whole activity from the moment one starts out to the moment one completes the trip. Yet in theological method, formal and material or substantive considerations overlap because the way in which the task is conceived inevitably shapes the way in which we approach and even organize the particular topics considered. Barth's work is a good modern example of this. He found himself unable to complete his projected *Christian Dogmatics* because he worried that he had made a methodological false step. So he began again with his task in the *Church Dogmatics*, which is very much an account of Christian doctrine in a christological key, Christ being the center from whom all other doctrines radiate out. A very different approach to the matter can be found in, say, Friedrich Schleiermacher, whose *Christian Faith* focused on the experience of the divine, the sense of absolute dependence upon God, and the articulation of this experience in Christian doctrine as a second order activity. Schleiermacher's method drove him to relegate the Trinity to an appendix—a significant dogmatic decision if ever there was one!

Another distinction often made in post-Reformation dogmatics is between archetypal and ectypal theology. Theology from a God's-eye view is archetypal, whereas theology that attempts to think God's thoughts after him is ectypal. If we think of theology in this second way, then the dogmatic task is about trying to ascertain God's thoughts after him. But, of course, this raises additional questions about where to find God speaking. Primarily, God speaks in Scripture (at least, according to *Christian* theology). But does he not also speak by means of the natural world? And may he not also speak in other ways—by means of the sense of divinity with which we are all born, for instance? John Calvin certainly thought so, and placed his discussion of the twofold knowledge of all things—of God and of ourselves—at the very beginning of his *Institutes of the Christian Religion*. Few have followed his lead, though it has been influential on much Reformed theology.

Faith seeks understanding. This too is a venerable theme in discussions of theological method that can be traced through Archbishop Anselm of Canterbury to Bishop Augustine of Hippo. For we begin with faith, standing within the faith, not as some disinterested spectator watching from the sidelines. Theologians seek to understand something of the faith that they have been given. They do not cogitate about religious matters independent of their own experience of the divine. What is more, the faith-seeking-understanding tradition of theology has the merit of intellectual humility in the face of the divine mystery as well. We seek to understand all right, but we do not presume that we will ever completely apprehend the divine. Perhaps all our theologizing will seem like "so much straw," as it did, in the end, to the great Thomas Aquinas. Faced with the brilliance of the divine presence, as Isaiah was when he found himself in the courtroom vision recorded in chapter 6 of that book, we may well find ourselves unable to say anything more than "Woe to me! I am ruined! For I am a man of unclean lips, and I live among a people of unclean lips, and my eyes have seen the King, the Lord Almighty" (Isa 6:5).

Does that mean we should not even try to understand something of the mystery of divinity? Not at all. But it should chasten our attempts to do so. The contributors to this volume would, we think, agree with that particular sentiment.

A final thought about theological method: the preoccupation with theological method is a very modern concern. When one reads much classical theology, it is striking how few discussions of method there actually are. In recent times Jeffrey Stout, among others, has worried about the interminable theological "throat-clearing" that is discussion of methodological matters. Will we ever get to the substance of theology? We have already indicated one reason why such hard-and-fast distinctions may be misplaced. But also, in a postmodern world with multiple approaches to knowing and to the theological task, it is not surprising that methodological discussion has taken a much more prominent place in dogmatics. Nevertheless, it might be objected that discussion of theological method, and of prolegomena more generally, is not theology as such. It is more like discussion of how to proceed in theology, or what we might call metatheology—or even, as some recent authors have put it, the philosophy of theology. But metatheology is not theology any more than planning a journey is the same as journeying. Some of the essays collected here reflect this tension. There are methodological essays here that do include both formal and material elements, moving from metatheology to theology proper. Others are more clearly just about method (and therefore more obviously candidates for the term "metatheology"). Even this distinction is not perhaps as hard-and-fast as has sometimes been thought. But whether it is metatheology or dogmatics that is being engaged in, the theological task is the focus of attention.

This brings us to the essays themselves. In chapter 1, Kevin Vanhoozer undertakes the ambitious task of defining what dogmatic statements are. He argues that dogmatic statements occur somewhere between what he calls the analytics and the poetics of dogmatics. If the analytics of dogmatics emphasizes producing a conceptual representation of what reason has learned from following the text exegetically (Vanhoozer cites John Webster's work as one of the best examples), then the poetics of dogmatics adds to this an equal preoccupation with the form and genre in which this representation is communicated (examples of this include von Balthasar and Vanhoozer himself). The approach by analytics risks giving the impression that theology has improved on Scripture's own witness; the approach by poetics risks being untranslatably fixated on given forms. Vanhoozer proposes that the entire project of pronouncing dogmatic judgments is best comprehended by the category of mission. Dogmatic statements, on this model, are "statements on a mission." They draw the church into the communicative acts of the triune God's mission, pressing the church to witness to that work in its indicative judgments about "what is in Christ." Chief among the benefits of conceiving dogmatics as witness is that it draws attention to the corporate and active character of dogmatics, which includes the gestures and forms of community life as well as statements.

In chapter 2, Scott Swain asks about the systematic character of dogmatics. He considers dogmatics a mixed species of wisdom, including a practical and a theoretical aspect, both *phronesis* and *sophia*. This mixed character derives from its status as a response to God's self-revelation as recorded in Scripture. Because the ultimate object of theological understanding is the triune God, the entire project has its ultimate basis in wonder in the face of mystery. In commending the fruits of its contemplation to others, dogmatic formulations take on a systematic character; indeed, when dogmatics elaborates its wisdom as knowledge of God on the one hand and knowledge of all things relative to God on the other hand, it approaches its own systematic potential. When dogmatics does this, it is best equipped not only to tend to its own affairs but also to serve other disciplines. Dogmatics, on Swain's account, is not a view from nowhere. It is instead "a view of God from God in the presence of God."

In chapter 3, Sameer Yadav argues that the nature of Christian doctrine is a form of ontological commitment to an overarching biblical narrative of creation and redemption. The function of a doctrine is to state what must or may be the case if indeed the narrative corresponds to the way things are. Fundamental doctrines that are defining of a Christian identity are those that must be the case on pain of denying the correctness of the narrative, while nonfundamental doctrines are those that merely may be the case if that narrative is correct. After Yadav characterizes this conception and meets some objections, he shows how it situates the Bible as a norming norm in formulating doctrine, as well as how it can accommodate various competing intuitions about the nature of doctrine (e.g., as a cultural-linguistic rule, as an expression of lived religious experience, and as a recapitulation of scriptural assertions). He believes that adopting this analysis could facilitate engagement across boundaries of deep theological disagreement, since disputants could proceed from a shared conception of theology's evidence base and its primary mode of reasoning from that evidence.

Chapter 4 turns to the interface between biblical studies and systematic theology. Chris Tilling's chapter explores the task of dogmatics in light of the apostle Paul's deployment of a framing *theologoumenon* in 1 Corinthians 8–10. Tilling argues that Paul responded to the "knowledgeable" Corinthians, and particularly their understanding of the nature of theology (mediated to us in the propositions in 8:4), by redirecting them to the self-involving, covenantal, and love-for-God orientated nature of monotheistic rhetoric (see 8:2–3). This is then taken in a christological direction in 8:6, 12 and 10:1–22. The christological monotheism that unfolds in this section of Paul's letter bespeaks a relational, lived reality that penetrates interpersonal practices, goals, and desires. This corresponds with Paul's "relational" epistemological tendencies which, taken with his argument in 1 Corinthians 8–10, informs Christian explication of the task of dogmatics. This is brought into conversation with claims about the task of the doctrine of the Trinity in the scholarship of British historical theologian Stephen Holmes, thereby providing a case study of "joined up" biblical and historical systematic theology.

In chapter 5, the French evangelical theologian Henri Blocher addresses himself to the issue of the permanent validity and contextual relativity of doctrinal statements. Blocher is conversant with a wide range of historical and social contexts that call dogma into question, and he provides an insightful survey of the relativizing influences of modern intellectual culture. When these other voices have had their say, however, Blocher maintains that Christian doctrine continues to be valid, not only because of its ultimately transcendent source in divine revelation but also because of the unity of creation. While intellectuals may let each other get away with using tropes and metaphors claiming that humans live in different worlds from each other, the truth is that we live today in the same world as Abraham. Blocher appeals to canon sense and common sense (though his common sense is informed by theorists like Ricouer and his canon sense is similarly sophisticated) in defense of what he calls "present truth," echoing the formulation found in 2 Peter 1:12.

Katherine Sonderegger returned to the LA Theology Conference to give the paper that became chapter 6. It is a highly constructive account of the nature of Scripture as a source of theological authority in dogmatics. Sonderegger has already published the first volume of her *Systematic Theology*, which deliberately eschewed extensive reflection on methodology and instead included a number of implicit commitments regarding the nature of theology. In this chapter, "Holy Scripture as Sacred Ground," she gives a public account of the doctrine of Scripture that undergirds her work. After showing that Holy Scripture cannot be contained in any available categories, genres, or contexts, Sonderegger argues that it is not only an incomparable book literarily or historically considered; Scripture is "strongly unique." As a sheerly given reality in God's economy, it is perhaps a mode of divine presence, or at the very least the crucial place of divine presence. Theologians do their work in its presence in a way analogous to how Moses behaves before the burning bush; or they should.

In chapter 7, Darren Sumner focuses on whether the procedure and content of systematic theology should be Christocentric. Karl Barth famously stated that all theology must finally be Christology, that is, at every point beginning from and normed by the event of Jesus Christ. John Webster, in contrast, suggests that taking one's departure always from the immanent Trinity makes for a more well-rounded and capacious theology. This chapter seeks to adjudicate the relationship between Trinity and Christology in theological method, inquiring as to whether one of these ought to serve to the other. In a constructive proposal, Sumner suggests that the pattern of proper systematic discourse is not linear or progressive but rather fractal, that is, the repetition of a set pattern producing an increasingly complex symmetry, wherein the microcosm replicates the macrocosm perfectly in scale. This has a number of advantages over more linear models. Here Christology serves not as the starting point but the "pattern" that is reproduced in different ways (i.e., nonrecursively) at every point throughout the whole. The doctrine of the Trinity is the starting point in this proposal, so that dogmatics begins from God and God's works, and proceeds in an unavoidably christological key.

In chapter 8, James Arcadi argues that truthmaker theory illuminates Barth's discussion of the relations among church proclamation, dogmatics, and the Word of God, in his *Church Dogmatics*. A standard principle in truthmaker theory is as follows: *a truthmaker is that in virtue of which something is true*. Arcadi argues that one interpretation of the "in virtue of" relation— that of an entailment relation—aptly clarifies what Barth means by the "agreement" relation between church proclamation and the Word of God in *Church Dogmatics* I/1. The task of dogmatics, then, is to evaluate when and how talk about God is entailed by the Word of God and thus has the Word of God as its truthmaker. One extension of this notion is the way that persons stand as truthmakers for propositions about themselves. These propositions can be distinguished into third- and second-personal nuances due to the intentional stance of the proposition's issuer. This further clarifies Barth's concern to maintain the second-personal nature of proclamation because "the Word of God is spoken to man."

In chapter 9, Joshua Malone and Brannon Ellis consider the divine perfections and the shape of dogmatics. The chapter begins to develop an approach to the doctrine of the divine attributes that fully affirms both the boundless uniqueness of the one God and the christological location of God's self-disclosure as our Father in his Son and by his Spirit. Taking their cue from John Webster, the authors argue that God's aseity and simplicity should form our scriptural reasoning about the divine attributes, in the sense of bracketing the scope and shape of all our theological claims. At the same time, Trinity and Christology should inform theological reasoning, in the sense of pervasively characterizing the content of those claims and governing their interrelations. The chapter ends with applications for the practice of dogmatics beyond the doctrine of God.

In chapter 10, Michael Allen takes up the issue of dogmatics as ascetics. He argues that the sanctifying ends of ascetic discipline are not simply a set of spiritual supplements that ought to be added to the theological task. Instead, fruits of sanctification like worship and discernment ought to be located within the theological task itself, and especially in the theological task conceived of as dogmatics within the church. Allen's recommendation of a theology with self-renunciatory and purgative effects has much in common with Sarah Coakley's *théologie totale*, one of the most ambitious projects on the current theological scene. Allen develops his own theses in a running critique of Coakley's project, in order to bring out what is distinctive about the kind of Reformed dogmatics that have an eye on the holiness appropriate to theology and its practitioners. Where Coakley engages a stunning profusion of cognate disciplines and literatures, using their insights to disrupt theology's conventional narrowness, Allen instead commends John Webster's intentional limitation of the dogmatic task to a narrow set of sources and texts. In a set of theses for a Reformed dogmatics that achieves ascetic ends, Allen spells out some implications for the doctrine of God and for theological anthropology.

In the last chapter of the volume, Gavin Ortlund asks, "Why Should Protestants Retrieve Patristic and Medieval Theology?" Locating his essay within the growing body of literature on theological retrieval, Ortlund notes that the retrieval of patristic and medieval theology has been an underexplored and underappreciated task among Protestant Christians, particularly evangelical Protestants in the United States. Identifying B. B. Warfield's retrieval of Augustine as an example various modern Protestant tendencies, he points to the retrieval practices of the Reformers as a more helpful model, suggesting that Protestant theology can and should be rooted in the entire history of the church. He then offers a taxonomy of four particular ways that patristic and medieval theology can resource contemporary Protestant theology, each with a metaphor and then an example or case study. The chapter concludes with three specific case studies of early medieval texts that may be especially helpful to retrieve: Boethius's *The Consolation of Philosophy*, Gregory the Great's *The Book of Pastoral Rule*, and John of Damascus's writings on the iconoclast controversy.

May these essays extend discussion of the task of dogmatics, *ad maiorem dei gloriam*.

Oliver D. Crisp and Fred Sanders, March 2017

CHAPTER 1

ANALYTICS, POETICS, AND THE MISSION OF DOGMATIC DISCOURSE

KEVIN J. VANHOOZER

THE DISCOURSE OF DOGMATICS: SAYING WHAT IS "IN CHRIST"

Of talking about many things, as the making of many books, there is no end (see Eccl 12:12). Theology is "talk about God" (the *logos* of *theos*), yet there are many kinds of theology, including pastoral, biblical, historical, and systematic. There is also misleading talk of God, not only the idle talk of idolaters but also the false "teachings of demons" (1 Tim 4:1).[1] This essay treats yet another variety of theology, dogmatics. Indeed, the goal is to give a dogmatic account of the project of dogmatics itself, along the lines of John Webster's theological account of theology.[2]

Let me define dogmatics provisionally as the church's attempt to employ its own resources (e.g., Scripture, tradition) to issue binding statements concerning who God *is* and what God *is doing*.[3] In particular, dogmatics sets

---

1. Unless otherwise noted, Scripture quotations in this chapter come from the ESV.

2. John Webster, "Theological Theology," in *Confessing God: Essays in Christian Dogmatics II* (London: T&T Clark, 2005), 11–32. Webster acknowledges a distinction between systematic and dogmatic theology, but in his own work often uses the terms interchangeably (see "Introduction: Systematic Theology," in *The Oxford Handbook of Systematic Theology*, ed. John Webster, Kathryn Tanner, and Iain Torrance (Oxford: Oxford University Press, 2007), 1–15, esp. 1–2.

3. By way of contrast, some systematic theologies employ extrabiblical, often philosophical resources and conceptual schemes as their unifying principles (e.g., Paul Tillich's use of existentialism in *Systematic Theology*, 3 vols. [Chicago: University of Chicago Press, 1951–63]).

forth in speech what God is doing in Christ. Stated even more succinctly: dogmatics says *what is* "in Christ." As we shall see, however, saying what is in Christ cannot be abstracted from having the mind of Christ and walking in the way of Christ. While the task of dogmatics involves setting out faith's *content* ("the good deposit," 2 Tim 1:14), it also involves the *forms* of language, experience, and thought that communicate it. Dogmatic discourse involves not only *what* we say about God (content) but *how* we say it (form).

Which comes first in dogmatics: a certain kind of experience, reflection, or language? The relationship between concepts (thought), percepts (experience), and words (language) has been at the center of modern debates about meaning and truth. The poet Christian Wiman wonders whether the decay of belief among educated Westerners precedes the decay of language: "Do we find the fire of belief fading in us only because the words are sodden with overuse and imprecision, and will not burn?"[4] Immanuel Kant complicated the dogmatic task by claiming that experience and language, especially concepts, only get as far as a knowledge of appearances, not reality. Consequently, content-oriented dogmatics has been in the doghouse for much of modernity. Friedrich Schleiermacher accepted the Kantian limits, insisting that the piety that forms the basis of the church is a matter neither of knowing or doing, but rather of feeling (i.e., the consciousness of being related to God).[5] Hence his famous definition: "Christian doctrines are accounts of the Christian religious affections set forth in speech."[6] Feelings, religious affections, and consciousness are all modes of human subjectivity, and sure enough Schleiermacher declares, "the description of human states of mind to be the fundamental dogmatic form."[7]

Schleiermacher falls easy prey to Ludwig Feuerbach's suspicion that underneath every theological statement there lurks an anthropological truth.[8] By way of contrast, the present essay views the task of Christian dogmatics as speaking and reflecting not about our own experience primarily—even if those experiences are experiences of redemption by Jesus Christ—but rather about who God is and what God is doing. Dogmatics obliges us to

---

4. Christian Wiman, *My Bright Abyss: Meditations of a Modern Believer* (New York: Farrar, Strauss, and Giroux, 2013), 124.
5. Friedrich Schleiermacher, *The Christian Faith,* ed. H. R. Mackintosh and J. S. Stewart (Edinburgh: T&T Clark, 1928), 5.
6. Ibid., 76.
7. Ibid., 126.
8. See Ludwig Feuerbach, *The Essence of Christianity,* trans. George Eliot (Buffalo, NY: Prometheus 1989). For a response to Feuerbach's suspicion, see my *Remythologizing Theology: Divine Action, Passion, and Authorship* (Cambridge: Cambridge University Press, 2010), 18–21, 388–90.

do more (but not less) than talk about ourselves.[9] I agree with John Webster: dogmatics is the study that has the being and agency of God not only for its subject matter but also for its very condition of possibility. What we need, perhaps going beyond Webster, is a dogmatic account of how all three—experience, thought, and language—come together in statements of what is in Christ.[10] In sum, what we need is a *poetics* of dogmatics.

THE ISSUE: THE RELATIONSHIP OF EXPERIENCE, THINKING, AND SPEAKING IN KNOWING GOD

Robert Jenson says the church's mission is "to see to the speaking of the gospel."[11] The material content of the gospel deserves pride of place, although in a "post-truth" age we do well "to see to the speaking," that is, both what is said and how it is said—hence the present reflection on the nature and function of language in dogmatic reasoning and, in particular, the ways in which language brokers the complex relationships between experience and thought. To see what I'm talking about, consider an example from another discipline: mathematics.

The Man Who Knew Infinity is a novel (now a major motion picture with Dev Patel and Jeremy Irons) that tells the true story of Srinivasa Ramanujan, a self-taught mathematician who gained admittance to Cambridge University to work with the renowned Englishman Professor G. H. Hardy. Ramanujan was a devout Hindu for whom mathematical discovery resembled a process of mystical vision. He claimed that all his discoveries were revealed: "An equation to me," he famously said, "has no meaning unless it expresses a thought of God." By contrast, his Cambridge mentor, while recognizing Ramanujan's genius, insisted on his supplying step-by-step clarifications of his seminal ideas about numbers. The novel details the way in which Hardy, "the Apostle of Proof," engaged Ramanujan, "the Prince of Intuition."

The story turns largely on what we might describe as a conflict of mathematical poetics: an intuitive imagination that yearns for not a beatific but an arithmetic vision on the one hand, and an analytic reason satisfied with

---

9. Here I am thinking of the claim with which John Calvin opens his *Institutes*: "Nearly all the wisdom we possess . . . consists of two parts: the knowledge of God and of ourselves" (*Inst.* 1.1.1).
10. As opposed to privileging one over the others, as Charles Hodge (content), Schleiermacher (experience), and George Lindbeck (language) tend to do in their respective theologies.
11. Robert Jenson, *Systematic Theology*, vol. 1, *The Triune God* (New York: Oxford University Press, 1997), 11.

nothing less than the long way of axiomatic demonstration on the other. Hardy once said that Ramanujan had "a feeling for form," and this is a good description of poetic sensibility. Even in a discipline like mathematics there are connections between forms of seeing, experiencing, and thinking. Well, what about dogmatics? Where should we locate its discourse on the linguistic spectrum between analytic demonstration and poetic intuition?

THE NATURE OF DOGMATIC DISCOURSE

There is a poetics of theology as there is in mathematics—a variety of ways to experience, think, and speak about the infinity (of God). Perfect being theologians purport to set forth in speech the properties of a being so great that none greater can be conceived—a being of infinite perfection.[12] Setting forth in speech the properties of such a being is not quite the project of dogmatics, which attends not merely to the concept of infinite perfection but, more specifically, the triune God—and to what Emily Dickinson describes as "the infinite a sudden guest" (a reference to the historical incarnation), and what Ed Oakes's recent Christology describes as "infinity dwindled to infancy."[13]

Neither can dogmatics be content with an apophaticism that speaks of infinity only by saying what it is not. For the biblical discourse of the prophets and apostles that generates and governs Christian dogmatics is largely cataphatic, describing in positive terms (even if they are anthropomorphisms) "that which was from the beginning, which we have heard, which we have seen with our eyes, which we looked upon and have touched with our hands, concerning the word of life" (1 John 1:1).

Christian dogmatics is not a speculative discourse that begins from or limits itself by means of an abstract concept of infinity. It is rather a response to a prior divine communicative initiative.[14] We speak truly of God because God first spoke to us. Dogmatics exists in and under what John Webster calls "the domain of the Word": God's communicative and self-communicative activity. Defining dogmatics as "talk about God" does not go far enough; other forms of discourse speak of God (often in vain).

---

12. See, for example, Katherin A. Rogers, *Perfect Being Theology* (Edinburgh: Edinburgh University Press, 2000).

13. Edward T. Oakes, *Infinity Dwindled to Infancy: A Catholic and Evangelical Christology* (Grand Rapids: Eerdmans, 2011).

14. Speculative discourse differs from contemplative discourse (see Scott Swain's essay in the present volume), for the focus of the latter is on God's self-presentation. For a critique of speculative theology, see James Gordon, "A 'Glaring Misunderstanding'? Schleiermacher, Barth and the Nature of Speculative Theology," *IJST* 16 (2014): 313–30.

Webster rightly identifies the distinctiveness of dogmatics "in its invocation of God as agent in the intellectual practice of theology."[15] God is Lord of his Word—its form (poetics) and content (analytics)—as well as its hearing. And, out of his lordly love and freedom, God has decided to communicate a share of his infinite knowledge of himself with those he created in his image.[16]

Humans may not be capable of experiencing, knowing, and saying the infinite, yet the infinite is capable of humanity: *infinitum capax finiti*, or rather "the Word became flesh" (John 1:14). Specifically, God the Son, the "form of God" (Phil 2:6), took on the "form of a servant" (Phil 2:7). The communicative agency of the triune God is the enabling condition of Christian dogmatics: not philosophical anthropology, epistemology, or even hermeneutics. In the economy of divine light, Christ is the human surface that mirrors the Father, who otherwise dwells in unapproachable light (1 Tim 6:16). God is both subject matter (object) and active agent (subject) of dogmatics. Theologians too are subjects of intellectual acts—of biblical interpretation, historical inquiry, conceptual elaboration, and as we shall see, confessions of faith—but their activity originates, is sustained, and is illumined by a divine communicative activity that encompasses them.

THE TASK OF DOGMATIC DISCOURSE (ACCORDING TO BARTH, BAVINCK, AND WEBSTER)

For Karl Barth, the task of dogmatics is to examine how far church proclamation corresponds to or agrees with the Word of God: "Dogmatics is the church's evaluation of its own utterance by its own given norm of revelation."[17] Dogmatics is a function of the hearing and teaching church. In hearing, the church must hearken first and foremost to God's Word: no dogmatics can serve two masters. In teaching, the church must speak. It must proclaim and exposit the content of the gospel: the self-communicative action of the triune God, the revelation of the Father's reconciliation in Jesus Christ by the Holy Spirit. Barth views dogmatics as the science of the Word of God, whose form and content is Jesus Christ.[18] Dogmatics is

---

15. Webster, "Theological Theology," 25.

16. John Webster, *God without Measure: Working Papers in Christian Theology*, 2 vols. (London: Bloomsbury T&T Clark, 2016), 1:216.

17. John Webster, *Karl Barth*, 2nd ed. (London: Continuum, 2004), 53.

18. Barth views Christian doctrine as the description of the movement of the Word of God (*CD* IV/1, [Edinburgh; T&T Clark, 1956], 55).

scientific to the extent that it lets its object determine the way it comes to be known and spoken of.

Similarly, Herman Bavinck conceives dogmatic theology as the science of the knowledge of God and his creatures as they stand in relation to him. God reveals this knowledge, humans receive it by faith through the Spirit, and this faith is nurtured in particular ecclesial contexts. However, Bavinck distinguishes "symbolics" (the exposition of what a church in fact confesses) from dogmatics, the assessment what the church *ought* to confess. In Bavinck's words: "dogmatic theology dogmatizes, i.e., it sets forth . . . what ought to count as truth."[19] Both Barth and Bavinck would agree with Jaroslav Pelikan's definition of dogma as "a formal, official, public, and binding statement of what is believed and confessed by the church."[20]

John Webster has roused many of us from our nondogmatic slumbers, awakening us to the bracing prospect of speaking of God in himself (i.e., his perfect life as a fellowship of Father, Son, and Spirit) as well as speaking of his external operations (e.g., creation, providence, redemption). Here too, the focus is on God's communicative agency, and on "the continuous identity of the acting subject in God's inner and outer works."[21] This is heady stuff, for theology under the house arrest of modernity was not allowed to make claims that transcended human spatiotemporal experience. Webster does not deny the ectypal nature of human knowledge of God: we do not know God the way God knows God. Yet acknowledging theology as ectypal (i.e., accommodated to human minds and contexts) need not result in the self-destruction of dogmatics, much less its deconstruction. On the contrary, a dogmatic account of dogmatic discourse acknowledges the limitations of the human intellect "but places them within the sphere of God's communicative and saving causality."[22]

THE CHALLENGE OF DOGMATIC DISCOURSE

Hopefully by now I've established my Websterian bona fides. I am on board with his notion that while we may need to begin with the economy (God's external works in space and time), in a material sense "theology proper [the consideration of God's perfect life in itself] precedes and governs the

19. Bavinck, *Reformed Dogmatics*, ed. John Bolt, trans. John Vriend (Grand Rapids: Baker Academic, 2003), 1:88.
20. Jaroslav Pelikan, *Credo: Historical and Theological Guide to Creeds and Confessions of Faith in the Christian Tradition* (New Haven, CT: Yale University Press, 2003), 60.
21. Webster, *God without Measure*, 1:8.
22. Ibid., 10.

economy."[23] Webster insists that the God who is with us and for us in his works in the world is the one who enjoys perfect life in himself. Triune perfection establishes and enables triune presence.[24] Getting a better handle on this marvel—our ability to speak well of God's existence *in se*—is one of my reasons for attempting a dogmatic account of dogmatic discourse.

What makes talk of God count as properly dogmatic discourse? The Gospels include technically true statements about Jesus that fall short of the dogmatic mark. Consider, for example, Jesus's encounters with demons, like the one in Luke 4, where the evil spirits of a man possessed cry out "Go away! What have you to do with us, Jesus of Nazareth? . . . I know who you are—the Holy One of God" (Luke 4:34). This was hardly an isolated incident: "And demons also came out of many, crying, 'You are the Son of God!'" (Luke 4:41). James 2:19 says: "You believe that God is one; you do well. Even the demons believe—and shudder [from *phrissō* (cf. *frisson*)]." How, then, should we explain the difference between demonic and dogmatic discourse? As we shall see, it has something to do with the relationship between forms of experience, thought, and language. Dogmatics involves not only propositions but doxastic attitudes (i.e., faith) and obedient actions (i.e., works) too. By way of contrast, those who do not believe God "went after false idols and became false" (2 Kings 17:15), illustrating what we may call the poetics of unbelief.

Concepts stand at the intersection of language and thought and are the workhorses of dogmatic theology. What is the status of categories that are not explicitly used by biblical authors? We've all heard of the Hellenization thesis, according to which Greek philosophical categories corrupted the pure narrative simplicity of the Gospels, but Ann Moss's "Latinization" thesis may be less familiar.[25] Moss argues that language change was "of overriding importance in Renaissance humanism's refashioning of the mentality of Western Europe."[26] The Renaissance humanists introduced a new type of Latin, in contrast to the Latin of medieval scholasticism. Their goal was to have the humanist schoolboy "speak, write, and think as if he were an integrated member of the same speech community as Cicero

---

23. Ibid., 3.

24. See Webster's unpublished Kantzer Lectures on "Presence and Perfection."

25. I prefer to speak of the evangelization of Hellenism, for the development of the doctrine of the Trinity, though it used Greek concepts, is best understood as the biblical story taking every (Greek) thought captive (cf. 2 Cor 10:5).

26. Ann Moss, *Renaissance Truth and the Latin Language Turn* (Oxford: Oxford University Press, 2003), 5.

and Virgil."[27] Moss may be doing Renaissance history, but she has bought into, and imported, the twentieth-century turn to language: the idea that "our modes of perception and our ways of organizing our thoughts and experience [are] conditioned, determined even, by the language(s) in which they operate."[28]

Ought we to say something similar about dogmatics? Is its mission to train today's evangelical seminarians to speak, write, and think as if they were an integrated member of the same speech community as Athanasius or Calvin? One of my former doctoral students, now teaching in the Philippines, is wrestling with the degree to which insights from cross-cultural dialogue ought to inform dogmatic theology. He admires Webster's work but wonders whether it pulls theology out of the orbit of particular human cultures, with the unintended consequence of devaluing non-Western theologies as deviations from the Latin (i.e., Western) norm.

The way forward is to view concepts as mental habits that are not language specific. The "habit" in question is the association of ideas. Children learn to associate certain ideas with the concept "Christmas," for example, by participating in annual family celebrations. Christians, similarly, learn the concepts that order faith by participating in celebrations of the Lord's Supper and other worship practices and, more fundamentally, by reading Scripture and participating in what I have elsewhere called "canonical practices."[29] Doctrinal concepts thus function as shorthand for a whole set of associations (N. T. Wright compares them to suitcases). For example, think of how the doctrine of the atonement functions as shorthand for the much longer story of how God makes provision for the forgiveness of sins. As to the question of whether concepts are too tied to particular cultures, dogmatic theologians do well to remember that the same biblical judgments about who God is and what God is doing may be expressed in every language, sometimes with different concepts.[30]

A more fundamental question about concepts concerns the confidence with which dogmatic discourse can really speak of God's own perfect life. Modern theologians typically stumble over Kantian limits, acutely conscious that the categories with which we think about the world tell us more about

---

27. Ibid.
28. Ibid., 6.
29. Vanhoozer, *The Drama of Doctrine: A Canonical-Linguistic Account of Christian Theology* (Louisville: Westminster John Knox, 2005), 283–85.
30. For the important distinction between judgments and concepts, see the seminal essay by David S. Yeago, "The New Testament and the Nicene Dogma: A Contribution to the Recovery of Theological Exegesis," *Pro Ecclesia* 3, no. 10 (Spring 1994): 152–64.

the structures of human consciousness than they do the thing-in-itself: "To tour a town with a guidebook in hand is to see only what the guidebook permits."[31] If the thing-in-itself is always conceptually out of reach, how much more elusive is God-in-himself?

Forms of experience and thought are obviously relevant to thinking infinity and knowing God and are thus elements in dogmatic discourse. Yet it is language that brokers the relationships between experience and thought, and language that is used to make dogmatic statements. So it comes as some surprise to discover that theologians typically do not pause to consider the role of language in dogmatics. Because human persons are embodied communicative agents, however, we should not draw too rigid a distinction between language, life, and thought. Accordingly, the "analytics" and "poetics" of my title roughly parallel the two views of language that Charles Taylor labels "designative" and "constitutive" in his book *The Language Animal*.[32] The basic difference is between viewing language as a tool that subjects use to encode information, express thought, and represent things on the one hand, and as a medium of intersubjectivity, an enabling condition that makes certain kinds of experience and thought possible, on the other.

DOGMATIC DISCOURSE, PART 1: ANALYTICS

John Webster frequently sounds a distinctly analytic note: "Dogmatics is the schematic and analytic presentation of the matter of the gospel."[33] It is a species of reasoning, and one of his signal contributions is his dogmatic account of such reasoning. It involves viewing reason as created and redeemed intelligence caught up in an economy of grace that enables the saints to understand God's communicative acts. Whereas exegetical reasoning focuses on understanding the way the biblical words go, dogmatic reasoning yields "a conceptual representation of what reason has learned from its exegetical following of the scriptural text."[34] Is Websterian dogmatics therefore simply a species of analytic theology? Let's analyze that proposition.

---

31. Adam Roberts, *The Thing Itself* (London: Gollancz, 2015), 44.

32. Taylor, *The Language Animal: The Full Shape of the Human Linguistic Capacity* (Cambridge, MA: Belknap Press of Harvard University, 2016).

33. Webster, "Biblical Reasoning," in *The Domain of the Word: Scripture and Theological Reason* (London: T&T Clark International, 2012), 131. Webster also contributed an essay, "What Makes Theology Theological," to the *Journal of Analytic Theology* 3 (2015): 17–28 (also published in *God without Measure*, 1:213–24).

34. Webster, *Domain of the Word*, 130.

DOGMATIC DISCOURSE AS ANALYTIC

The "retrieval" of analytic philosophy for the purposes of constructive theology is one of the major developments of our time, boasting annual conferences, a manifesto, and an online journal.[35] To what extent does it serve the task of dogmatics? More pointedly, to what extent is dogmatic discourse essentially analytic?

William Abraham defines analytic theology as "systematic theology attuned to the deployment of the skills, resources, and virtues of analytic philosophy."[36] It is a method, says Oliver Crisp, "characterized by a logical rigour, clarity, and parsimony of expression."[37] Tom McCall's recent book, *Invitation to Analytic Theology*, goes a long way towards showing how analytic theology is both analytic and theological. He also calls analytic theology "to a deeper engagement with the traditional resources of the theological task,"[38] the very aim of Webster's dogmatics.

Webster clearly makes use of conceptual distinctions. Perhaps the most important is that between creature and Creator: "Dogmatics considers God absolutely and relatively,"[39] that is, in his self-existent internal perfection and economically in his external works. The external works of God are *his* works, "and this continuity of acting subject means that God's economic acts elucidate his inner being, even though they do not exhaust it."[40] Dogmatics begins by contemplating God's external works, then traces them back to their worker, the undivided Trinity. To stay on the level of the economy only risks treating God and created things as paired, thus forgetting the all-important creature/Creator distinction. Webster insists that theology proper "is oriented chiefly to invisible things, 'things that are unseen' (2 Cor. 4:18)."[41] But not necessarily *unheard*. Indeed, dogmatic theology speaks of these unseen things precisely by attending to what is spoken in Scripture, offering a conceptual analysis and elaboration of biblical discourse.

---

35. *The Journal of Analytic Theology*, http://journalofanalytictheology.com/jat/index.php/jat, accessed April 19, 2017.
36. Abraham, "Systematic Theology as Analytic Theology," in *Analytic Theology: New Essays in the Philosophy of Theology*, ed. Oliver Crisp and Michael Rea (Oxford: Oxford University Press, 2009), 54.
37. Crisp, "On Analytic Theology," in *Analytic Theology*, 35.
38. McCall, *An Invitation to Analytic Christian Theology* (Downers Grove, IL: IVP Academic, 2015), 10.
39. Webster, *God without Measure*, 1:7.
40. Webster, "Christology, Theology, Economy. The Place of Christology in Systematic Theology," in *God without Measure*, 1:46.
41. Ibid., 6.

DOGMATIC DISCOURSES AS PHENOMENOLOGICAL

One underappreciated influence on analytic philosophy is phenomenology.[42] Phenomenology is a descriptive discipline that brackets out what we think we know about things, observes closely how they appear to consciousness, and then abstracts essences from the appearances. Edmund Husserl's famous battle-cry—"back to the 'things themselves'"[43]—sums up phenomenology's descriptive aim. His famous eidetic reduction attempts to identify the essential components of phenomena by eliminating contingent aspects of things in order to imagine "the invariant, the necessary, universal form, the essential form, without which something of that kind . . . would be altogether inconceivable,"[44] thereby identifying the absolute in the relative.

Whereas phenomenology describes the essences of things that appear in consciousness, dogmatics describes the essences of things that happen in space-time, namely, the history of redemption attested by the biblical authors. Webster is a phenomenologist of the triune economy, concerned with describing not simply the phenomena—God's space-time appearances—but his eternal essence as well. Webster's aim is not the thing-in-itself but God-in-himself and all things-in-relation-to-God. Webster sounds like a phenomenologist when he speaks of dogmatic theology as a "reduction of elements to their founding principles."[45] By "principles" Webster means the beginning of things (from the Latin *principium* for "beginning, foundation"), referring to their origin and nature as creatures in relation to God. The ultimate origin and end of all things is the triune God, which is why Webster insists, "There is one principal Christian doctrine, the doctrine of God the Holy Trinity."[46] To give a dogmatic account of something is thus to locate the origin, nature, and end of that entity in relation to the triune God. The foundational principle of Christian dogmatics is the communicative being and activity of the triune God: "The principles of theology are thus a conceptual rendering of the work of divine charity, in which at the Son's behest the Father sends the Spirit to instruct the church (John 14:26)."[47]

---

42. See David Woodruff Smith and Amie L. Thomasson, eds., *Phenomenology and Philosophy of Mind* (Oxford: Clarendon Press, 2005).

43. Husserl, *Logical Investigations*, 2nd ed. (London: Routledge, 2001), 168.

44. Husserl, *Phenomenological Psychology: Lectures, Summer Semester, 1925* (The Hague: Nijhoff, 1977), sec. 9a.

45. Webster, *God without Measure*, 1:7. Cf. Webster's comment that even in moral theology, dogmatic theology operates by "reduction to *principia*" or first principles (*God without Measure*, 2:2).

46. Ibid., 2:2.

47. Webster, *Domain of the Word*, 136.

Dogmatics is the result of created intelligence contemplating, reflecting on, and describing the economy of God's self-communication: "Contemplation—what Aquinas calls 'a simple gaze'—requires the mind to move through created things to the divine reality of whose self-communication they are signs and bearers."[48] This is similar to the eidetic reduction, a movement of thought from the economy (e.g., the missions) to the Trinitarian things themselves (e.g., the processions). As the *Catechism of the Catholic Church* puts it: "Through the *oikonomia* the *theologia* is revealed to us; but conversely, the *theologia* illuminates the whole *oikonomia*. God's works reveal who he is in himself; the mystery of his inmost being enlightens our understanding of all his works."[49] Again, Webster insists that dogmatics is possible only because the exercise of theological intelligence is "a moved movement"[50]: our intellectual capacities themselves have their origin in God, and it is God who sustains them and determines their proper ends.[51]

The proximate object of dogmatic contemplation, reflection, and description is Holy Scripture, whose verbal testimony is itself an element in the economies of revelation and redemption. Interestingly, the philosopher J. L. Austin likened his analytic approach to a phenomenology of ordinary language:

> When we examine what we should say when, what words we should use in what situations, we are looking again not merely at words . . . but also at the realities we use the words to talk about. . . . For this reason, I think it might be better to use, for this way of doing philosophy, some less misunderstanding name than those given above—for instance, "linguistic phenomenology," only that is rather a mouthful.[52]

We can similarly describe Webster's dogmatic discourse as a linguistic phenomenology, not of ordinary but biblical language, a description and contemplation of God's Word written by the regenerated and illumined intellect. Biblical reasoning gives way to dogmatic reasoning, namely, a phenomenological description of the economic Trinity, whose "principle" or essence is God's own perfect life in himself.

---

48. Webster, *God without Measure*, 1:220.
49. *Catechism of the Catholic Church* (New York and London: Doubleday, 1995), 70.
50. Webster, *God without Measure*, 1:218.
51. Webster insists that "the order of [God's] being precedes and is actively present to the order of [human] knowing" (*Domain of the Word*, 135).
52. J. L. Austin, "A Plea for Excuses," in *Philosophical Papers*, 3rd ed. (Oxford: Oxford University Press, 1979), 182. On ordinary language analysis as linguistic phenomenology, see Jerry Gill, "Linguistic Phenomenology," *International Philosophical Quarterly* 13 (1973): 535–50.

CAUTIONS

Is analysis—be it propositional, principial, or phenomenological—thus the primary mode of dogmatic discourse? Is the mission of dogmatic statements to achieve conceptual clarity and precision only? Several people warn against reducing dogmatics to analytics, including Webster himself.

Khaled Anatolios, thinking of fourth-century Trinitarian controversies, argues that the church's doctrine arises not merely from abstract logic applied to Scripture, but from Scripture as lived out in "the entirety of Christian faith and life," including the liturgy, prayer, the moral life, and so forth.[53]

T. F. Torrance, thinking of the gospel, says that "the ultimate mystery of the atonement recedes into the eternal being of God far beyond our human grasp."[54] This kind of conclusion "is often found in his writing when he becomes aware that our forms of thought and speech break off in wonder, as he refuses to advance along the path laid out by logico-causal attempts at explanation" (i.e., analytic theology!).[55]

John Webster's caution appears in his essay "Principles of Systematic Theology," in connection with his discussion of Geerhardus Vos's distinction between biblical and systematic theology. According to Vos, biblical theology considers "both the form and the contours of revelation as . . . parts and products of a divine work. In Systematic Theology these same contents of revelation appear . . . rather as the material for a human work of classifying and systematizing according to logical principles."[56] Webster says this division of labor generates two problems. First, it turns the biblical texts into raw material for systematic processing, leaving the canonical form to be studied by another discipline (viz., biblical theology). Hence, "The idiom of systematic theology drifts away from Scripture. . . . Indeed, systematic theology becomes a kind of analytic theology, operating at some distance from the idiom of Scripture and heavily conceptual in tone and structure."[57] Second, it gives rise to the dangerous idea "of dogma as an improvement upon Holy Scripture—as the replacement of the informal and

---

53. Khaled Anatolios, *Retrieving Nicaea: The Development and Meaning of Trinitarian Doctrine* (Grand Rapids: Baker Academic, 2011), 283–84.

54. T. F. Torrance, *Atonement: The Person and Work of Christ* (Downers Grove, IL: InterVarsity, 2009), 88.

55. Andrew Purves, *Exploring Christology and Atonement: Conversations with John McLeod Campbell, H. R. Mackintosh and T. F. Torrance* (Downers Grove, IL: InterVarsity, 2015), 214.

56. Vos, "The Idea of Biblical Theology as a Science and as a Theological Discipline," in *Redemptive History and Biblical Interpretation: The Shorter Writings of Geerhardus Vos*, ed. Richard B. Gaffin (Phillipsburg, NJ: P&R, 1980), 7.

57. Webster, *Domain of the Word*, 148.

occasional language of Scripture by conceptual forms at once more clearly organized, better warranted and betraying a greater degree of sophistication."[58] Webster prefers a kinder, gentler, more "lightweight" understanding of the dogmatic task—and, we might add, one that is more nimble when it comes to forms of discourse.

Taylor's concern with the designative view of discourse assumed by analytic philosophy and theology is that it views language as purely instrumental: a matter of encoding what is already known.[59] In other words, language comes too late to contribute anything to the discussion; it simply expresses what thought has already discovered. For Taylor, however, language is not merely a matter of words, labels, and conceptual tools that we acquire one at a time; it is rather something we learn in relation to learning forms of life. Stated differently: it is not as though we first relate to and analyze things and then say what we have discovered; it is rather that certain forms of language enable certain kinds of experience and thought.[60]

DOGMATIC DISCOURSE, PART 2: POETICS

This brings us to the poetics of dogmatics, by which I mean a concern not only for *what* is said, but also *how*.[61] The task of dogmatics involves content, to be sure, but also the forms of language, experience, and thought that communicate it. Webster tends to use the term "poetics" pejoratively, as a catchall term for approaches that put too much emphasis on human creativity and invention.[62] Yet he also says positive things about what I mean by poetics, namely, the relationship of forms of language and literature to forms of experience and thought. For example, he acknowledges the importance of Scripture's own forms of discourse: "Scripture is doing real work, not simply furnishing topics to be handled in a non-Scriptural idiom."[63]

Webster manifests a concern for what I am calling poetics when he

---

58. Webster, "Discovering Dogmatics," 135.
59. Taylor, *The Language Animal*, 86.
60. In Taylor's words, "Being constitutive means that language makes possible its own content, in a sense, or opens us to the domain it encodes" (*The Language Animal*, 40).
61. Broadly defined, poetics is the theory of literary discourse or communication, with special attention to the distinct function and contribution of forms of discourse and communication. In the present context, I am interested above all in the forms and functions of dogmatic discourse. See T. V. F. Brogan, "Poetics," in *The New Princeton Encyclopedia of Poetry and Poetics*, 3rd ed., ed. Alex Preminger and T. V. F. Brogan (Princeton: Princeton University Press, 1993), 929–34.
62. See, for example, his association of poetics with readers co-constituting the text (*Word and Church: Essays in Christian Dogmatics*[Edinburgh: T&T Clark, 2001], 43), or interpreters being creative rather than receptive as concerns Scripture (*Confessing God*, 57).
63. Webster, *Domain of the Word*, 148.

says that the history of the various genres of theological writing "is still largely unexplored in any systematic way; yet the importance of such a study for interpreting the situation of theology in modernity can scarcely be over-emphasized."[64] What happens to dogmatics, he wonders, when *Wissenschaft* replaces biblical commentary? David Tracy describes modern theology as the triumph of *logos* (by which he means propositions and the conceptual form) over *theos* and the various ways in which Scripture names God.[65] The contrast with the earlier modes of dogmatic discourse Webster wants to retrieve is striking: "When citation is in the ascendant, the literary forms of theology are generally governed by the fact that the Christian worlds of meaning are shaped by biblical, creedal and doxological texts and by the practices which both carry and are themselves carried by those texts."[66] Webster never comes closer to a call for a properly Protestant poetics than that.[67]

THE POETICS OF DOGMATICS, PART 1: A BRIEF HISTORICAL SAMPLING

This is not the place to respond to Webster's call to explore the history of genres of theological writing. I have time merely to list a few examples.

Gregory of Nazianzus's *Poemata Arcana*

You know Gregory, "the Theologian," one of the Cappadocians, a bishop, and chairman of the Council in 381 that produced the Nicene Creed. But did you know that he was also a poet?[68] According to Frederick Norris, "The poems present Christian claims in Hellenistic verses at the same time that they specifically avoid the elegant buffoonery of classical rhetoric—cute words without content—that Gregory so despised. They provide simple, appealing aspects of Christian confession that meet the needs of common people"[69] or, to use the title of Norris's essay, a poetic, musical catechism.[70]

---

64. Webster, "Theological Theology," 20.

65. Tracy, "Literary Theory and Naming God," *Journal of Religion* 74 (1994), 307.

66. Webster, "Theological Theology," 20.

67. See further Barbara Kiefer Lewalski, *Protestant Poetics and the Seventeenth-Century Religious Lyric* (Princeton, NJ: Princeton University Press, 1979).

68. See Gregory of Nazianzus, *Poemata Arcana*, ed. C. Moreschini and D. A. Sykes (Oxford: Clarendon, 1997).

69. Frederick Norris, "Gregory Nazianzus' *Poemata Arcana*: A Poetic, Musical Catechism?" *Union Seminary Quarterly Review* 63, no. 3 (2012): 71.

70. See further John McGuckin, "Gregory: The Rhetorician as Poet," in *Gregory of Nazianzus: Images and Reflections*, ed. Jostein Børtness and Tomas Hägg (Copenhagen: Museum Tusculanum, 2006), 193–212.

Friedrich Schleiermacher's *Christmas Eve Celebration: A Dialogue*

Schleiermacher is "the only major theologian to produce a distinctive book on Christmas for the general public."[71] It's similar to a Platonic dialogue, but with women and children. Schleiermacher sets his dramatic dialogue showcasing different perspectives on the incarnation in an ordinary German household on Christmas Eve. Of particular interest is the way the four men tend to give academic interpretations while the women tell stories. There is singing and an exchange of gifts as well. This is a fascinating example of theological communication that allows Schleiermacher to make his point indirectly about the commingling of love and joy. The style matches the substance, for the way in which Schleiermacher shows the competing voices amiably engaging one another speaks volumes about what he takes to be the meaning of Christmas itself.[72]

Hans Urs von Balthasar's *Theo-Drama*

Hans Urs von Balthasar represents what is probably the most impressive twentieth-century attempt to explore the poetics of dogmatics. He unfolds God's revelatory Word in terms of Plato's transcendentals—the true, good, and beautiful—over a dozen volumes in three series: "Balthasar insisted that there can be no reflection on the *truth* of Christian revelation (Part 3) until it is lived out in committed *action* (Part 2), which a Christian will never feel called to do without having first perceived revelation in all its inherent *beauty* (Part 1)."[73] Interestingly, Balthasar begins with the perception of beauty in his seven volume *Glory of the Lord: A Theological Aesthetics* where the incarnate "form" of divine self-communication, Jesus Christ, takes pride of place.[74]

In *Theo-Drama*, Balthasar focuses on God's saving action in Christ under the rubric of the "good" (as in good news).[75] Here God's self-communication takes dramatic form in the form of a servant, the lived humanity of Jesus—the drama of the Christ.

I have suggested in my own work that if the method of Christian dog-

---

71. Terrance Tice, "Editor's Foreword," in Friedrich Schleiermacher, *Christmas Eve Celebration: A Dialogue* (Eugene, OR: Cascade, 2010), vii.

72. See Schleiermacher's "Preface to the Second Edition," in *Christmas Eve Celebration*, xxx.

73. Edward T. Oakes, "Hans Urs von Balthasar," in *The Oxford Companion to Christian Thought*, ed. Adrian Hastings et al. (Oxford: Oxford University Press, 2000), 744.

74. See Hans Urs von Balthasar, *The Glory of the Lord: A Theological Aesthetics*, vol. 1, *Seeing the Form*, 2nd ed. (San Francisco: Ignatius, 2009).

75. Hans Urs von Balthasar, *Theo-Drama: Theological Dramatic Theory*, 5 vols. (San Francisco: Ignatius, 1988–98).

matics is to correspond to its subject matter, then it ought to take the form of a theodramatics. This is my way of doing justice to the full scope of dogmatics, insofar as the discipline, in Webster's words, "requires consideration of both *credenda* and agenda."[76] The gospel is not an idea but a communicative activity, a divine word and deed, spoken and enacted on the stage of world history. To provide a "schematic and analytical presentation of the matter of the gospel"[77] is thus to explain the agent and the action at the heart of the drama of redemption: "conceived . . . born . . . suffered . . . was crucified, died, buried . . . rose again . . . ascended . . . will come again." The dogmatic exposition of those crucial verbs helps disciples understand what God is doing in Christ, and then to demonstrate their understanding by living out its truth. The etymology of the Greek term *dogma* connotes "what seems good, fitting, becoming,"[78] and I have argued that the task of dogmatics is to instruct the church in theodramatic fittingness.[79] To speak and show faith's understanding—this too is high historical drama, and as Dorothy Sayers says, "the dogma is the drama."[80] Dogmatics directs disciples to show and tell the greatest story ever told.

I got Webster's endorsement on the back of a book, but what he gave with a right-hand blurb, he partially took back with a left-hand footnote: "I remain agnostic about whether the task of theological identity description of moral agents is helped by a 'theodramatic' conception of the Christian faith."[81] I wish I had had the opportunity to convert him from agnosticism into whole-hearted belief, perhaps by arguing that theodrama is a "form of forms" that allows us to coordinate the form of Jesus Christ with the various literary forms of Scripture that attest him, and which generate and govern forms of Christian experience, thinking, and practice.

THE POETICS OF DOGMATICS, PART 2: BIBLICAL REASONING REVISITED

Let's return to Webster's exhortation not to let systematic theology drift away from the idioms of Scripture so that its mode of argument is exclusively logical analysis.[82] Scripture is doing "real work," he says, real argumentative work. Elsewhere I have argued that the imagination too is a cognitive

---

76. Webster, "Introduction: Systematic Theology," 6.
77. Webster, *Domain of the Word*, 131.
78. See Kathleen Norris, *Amazing Grace: A Vocabulary of Faith* (New York: Riverhead, 1998), 324.
79. See my *The Drama of Doctrine*, esp. chap. 8.
80. Dorothy L. Sayers, *Creed or Chaos?* (New York: Harcourt, Brace, 1949), 3.
81. Webster, "'Where Christ Is': Christology and Ethics," in *God without Measure*, 2:11n9.
82. See Webster, *Domain of the Word*, 148.

capacity, something God creates, regenerates, and redeems along with the creaturely intellect.[83] It is important to hearken to the several ways Scripture says what is in Christ.

The Biblical Imagination: Enlarging the Domain of the Word

Combining Webster's concern for the idioms of Scripture with Charles Taylor's conviction that language creates a context for human life and action yields a greater appreciation of the theologically formative biblical imagination, and ultimately an enlargement of the domain of the Word.

As we have seen, the analytic impulse is to break things up into their component parts and the phenomenological impulse is to reduce things to their essential principles. In both cases, the aim is to describe a certain objective content with concepts that are as clear as they are clean. There is no question that dogmatics aspires to be "the *scientia* of what faith knows."[84] The question is whether dogmatic discourse does more than simply encode information and designate things.

The nature of Scripture, and hence biblical authority, is a matter of form as well as content. God in his wisdom saw fit to employ many forms of human discourse to communicate his Word. Take narrative, for example: stories are not simply delivery systems for transmitting factual content but cognitive strategies in their own right that help us organize events in orderly patterns and meaningful wholes.[85] This is the distinct poetics of biblical narrative, its particular way of handling the part/whole relationship: explanation by emplotment. To invoke poetics, then, is to call attention not simply to bits of revealed information (content) but to larger-scale patterns of information processing (form).[86]

Martha Nussbaum says we need poets and novelists because "in today's political life we lack the capacity to see one another as fully human."[87] How much more do we need biblical narrative to see Jesus Christ as fully human and fully divine, and to cultivate not simply right opinion but right

---

83. Vanhoozer, *Pictures at a Theological Exhibition: Scenes of the Church's Worship, Witness, and Wisdom* (Downers Grove, IL: InterVarsity, 2016). See esp. the introduction, "The Discarded Imagination: Metaphors by Which a Holy Nation Lives."

84. Webster, *Domain of the Word*, vii.

85. See my "Love's Wisdom: The Authority of Scripture's Form and Content for Faith's Understanding and Theological Judgment," in *Journal of Reformed Theology* 5 (2011): 247–75. See also Eleonore Stump, *Wandering in Darkness: Narrative and the Problem of Suffering* (Oxford: Oxford University Press, 2010), for an excellent example of an analytic theologian who believes that some things are best known through narrative rather than logical analysis.

86. See further my *Pictures at a Theological Exhibition*.

87. Nussbaum, *Poetic Justice: The Literary Imagination and Public Life* (Boston: Beacon, 1995), xiii.

affections: the fear of the Lord. The demons believe, but their hearts have not been formed to respond to the truth in the right way. It is one thing to assent to propositions, quite another to confess and live them out. The imagination at work in the various forms of biblical literature addresses the heart as well as the intellect. The illumination of the Spirit turns the forms of biblical discourse into means of grace which not only inform but reform human cognition, volition, and affection alike. The Bible makes possible the common focus of the gathered assembly on the gospel. The Bible exercises a constitutive function as canon, gathering and governing the people of God, which is why the Reformers treat the church as a creature of the Word.[88]

The Christian Imaginary: From Biblical Forms to Dogmatic Formulations

Much more could be said about the poetics of biblical discourse, but what is the moral for dogmatics? It is one thing to acknowledge the cognitive function of narrative, another thing to adopt its form. Should dogmatic theology look more like a science textbook, a system of ideas, or a story? Three brief points:

First, we must not confuse propositional content with propositional form. All discourse is propositional insofar as it has content (subject and predicate). Poetics calls attention to the diverse ways that various forms of discourse propose some content for our consideration. Some forms of discourse (call them analytic) excel in clarifying what it is we're talking about by breaking it down into its smallest components; others (call them imaginative) excel in helping us view things synthetically, as parts of a larger whole that provides meaning (remember Ramanujan, the "Prince of Intuition"). Both modes are broadly propositional.

Second, let's not commit the "fallacy of imitative form," namely, the mistake of thinking that dogmatics has to adopt the actual styles of biblical discourse in order to think biblically. You can talk about Plato's dialogues monologically, just as you can talk about narrative without having to tell a story.[89]

---

88. Christoph Schwöbel, "The Creature of the Word: Recovering the Ecclesiology of the Reformers," in *On Being the Church: Essays on the Christian Community*, ed. Colin E. Gunton and Daniel W. Hardy (Edinburgh: T&T Clark, 1989), 110–55, esp. 122.

89. I am indebted to Martin Warner for this point. See his *The Aesthetics of Argument* (Oxford: Oxford University Press, 2016), xiii. Warner is drawing on Yvor Winters, *In Defense of Reason* (Chicago: Swallow, 1947), 62.

And third, the rationality of arguments is not always a matter of deductive validity or logical inference. The narrative form of the Fourth Gospel is a kind of courtroom drama where readers are presented with various kinds of evidence or testimony in word and deed: "But these are written so that you may believe that Jesus is the Christ, the Son of God, and that by believing you may have life in his name" (John 20:31). To do justice to this kind of biblical discourse, we require both analytic skills and poetic sensibilities: the ability *conceptually to elaborate* what is said and the ability *imaginatively to feel* the particular force with which it is said. Even the demons can do analytic theology.

Colin Gunton, in his essay "Dogma, the Church, and the Task of Theology," cites Isidore of Seville, "the last Western church father," who says that dogma means "I judge this to be good, this to be true" (and we could add, "this to be beautiful").[90] Dogmatic discourse articulates what the church judges to be true, good, and beautiful on the basis of the Scriptures. In particular, says Gunton, "the function of dogma is the articulation of the whole,"[91] namely, God's plan to unite all things in Christ (Eph 1:10). Whereas analytic theology concerns clarifying "the parts," what I am calling poetics treats the ways dogmas articulate "the whole."

Dogmas are ecclesial judgments about who God is and what God has done, is now doing, and will do in Christ, based on the observation and contemplation of the form and content of biblical discourse. They are judgments that discern the truth, goodness, and beauty of the unified plot of redemptive history and triune identity of the Redeemer. The "whole" that dogmas articulate is the gospel of God and the God of the gospel. Dogmas are "summaries of gospel material,"[92] identifications of the actors and précis of the plot expressed in the economy of salvation, an economy that communicates in time the way God is in eternity.

Gerhard Sauter says that dogmas "are statements to which we can and must refer because they express linguistically the valid and provisionally enduring content of theological knowledge."[93] Dogmatic discourse characteristically refers everything back to the gospel of God and the God of the gospel. The life and work of the triune God constitute the framework,

---

90. Colin Gunton, "Dogma, the Church, and the Task of Theology," in *the Task of Theology Today*, ed. Victor Pfitzner and Hilary Regan (Edinburgh: T&T Clark, 1999), 3.

91. Ibid., 5.

92. Ibid., 21.

93. Gerhard Sauter, *Gateways to Dogmatics: Reasoning Theologically for the Life of the Church* (Grand Rapids: Eerdmans, 2003), 36.

principium, and whole under which everything else is to be understood. To give a dogmatic account of something, therefore, is ultimately to relate that thing to its origin in creation through Christ and to the redemptive plan of the Father enacted in the Son by the Spirit.

This drama of redemption—the action and its divine players—serves as what we might call, with a nod to Charles Taylor, the Christian social imaginary, that prereflective "doxa" or inherited opinion that theologians inhabit before they examine critically. The Christian imaginary is the biblically normed imaginary of the church, the society of Jesus Christ. It is this storied understanding that frames the church's most important convictions and shapes its most important practices.[94] Dogmatics proves itself in its service to the gospel of Jesus Christ: preserving the integrity of the story, expositing what gives unity to the story, and in general giving direction for understanding, seeing, tasting, and judging everything that is in relation to the drama of redemption and its principal agent, the triune God.

THE MISSION OF DOGMATIC STATEMENTS: A DOGMATIC ACCOUNT

It is out of this Christian imaginary, sourced and normed by the Scriptures, that the church produces dogmatic statements—what Webster calls "astonished indications."[95]

DOGMATIC INDICATIVES: STATEMENTS ON A MISSION

Dogmatic statements are statements on a mission, namely, to state what is happening in the missions of the Son and the Spirit. The risen Jesus assures his disciples that they will receive "power" when the Holy Spirit comes upon them. He also says they will be his witnesses in Jerusalem and to all the ends of the earth (Acts 1:8). The two points are linked: the Spirit enables true witness. We can go further: the Holy Spirit enlists dogmatic statements in his own mission to bear witness to the mission of the Son. How else should we construe Nicene Trinitarianism?

To bear witness is to confess what one has seen, heard, and believed to be true. Paul says that Timothy "made the good [*kalēn*, "wise" or "beautiful"]

---

94. See Charles Taylor, *A Secular Age* (Cambridge, MA: Harvard University Press, 2007), esp. chap. 4; and Taylor, *Modern Social Imaginaries* (Durham, NC: Duke University Press, 2004).

95. "Testimony is astonished indication. Arrested by the wholly disorienting grace of God in Christ and the Spirit, the church simply *points*" (Webster, "On Evangelical Ecclesiology," in *Confessing God*, 185).

confession in the presence of many witnesses" (1 Tim 6:12), and did so in imitation of Christ, "who in his testimony before Pontius Pilate made the good confession" (1 Tim 6:13). The witness is a martyr: one whose life is often at stake because of one's confession. Dogmatic theology is instruction in bearing right witness to the God of the gospel—call it orthomartyrology: to say of what is in Christ that it is.

For Barth, no topic in dogmatics ever really gets beyond the "utterly minimal" statement, "God is."[96] Yet *is* can be said in many ways. There is a poetics of testimony.[97] Consider: the metaphorical is ("is and is not"); the narrative is ("now is, and then is"); the eschatological is ("is already and is not yet"); and, finally, the eternal is ("is now and ever shall be"). The point is that dogmatics guides the church in saying what is in Christ.

Jesus Christ is the first and foremost witness. He is alive, and his presence is communicative. It was he who commissioned John's testimony in the book of Revelation: "I heard behind me a loud voice like a trumpet saying, 'Write what you see in a book'" (Rev 1:12). Everything in Scripture is testimony commissioned by the risen Christ. Dogmatic theology is the church's verbal testimony to the verbal testimony of the prophets and apostles to Jesus Christ. Dogmatic theologians are part not only of a cloud but also a chain of witnesses commissioned to teach the truth of Jesus Christ. A dogmatic statement says what is in Jesus Christ, and it does so only because the church has heard what Christ says about himself in the Scriptures. Demonic discourse may be indicative, technically correct, and perhaps even astonished, but it cannot be joyful, faithful, and adoring, as is dogmatic discourse. Clarity on this point allows us to specify the dogmatic location of Christian dogmatics: it is a part of the economy of light by which the risen Son distributes truth through word and Spirit.

DOGMATICS AT JERUSALEM: A MISSION(S) STATEMENT

One particular beam of light shines through in Acts 15, the episode of the Jerusalem Council. It all started with some men from Judea saying that salvation required circumcision. You see, the circumcision party failed to understand the drama of redemption. They were stuck in "act 2," apparently unaware that the cross did away with the wall of hostility that divided Jew

---

96. See *CD* §28 on "The Reality of God." In one sense, dogmatics is simply (!) the exegesis of this simple statement: "God is" (*CD* II/1, 257).

97. See Paul Ricoeur, "The Hermeneutics of Testimony," in *Essays on Biblical Interpretation*, ed. Lewis S. Mudge (Philadelphia: Fortress, 1980), 119–53.

and Gentile. What was at stake at the Jerusalem Council was nothing less than the integrity of the gospel, and how rightly to represent the God of the gospel by living out its implications.

After much debate (Acts 15:7), Peter testified to a game-changing divine deed: God gave believing Gentiles the Holy Spirit (Acts 15:8). Barnabas and Paul corroborate Peter's story (Acts 15:12). James then cites Amos 9:11–12 and pronounces his judgment: "we should not trouble those of the Gentiles who turn to God" (Acts 15:19). Luke says, "It seemed good to the apostles" (Acts 15:22, 25) and "to the Holy Spirit" (Acts 15:28). Recall that *dogmas* pertain to judgments that something is or is not true, good, and beautiful. Luke uses the term in Acts 16:4 when he mentions "the decisions [*ta dogmata*] that had been reached by the apostles and elders who were in Jerusalem." The Jerusalem Council produced a judgment about what God was doing in Christ. As a result, they were able to agree that requiring circumcision of believing Gentiles lacked fittingness with the drama of redemption. This corporate judgment marks the genesis of dogmatics.

The mission of dogmatic statements is to understand the mission of God and, by implication, the mission of the church. The church's mission is to confess the truth of Jesus Christ. "Confession," says Webster, ". . . is that event in which the speech of the church is arrested, grasped, and transfigured by the self-giving presence of God."[98] Confession is responsive rather than spontaneous; it's an episode in the conflict whereby God overcomes sin, in particular the demonic tendency to say it like you don't mean it. The demons can only acknowledge Jesus as the Son of God, not confess him as Lord: "Without personal identification with Jesus Christ, cognitive specification of who he is remains empty; without cognitive specification of who Jesus Christ is, however, personal identification with him is blind."[99] When the church confesses, it does not simply designate things, it inhabits the language of faith: "it does not convert the drama of redemption into a set of propositions to be policed."[100] To confess is to participate rightly in the economy of testimony. To confess is joyfully to acknowledge Jesus as Lord (cf. Rom 10:9).[101] The demons believe; they cannot confess.

---

98. Webster, "Confession and Confessions," in *Nicene Christianity: The Future for a New Ecumenism*, ed. Christopher Seitz (Grand Rapids: Brazos, 2001), 121.

99. Miroslav Volf, *After Our Likeness: The Church as the Image of the Trinity* (Grand Rapids: Eerdmans, 1998), 148.

100. Webster, "Confession and Confessions," 130. I note with pleasure Webster's positive mention of "the drama of redemption"!

101. Pelikan, *Credo*, 59.

KEVIN J. VANHOOZER

CAN I GET A WITNESS? THE DISCOURSE OF DOGMATICS AND THE GESTURES OF DISCIPLESHIP

Why is there dogmatics rather than nothing? The short answer: to point to what God is doing in Christ and direct disciples to do the same. Barth was impressed by the quasi-miraculous way that Grünewald's Isenheim altarpiece depicts John the Baptist's finger pointing to Jesus. It's also a metaphor for my final point, about the importance of including gestures in dogmatic discourse. Saying what is in Christ involves a certain kind of body language too, namely, action on the part of the body of Christ, the church. This too is part of the poetics of dogmatic discourse. Indeed, the characteristic gesture of Protestant dogmatics is not a fist raised in protest but a finger—or rather, a whole body—that indicates Jesus Christ.[102]

Certain ways of being together would not be possible without language. Without language, says Charles Taylor, humans would lack the crucial capacity "for joint attention, or communion."[103] If this is the case in general, how much more is it the case in that bodily gathering we call the church. Dogmatic discourse does not simply refer to things; it makes possible "a shared consciousness of the world."[104] Specifically, dogmatic discourse enables the church's joint attention on God, the communion of the saints, the coordinated action of Christian witness, and a common confession. Learning the language (dogmatics) is inseparable from learning the life (discipleship).

Dogmatics takes not a village but a body: the church. Recent work in linguistics suggests that gestures—bodily movements that are not mere expressions of experience but communicative actions in their own right— are vital ingredients in both speaking and thinking.[105] Gestures do not simply express thought or language but are part of language.[106] Just as forms of language become intelligible in the context of forms of life, so also gestures disambiguate speech (and vice versa): "Speech acts involve more than emitting the appropriate words. They also involve bodily action, stance, gesture."[107] This should not be entirely foreign to those who confess the

---

102. Interestingly, Pelikan notes that the first example that Basil of Caesarea cites in his treatise *On the Holy Spirit* is "to sign with the sign of the cross" (*On the Holy Spirit*, 27.66, cited in Pelikan, *Credo*, 89).
103. Taylor, *The Language Animal*, 335.
104. Ibid., 333.
105. See Jürgen Streeck, *Gesturecraft: The Manu-facture of Meaning* (Philadelphia: Benjamins, 2009); Jürgen Streeck, Charles Goodwin, and Curtis LeBaron, eds., *Embodied Interaction: Language and Body in the Material World* (New York: Cambridge University Press, 2011).
106. David McNeill, *Gesture & Thought* (Chicago: University of Chicago Press, 2005), 5.
107. Taylor, *The Language Animal*, 98.

46

Word made flesh (John 1:14). The astonished indications that comprise the poetics of dogmatic discourse involve concepts (propositions) and body-language (practices) alike.

In 2 Corinthians 9:13, Paul links the Corinthians glorifying God both to their confession of the gospel and to their generosity in contributing to a gift for the Jerusalem church. This concrete gesture helped the early church express what it meant to be one body. Another characteristic gesture is genuflection, by which a worshiper embodies submission to God by bowing. Hugh of St. Victor wrote a whole book on the pedagogy of gestures, which he defined as a movement of the whole body.[108] For Hugh, gestures speak, and speech is expressive. Dogmatics is as much about learning to imitate God's gestures after him as it is thinking God's thoughts after him.

Dogmatic discourse orients the church's corporate witness and gives guidance to the speech and gestures of the body of Christ. What we do with our bodies in the body of Christ is part and parcel of our Christian witness. To be a disciple is, in part, to have one's embodied experience transformed to show forth Christ's body."[109] Dogmatics helps the church make "Christly gestures."[110]

One particular Christly gesture, replete with theological significance, is the celebration of the Lord's Supper, an enacted summa of the gospel.[111] In sharing the loaf, the church performs its union and communion in Christ. I won't here get into what kind of *is* Jesus had in mind in saying, "This is my body." Suffice it to say that a dogmatic account of the Lord's Supper enables disciples to discern the body (1 Cor 11:29), and in so discerning, to become the body: an instantiation of dogmatic discourse and compelling gesture of dogmatic truth.

In conclusion, dogmatics is the cognitive science or mind of the body of Christ, and exists to build up and help form the church into a holy nation: the city of God. Just as the medieval cathedral was a *summa theologia* that witnessed in the form of stone and glass to the invisible things above, so the forms of experience, thought, and language of the people of

---

108. See Hugh of St. Victor, "On the Formation of Novices" (*De institutione novitorium*). See further Emmanuel Falque, "Le geste et la parole chez Hugues de Saint-Victor: l'Institution des novices," *Revue des sciences philosophiques et théologiques* 95, no. 2 (2011): 383–412.

109. Dan McClain, "Repurposing the Body: Sacramentality and the Poetics of Discipleship," *Anglican Theological Review* 96, no. 2 (2014): 343.

110. See further Brett P. Webb-Mitchell, *Christly Gestures: Learning to be Members of the Body of Christ* (Grand Rapids: Eerdmans, 2004).

111. I have treated this theme more extensively in *Faith Speaking Understanding: Performing the Drama of Doctrine* (Louisville: Westminster John Knox, 2014), 160–66.

God constitute a temple made of living stones (1 Pet 2:5), a living *summa theologia*. Dogmatics aims to re-form minds and hearts, language and lives in order better to conform them to the form of Jesus Christ, the *logos* of God.[112] Forms of biblical discourse and interpretation give rise to forms of right dogmatic thinking and speaking which in turn give rise to right forms of Christian worship and living: "Christly gestures." Dogmatics is a conceptual gesture set forth in speech: an adoring indication of the truth, goodness, and beauty of what is in Christ, and thus a grammatical rule for the body-language of the body of Christ as it seeks to show and tell the glories of the Lord.[113]

---

112. On the importance of reading Scripture, dogmatics, and discipleship as forms for the re-formation of God's likeness in human creatures, see Boyd Taylor Coolman, *The Theology of Hugh of St. Victor: An Interpretation* (Cambridge: Cambridge University Press, 2010), esp. 1–29.

113. I wish to thank the Deerfield Dialogue Group and Ryan Fields for their comments on an earlier draft.

CHAPTER 2

DOGMATICS AS SYSTEMATIC THEOLOGY

Scott R. Swain

INTRODUCTION

Dogmatic theology is "the knowledge that God has revealed in his Word to the church concerning himself and all creatures as they stand in relation to him."[1] Dogmatic theology exists because the God who knows and loves himself in the bliss of his triune life wills to grant creatures a share in his triune bliss by making himself an object of creaturely knowledge and love through revelation. To put the matter in biblical idiom, dogmatics exists because of "the gospel of the glory of the blessed God" (1 Tim 1:11).[2] Accordingly, dogmatics is a subaltern science: the creature's happiness in knowing and loving the triune God flows from and is generated by the triune God's knowledge and love of himself and by his willingness to communicate himself to others. Holy Scripture is the divinely inspired instrument by which the triune God communicates to creatures a share in his knowledge and love. Holy Scripture therefore functions as the supreme source and norm of what is to be believed, what is to be done, and what is to be hoped for according to dogmatic theology.[3] Dogmatics, further-

---

1. Bavinck, *Reformed Dogmatics*, ed. John Bolt, trans. John Vriend (Grand Rapids: Baker Academic, 2003), 1:38.
2. Unless noted otherwise, English Scripture quotations come from the ESV.
3. Dolf te Velde, ed., *Synopsis Purioris Theologiae*, vol. 1, disp. 1–23 (Leiden: Brill, 2014), 1.14; 2.1, 3.

more, has an irreducibly "social element."[4] Dogmatic theology concerns the knowledge of God revealed in and authorized by God's Word in Holy Scripture, and received and recognized by the church in its creeds and confessions, as well as its prayer and praise.[5] Dogmatics, in this regard, is "that movement of believing intelligence by which the church today attends to the instruction of the church past, submitting its received teaching to the rule of Holy Scripture in prayer that we may be of 'the same mind with one another according to Christ Jesus,' and that we may 'with one voice glorify the God and Father of our Lord Jesus Christ' (Rom. 15:4–6)."[6] The subject of theology is the regenerate creaturely intelligence that receives, studies, contemplates, follows, and commends that which God has revealed in Holy Scripture and which has been confessed by the church. The ends of dogmatic theology are the glory of the blessed Trinity and the happiness of the people whose God is the Lord.

Dogmatic theology, thus understood, has a concern for being "systematic." There is a concern for *unity*: for coordinating the teaching found across the various authors, redemptive historical epochs, literary genres, and testaments of the Bible, and for coordinating that teaching with whatever wisdom may be found outside of the Bible. Indeed, some of the most important judgments within a system of dogmatics concern how to relate the wisdom of Holy Scripture with what is known, or what is purported to be known, outside of Holy Scripture. There is also a concern for *scope*: considering the fullness of divine revelation in Holy Scripture, "the whole counsel of God" (Acts 20:27). "The whole of Scripture must prove the whole system," Bavinck declares. And failure to take into account the fullness of biblical teaching "leads to one-sidedness and error in theology and pathology in the religious life."[7] Dogmatics, furthermore, has a concern for *proportion*: "Theology is a comprehensive science, a science of everything. But it is not a science of everything about everything."[8] The Bible has matters of "first importance"—"gospel issues" (1 Cor 15:3), and the Bible has matters of secondary importance (Matt 23:23). Dogmatics cannot afford to neglect matters of either primary or secondary importance. But it must attempt to reflect scriptural priorities within its own conceptual

4. Bavinck, *Reformed Dogmatics*, 1:30.
5. For dogmatic description of the place and function of the church in theology, see Michael Allen and Scott R. Swain, *Reformed Catholicity: The Promise of Retrieval for Theology and Biblical Interpretation* (Grand Rapids: Baker Academic, 2015).
6. Donald Wood, "Maker of Heaven and Earth," *IJST* 14 (2012): 381–82.
7. Bavinck, *Reformed Dogmatics*, 1:617.
8. Webster, "What Makes Theology Theological?," *Journal of Analytic Theology* 3 (2015): 19.

representation of biblical teaching. Finally, there is a concern in dogmatics for *relations* between various elements of Christian teaching. According to Sarah Coakley, dogmatics embraces "the necessary challenge of presenting the gospel afresh in all its ramifications—systematically unfolding the connections of the parts of the vision that is set before us."[9] In giving attention to the unity, scope, proportions, and relations of Christian teaching about God and all things relative to God, dogmatic theology as systematic theology gives attention to the *beauty* of Christian teaching, the doxological character of Christian doctrine.[10]

Systematic theology in the sense described above has been a central feature of Christian teaching throughout much of the church's history. Not only in what Karl Barth calls the "regular dogmatics" of Christian schools, universities, and seminaries, but also in the "irregular dogmatics" of pastoral catechesis and polemics, the church has inherited an embarrassment of riches in the form of books and articles, disputations and treatises that excel in expounding biblical teaching in a systematic manner for the good of the church and the glory of God. At times, systematic theology has even played the role of ruler amid the kingdom of human learning.

The history of systematic theology is not an uncontested one, however. A little over a century ago, B. B. Warfield found he could no longer take for granted systematic theology's right to rule as "queen of the sciences," and found it necessary to defend the discipline's right to exist. Several decades later, Barth would lament the state of academic systematic theology. Speaking of the decline of dogmatic theology in the Ritschlian tradition, Barth concludes, "Nothing we are producing now can stand comparison with the achievements of mediaeval and post-Reformation dogmatics, nor with Idealistic dogmatics, nor with Thomistic, let alone with the dogmatics of the Reformation. Would that we had even reached the point where we again regarded regular dogmatics as at least an admonitory ideal worth striving after!"[11]

Though it has not arrived at its former glory, systematic theology has witnessed something of a revival over the past several decades.[12] Due in part to institutional centers such as the Research Institute for Systematic

---

9. Sarah Coakley, *God, Sexuality, and the Self: An Essay 'On the Trinity'* (Cambridge: Cambridge University Press, 2013), 41.

10. As Aidan Nichols observes, *being* is "encountered most strikingly in aesthetic appearance" (*Chalice of God: A Systematic Theology in Outline* [Collegeville, MN: Order of Saint Benedict, 2012], 13).

11. *CD* I/1, 277.

12. Coakley, *God, Sexuality, and the Self*, 42.

Theology at King's College, London in the 1990s, journals like the *International Journal of Systematic Theology*, and the efforts of leading theologians in the field both to publish and to supervise at a doctoral level high quality academic work, systematic theology today enjoys some degree of prominence as an academic discipline in the English-speaking world. The recent spate of stand-alone and multivolume systematic theologies, which are beginning to appear in print, bodes well for the future of the discipline.

The contemporary ascendancy of systematic theology has not met a completely warm reception among evangelicals. Already in his aforementioned 1897 essay, Warfield observes that systematic theology's "sister discipline" biblical theology is "sometimes found resisting her [systematic theology's] high pretensions and declaring that [she] will no longer have her to rule over [her]." Warfield responds with an end-of-the-nineteenth-century equivalent of the "sick burn." He states, "Systematic Theology may look on with an amused tolerance and a certain older-sister's pleased recognition of powers just now perhaps a little too conscious of themselves, when the new discipline of Bible Theology . . . tosses her fine young head and announces of her more settled sister that her day is over."[13]

Warfield may have underestimated the little sister's potential for disruption within the kingdom of theological disciplines. Her resistance to systematic theology's right to rule among the theological disciplines has not waned among evangelicals since Warfield's day. In fact, as she has further matured, evangelical biblical theology has found further reasons, if not to question systematic theology's right to exist, to question her reliability as a pathway into Holy Scripture. Systematic theology's attempt to "organize" the biblical material in a systematic manner, and its commitment to engaging the doctrinal questions and formulas of the church, one leading biblical theologian argues, tends "to impose a structure not transparently given in Scripture itself" and risks allowing doctrinal debates, rather than the "categories" and "priorities" of the biblical text, to shape the discipline. Because its "ordering principles" are "topical, logical, and hierarchical, and as synchronic as possible," systematic theology "does not encourage the exploration of the Bible's plot-line, except incidentally." "Thus systematic theology tends to be a little further removed from the biblical text than does biblical theology."[14] And this is precisely where little sister has something to

---

13. B. B. Warfield, *The Right of Systematic Theology*, (Edinburgh: T&T Clark, 1897), 15.
14. D. A. Carson, "Systematic Theology and Biblical Theology," in *New Dictionary of Biblical Theology*, ed., T. Desmond Alexander and Brian S. Rosner (Downers Grove, IL: InterVarsity, 2000), 101–3.

offer. "Biblical theology tends to seek out the rationality and communicative genius of each literary genre."[15] Furthermore, biblical theology prevents a "de-historicizing of the gospel by anchoring the person and work of Christ into the continuum of redemptive history."[16] Given its focus on the literary genius of the Bible, and upon the unfolding drama of redemptive history, biblical theology is thus well-equipped to "rescue" her big sister from the bane of theological "abstraction."[17]

More recently, biblical theology's younger cousin, "missional theology," has arrived on the scene at the royal court of theological disciplines. Having been raised by the same historicist nannies, and having sat at the feet of some of the same antispeculative tutors, she too wonders whether her ailing older relative might need a little help in reading and applying the teaching of Holy Scripture. Specifically, missional theology would direct systematic theology to attend more directly to the missional dimension of biblical theology and to order its theological reflection to the church's missional end.[18] Refusal to accept such help, one leading missional theologian suggests, threatens to relegate dogmatics to a state of "sacred egocentricity," to borrow a phrase from Barth.[19] A sanctified systematic theology is one that is on the move with the mission of God.

This game of thrones is admittedly nonviolent. And it is not clear that biblical theology, or missional theology for that matter, has pretensions of assuming systematic theology's now vacant ruling position among the theological disciplines. Still, I hear in the younger relatives' evaluation of their elder the tune from *Annie Get Your Gun*: "Anything you can do, / I can do better."

My purpose in what follows is not to defend the right of systematic theology to exist, much less its right to rule the broader theological or university curricula. My aim is more modest in nature: to commend a particular conception of dogmatic theology as theoretical, contemplative wisdom, a conception that is often missing in the historical, literary, and practical emphases of other theological disciplines but that, more than anything else, accounts for dogmatic theology's "systematic" character. Along the way, I will

---

15. Carson, "Systematic Theology and Biblical Theology," 103.

16. Graeme Goldsworthy, "Ontology and Biblical Theology: A Response to Carl Trueman's Editorial: *A Revolutionary Balancing Act*," *Themelios* 28 (2002): 44–45.

17. Goldsworthy, "Ontology and Biblical Theology," 44.

18. For a thoughtful, recent presentation of these arguments, see Jason S. Sexton and Paul Weston, eds., *The End of Theology: Shaping Theology for the Sake of Mission* (Minneapolis: Fortress, 2016).

19. Michael Goheen, "A Missional Approach to Scripture for the Theology Task," in *The End of Theology*, 19. See also *CD* IV/3.2 (568).

address some of the most formidable objections that have been raised against such a conception of dogmatics in classical and contemporary theology. My argument will unfold in a series of four theses.

THESIS 1: God presents himself to us in his Word under the mode of a vision of glory. Theological wisdom is therefore supremely, but not exclusively, a wonder to behold, a truth to be known, and a doctrine to be believed.

Divine appearance and creaturely vision are characteristic modes of God's self-presentation to human beings in his Word. When God reveals himself to Moses in order to commission him as prophet and instrument of Israel's exodus from Egypt, he *"appears"* to him "in a flame of fire out of the midst of a bush" (Exod 3:2). And this wonder, the wonder of a bush that burns but is not consumed, causes Moses to "turn aside to *see* this great sight" (Exod 3:3).[20] In the context of this divine revelation and appearance, and in the context of Moses's gaze, God proclaims his name to Moses: "I AM WHO I AM" (Exod 3:14), YHWH, the self-existent one, the God of Israel, its maker, redeemer, and reward. When God later consoles his miserable people through the prophet Isaiah, once again we witness the coordination of divine appearance and creaturely vision. "The *glory* of YHWH shall be revealed," the prophet declares, "and all flesh shall *see* it together," for thus "the mouth of YHWH has spoken" (Isa 40:5). And God's commission that his herald proclaim "good news" of the new exodus includes the command to summon the people, *"Behold* your God! *Behold,* YHWH comes" (Isa 40:9–10).

The New Testament proclaims the realization of this Mosaic pattern and the fulfillment of this Isaianic prophecy in the coming of Jesus to save his people from their sins and to establish the dwelling place of the triune God among them. And this coming too is a revelation of divine glory and an endowment of creaturely vision. John the Baptist prepares the prophesied way of *the Lord* in his preaching (Mark 1:2–8), and *Jesus appears* as the beloved Son of the Father, as one baptized in the Holy Spirit that he might baptize others as well (Mark 1:9–11). In the light of John the Baptist's preaching and of Jesus's appearing, the Beloved Disciple confesses: "we have *seen* his *glory,* the glory as of the only begotten Son from the Father, full of grace

---

20. For a standard Reformed treatment of the nature and variety of creaturely visions of God, see Peter Martyr Vermigli's theological commentary on Judg 6:11 in John Patrick Donnelly, Frank A. James III, and Joseph C. McLelland, eds., *The Peter Martyr Reader* (Kirksville, MO: Truman State University Press, 1999), ch. 6. Emphasis added to the Scripture quotations here and those that follow.

and truth" (John 1:14).[21] This vision of divine glory, Peter tells us, at once confirms the prophetic expectation, grounds the apostolic witness, illumines our path in the time between Jesus's first and second advents, and beckons us toward the day when "the morning star" will rise in our hearts (2 Pet 1:16–19). In the brightness of that day, we will behold God's glory and see God's face in the unmediated splendor of blessed Trinity (Rev 22:1–5). This, according to the unified testimony of the prophets and apostles, is our "blessed hope" (Titus 2:13).

This is eternal life: to *know* the only true God, and Jesus Christ whom he has sent (John 17:3). For this reason, Peter Martyr Vermigli claims that "in the holy Scriptures contemplative [knowledge] hath the first place."[22] The Italian Reformer and father of Reformed Thomism adduces a host of biblical witnesses to the primacy of contemplative or theoretical wisdom in theology. Vermigli's first example comes in biblical teaching about justification: "We must first believe, and be justified by faith," he asserts; "afterward follow good works." He also appeals to the pedagogical pattern exhibited in Paul's Epistles: "First he handleth doctrine, afterward he descendeth to the instruction of manners, and to the order of life." Vermigli finds further warrant for his claim in the Old Testament example of Israel: "The children of Israel were first gathered together under the faith of one God the savior. Afterward in the desert they received laws which served unto actual knowledge. And in the table of the ten commandments the same order is observed. For first he sayeth, I am the Lord thy God: which belongeth to faith or speculative knowledge. Afterward follow the precepts, which belong to the works required by God."

Vermigli's claim that theoretical or contemplative wisdom "hath the first place" is not meant to deny the presence of practical wisdom in Holy Scripture: "In the holy Scriptures we have a knowledge of God contemplative, and that which consisteth in action." However, Vermigli insists that contemplative wisdom enjoys both first and final place in relation to practical wisdom. In "the order of sanctification," he argues, both faith and the renewal of the mind precede "just and honest deeds." Moreover, "the end of Christian godliness," he contends, is also contemplative in nature: "The end of Christian godliness is, that in us should be repaired

---

21. In John's theology, the phrase "grace and truth" alludes not only to the self-revelation of YHWH's glory at Sinai (Exod 34.6). It also anticipates the self-revelation of YHWH's glory on the cross (John 8.28; 12.41).

22. Peter Martyr Vermigli, *The Common Places of Peter Martyr Vermilius*, trans. Anthonie Marten (London, 1583), 1.2.13. All quotations below come from this section.

that image, whereunto we were made in righteousness and holiness of the truth, that we may every day grow up into the knowledge of God, until we be brought to see him with open face as he is." For these reasons, Vermigli concludes "that speculative knowledge is preferred above the active. For doing is ordained for contemplation, not contrariwise."

THESIS 2: From this mode of God's self-presentation in his Word arises the (partly) theoretical or contemplative nature of dogmatic theology.

Vermigli offers an early and influential Reformed defense of theology's status as a "mixed" species of wisdom, partly theoretical, partly practical, both *sophia* and *phronesis*. His view finds its root in Thomas Aquinas, who offers similar arguments in part 1, question 1 of the *Summa Theologiae*, and bears fruit later in the Reformed tradition in Franciscus Junius's *A Treatise on True Theology* and in Johannes Polyander's opening disputation in the *Synopsis of a Purer Theology*, "Concerning the Most Sacred Theology."

This view regarding the "mixed" character of dogmatic theology is not uncontested, even within the Reformed tradition.[23] Bartholomäus Keckermann, the first Reformed theologian to give the title of "systematic theology" to a book on Christian doctrine, argues that theology is a purely practical discipline, "the religious prudence to gain salvation."[24] The suggestion that theology is a "mixed" discipline, concerned with both theory and practice, Keckermann avers, "militates against the unity of the discipline of theology."[25]

A response to this objection already lies ready to hand in Thomas's treatment of the issue. The unity of the discipline of theology does not follow from its possession of *either* a purely theoretical object *or* a purely practical object. The unity of the discipline, Thomas insists, "is to be gauged by its object, not indeed, in its material aspect, but as regards the precise formality under which it is an object." "Therefore, because Sacred Scripture considers things precisely under the formality of being divinely revealed, whatever has been divinely revealed"—whether it is a matter of theoretical or practical wisdom—"possesses the one precise formality of the object of this science; and therefore is included under sacred doctrine as under one science."[26] In other words, because Holy Scripture speaks of doctrines and morals, of what

---

23. For the diversity of views, see Richard A. Muller, *Post-Reformation Reformed Dogmatics* (Grand Rapids: Baker Academic, 2003), 1:328–59. Hereafter *PRRD*.

24. Dolf te Velde, *The Doctrine of God in Reformed Orthodoxy, Karl Barth, and the Utrecht School* (Leiden: Brill, 2013), 89.

25. Bartholomaus Keckermann, *Systema sacrosanctae theologiae*, 67, cols. 1–2; cited in Muller, *PRRD*, 1:332.

26. *ST* 1.1.3, co., from (New York: Benzinger Bros, 1948).

is to be believed, of what is to be done, and of what is to be hoped for, and because Holy Scripture provides the precise formality that unifies theology as a discipline, the "mixed" nature of theology's object does not compromise the unity of the discipline. In Holy Scripture, *sophia* and *phronesis* are "like two streams flowing from one fountain."[27]

Objections to the theoretical or contemplative character of theology arise not only from formal concerns about the unity of the discipline. Objections also arise from fears that such a conception of theology renders it *irrelevant* to the concerns of practical Christianity or, worse, *idolatrous*.

In the preface to his classic book, *Knowing God*, J. I. Packer contrasts "two kinds of interest in Christian things" by drawing upon John Mackay's illustration of "persons sitting on the high front balcony of a Spanish house watching travelers go by on the road below."[28] "Balconeers," Packer explains, "can overhear the travelers' talk and chat with them; they may comment critically on the way that the travelers walk; or they may discuss questions about the road, how it can exist at all or lead anywhere, what might be seen from different points along it, and so forth; but they are onlookers, and their problems are theoretical only."[29] By contrast, "travelers . . . face problems which, though they have their theoretical angle, are essentially practical—problems of the 'which-way-to-go' and 'how-to-make-it' type, problems which call not merely for comprehension but for decision and action too."[30] "Balconeers and travelers may think over the same area," Packer observes, "yet their problems differ."[31]

Note well: Packer does not wholly exclude a theoretical dimension from theology. The theology of travelers has its "theoretical angle." But it is a theoretical angle that is oriented to practical concerns about how we should walk, where we should be going, and how we might get there from here. Moreover, Packer seems to suggest that any theoretical concern that is not wholly translatable into practical know-how is somehow suspect. Unprocessed theory is arcane and disinterested, laced with the vice of curiosity and lacking in self-commitment.

The sinister side of theoretical wisdom should not be denied or ignored. We might label theoretical wisdom in its vicious mode "speculation," that

---

27. Borrowing the imagery of Lactantius, cited in Francis Turretin, *Institutes of Elenctic Theology*, ed. James T. Denniston, trans. George Musgrave Giger (Phillipsburg, NJ: P&R, 1992), 1.7.6 (1:22).
28. J. I. Packer, *Knowing God* (Downers Grove, IL: InterVarsity, 1973), 11.
29. Ibid.
30. Ibid., 11–12.
31. Ibid., 12.

mode and product of reflection that goes beyond the bounds of what God has revealed in his Word.[32] Nevertheless, the existence of a vicious mode of contemplation is not remedied by forsaking the balcony of theory for the highway of practice. We should be "anti-speculative" in our theology. We cannot afford to be "anti-theoretical" or "anti-contemplative."[33]

While the objects of theoretical wisdom do indeed provide principles of conduct, informing prudence as it seeks to weigh the wisest course of action in a given situation, the objects of theoretical reason cannot be exhausted by their translation into principles of conduct. When the glory of the Lord descends upon the tabernacle, and later upon the temple, Moses is unable to enter the tent of meeting (Exod 40:34–35), and the priests are unable to minister in the temple because the glory of God overfills its creaturely dwelling place (1 Kgs 8:11). In similar fashion, Paul prays that God the Father, by his Spirit, might enthrone Christ in the hearts of his ecclesiastical temple (Eph 2:19–22) to the end that the knowledge of Christ's love would overfill the church "with all the fullness of God" (Eph 3:14–19). The revelation of God's glory in the face of Jesus Christ grants to contemplative wisdom a surplus, an excess that exceeds not only the possibilities of Christian comprehension, but also the requirements of Christian conduct. In the presence of the glory of the Lord as he presents himself to us in his Word there is wonder: a wonder that begets inquiry, that informs and outstrips our actions, and that finally resolves into greater wonder.[34] "Great is the Lord and greatly to be praised and his greatness is unsearchable" (Ps 145:3).

Theology's attention to this "surplus" dimension of theological wisdom is neither malign nor misanthropic; rather, it is fundamental to human flourishing in the courts of the Lord.

> One thing I have asked of the LORD,
>   that will I seek after:
> that I may dwell in the house of the LORD
>   all the days of my life,

---

32. John of Damascus, *An Exact Exposition of the Orthodox Faith* (New York: Fathers of the Church, 1958), 1.1.

33. The terms "speculative," "theoretical," and "contemplative" function largely as synonyms in the tradition. My pitting of "speculative" against "theoretical" and "contemplative," though meaningful I trust at a conceptual level, is thus contrived at a terminological level. "Speculative," as I use it here, closely approximates the vice of "curiosity," on which see John Webster, "Curiosity," in *The Domain of the Word: Scripture and Theological Reason* (London: T&T Clark, 2012), ch. 10.

34. Bavinck, *Reformed Dogmatics*, 1:619–21.

> to gaze upon the beauty of the LORD
> and to inquire in his temple. (Ps 27:4)

To J. I. Packer's fear of malign and misanthropic "theory," I would present Josef Pieper's *Happiness and Contemplation*.

The worry that characterizing theology in part as a species of contemplative wisdom might foster irrelevance is closely related to the worry that such a characterization might foster idolatry. Oswald Bayer ably articulates this worry in his study, *Theology the Lutheran Way*. Therein, Bayer takes no prisoners, assailing theoretical, existential, and moral conceptions of theology and in their place offering a conception of theology as essentially linguistic (and to this Vanhoozer protégé, quite compelling): a doctrine of the varied forms of the Word of God.[35] According to Bayer's conception, the object of theology is neither theoretical, as Hegel suggests, nor existential, as Schleiermacher suggests, nor moral, as Kant and his epigones suggest. The object of theology, as Luther defines it in his commentary on Psalm 51, is "the sinful human and the God who justifies."[36] God's encounter with the human being in his Word of law and gospel constitutes the unity of theology as a discipline.[37] Theology accordingly "suffers" the Word in its varied work, whether it be in the church as worship or in the academy as science, and in so doing theology is renewed in its thinking, feeling, and acting before God.[38]

Under the critical eye of Bayer, the problems with a theoretical or contemplative conception of theology are legion. Two stand out. First, such a conception attempts to mediate and reconcile all things under the umbrella of a single, totalizing theory of "the One, the True, the Good, and the Beautiful."[39] Second, such a conception threatens to abstract the theologian from his or her specific context as a creature of history.[40] In both cases, "it bypasses the cross of Jesus Christ," which shatters sinful humanity's totalizing illusions and situates him in God's presence, not as a generic human being but as a justified sinner.[41]

---

35. Oswald Bayer, *Theology the Lutheran Way*, ed. and trans. Jeffrey G. Silcock and Mark C. Mattes (Grand Rapids: Eerdmans, 2007), 94.

36. Ibid., 98.

37. Ibid., 105.

38. Ibid., 27, 105–106. The theme of the "pathos" of theology is further developed by Reinhard Hütter, *Suffering Divine Things: Theology as Church Practice*, trans. Doug Stott (Grand Rapids: Eerdmans, 1999).

39. Bayer, *Theology the Lutheran Way*, 26.

40. Ibid., 34.

41. Ibid., 26.

How should we respond to these concerns? With Bayer, we may grant that a theoretical conception of theology as enunciated in German ideal- ism and epitomized in Hegel is susceptible to these criticisms, along with a host of others. (I am reminded of Robert Jenson's famous comment that Hegel's only error was to confuse himself with the final judge of history!) However, the many errors of Hegel in particular and of German idealism in general are not addressed by *forsaking* the theoretical nature of theology but rather by *moderating* it. Bayer himself shows the path toward moderation in following the traditional Protestant orthodox example of locating "our theology" within its pilgrim context: *under* God, *short* of the beatific vision. Locating the creaturely contemplation of God and of all things relative to God within a pilgrim context allows us to admit, indeed insist upon, the limited nature of our contemplation as wayfarers (*viatores*) traveling east of Eden and short of the eternal kingdom. It also alerts us to the unavoidably contested nature of theology in the here and now and acknowledges the importance of lament in the space opened by the mismatch between God's promises and present circumstances. Finally, locating creaturely contem- plation within a pilgrim context directs us to expect perfect contemplation only in the beatific vision of the triune God.

Here I would note my own worry about Bayer's "Lutheran" proposal. Bayer's conception of the object of theology as "the sinful human and the God who justifies" (unwittingly) threatens to narrow the range of God's self-presentation in his Word.[42] God does indeed present himself in Holy Scripture as justifier of the ungodly (Rom 4:5)—to the praise of his match- less grace. But this does not exhaust the nature of God's self-presentation in his Word. Nor can God's identity as justifier of the ungodly finally be appreciated apart from a broader conception of God's triune identity and of God's triune works in nature, grace and glory.[43] God presents himself in Holy Scripture as thrice-holy wonder; as creator and providential ruler; as redeemer, justifier, and sanctifier of sinners; and as perfecting reward of the saints, along with the rest of the created world. And these varied forms of God's self-presentation in his Word must also find their place in

42. I say "unwittingly" because Bayer is mindful of the need to avoid reductionism and attempts to do so by following the Lutheran practice of defining the Word in its fourfold form of confron- tation with human beings and by identifying the topics of theology as God, self, and world (contra Rudolf Bultmann's reduction of the subject matter of theological understanding to God and the self).

43. John Webster, "*Rector et iudex super omnia genera doctrinarum?* The Place of the Doctrine of Justification," in *God without Measure: Working Papers in Christian Theology* (London: Bloomsbury T&T Clark, 2016), vol. 1, ch. 10; Michael Allen, *Justification and the Gospel: Understanding the Con- texts and Controversies* (Grand Rapids: Baker Academic, 2013).

our conception of the object of theology. "Great are the works of the Lord, studied by all who delight in them" (Ps 111:2).

This leads us to the primary reason for acknowledging the theoretical dimension of dogmatic theology. Dogmatics derives its character as theoretical, contemplative wisdom from its primary object: the triune God. The triune God who presents himself to us in his Word as an object of intelligent adoration presents himself to us under the name of YHWH, the self-existent, independent one. God's identity as the triune YHWH determines every feature of his being and activity *ad intra* and *ad extra*. God is "independent, not only in his existence but consequently also in all his attributes and perfections, in all his decrees and deeds. He is independent in his intellect (Rom. 11:34–35), in his will (Dan. 4:35; Rom. 9:19; Eph. 1:5; Rev. 4:11), in his counsel (Ps. 33:11; Isa. 46:10), in his love (Hos. 14:4), in his power (Ps. 115:3), and so forth."[44]

God in his being—and, through the revelation of his name, God in our reflection—exists in and of himself in the bliss of his triune life. God does not exist for any reason that lies outside of himself. Quite the contrary, "we exist for him" (1 Cor 8:6). Indeed "from him and through him and to him are all things" (Rom 11:36). Thus, while the study of God promotes innumerable practical ends and is of utmost relevance, comprising the supreme happiness of rational creatures, the study of God is not exhausted in its service of practical ends. God is not, as Ritschl suggests, "a 'Hülfsvorstellung'—a useful postulate for the validating of our practical ends."[45] The gospel reveals a truth that accords with godliness (Titus 1:1). And the godliness that gospel truth informs, in turn, prepares us for further contemplation of God and for the full realization of human happiness in the vision of God (1 Tim 4:7–10; Titus 2:11–14; Heb 12:14). "God is wisdom's goal, and that glimpse of God himself is saving and filled with glory, toward which we strive with this wisdom as our guide."[46]

THESIS 3: As theoretical or contemplative wisdom, theology is not a view from nowhere. Dogmatic theology is a view of God from God in the presence of God.

As a species of theoretical or contemplative wisdom, engaged by pilgrims as they are led by the Word out of the misery of sin into the bliss of God's

44. Bavinck, *Reformed Dogmatics*, 2:150.
45. Warfield, *Right of Systematic Theology*, 52, on Ritschl, Kant, and Hermann.
46. Franciscus Junius, *A Treatise on True Theology*, trans. David C. Noe (Grand Rapids: Reformation Heritage, 2014), 102.

eternal kingdom, dogmatic theology occupies itself with God. Dogmatic theology is a view *of God*.

Because God is not only the self-existent one but also the author and end of all things, theology's object is twofold. It fathoms the unsearchable depths of God's infinite and independent being, wisdom, goodness, and power: "Oh, the depth of the riches of the wisdom and knowledge of God! How unsearchable are his judgments and how inscrutable his ways! For who has known the mind of the Lord, or who has been his counselor? Or who has given a gift to him that he might be repaid?" (Rom 11:33–35). Theology also fathoms the unsearchable depths of God's works: "all things," which are "of him and through him and to him" (Rom 11:36). Theology's twofold object is the thrice-holy "Lord God Almighty" (Rev 4:8) and all things relative to God as "Alpha and Omega, the first and the last, the beginning and the end" (Rev 22:13).

Given its universal scope, theology contemplates objects also contemplated by other disciplines: philosophers contemplate God, anthropologists contemplate human beings, botanists contemplate the lilies of the field. What distinguishes dogmatic theology as a discipline is not the uniqueness of its objects, though theology certainly knows things about God, humanity, and even the lilies of the field that other disciplines fail to know. What distinguishes dogmatic theology as a discipline is the perspective from which it knows God, humanity, and the lilies of the field. Dogmatics knows these things from the perspective of divine revelation in Holy Scripture: from the perspective of God's self-naming as the triune YHWH (Matt 28:19), from the perspective of God's naming human beings "Adam" (Gen 5:2), from the perspective of God's teaching regarding the lilies of the field as objects of his fatherly care and providence (Matt 6:28–29).[47] Dogmatic theology is a view of God *from God*.

Theology's knowledge of God and all things relative to God is not derived, first and foremost, by ascending from creatures to their author and end (cf. Rom 1:19–20). Theology's knowledge of God is hidden from the wise of this world (Matt 11:25). The world by its wisdom does not know God (1 Cor 1:21). Theology knows God and all things relative to God because God stoops down to us and unfolds, from the inside out, the mystery of his triune life and of his triune purpose for all things: "All things have been handed over to me by my Father, and no one knows the Son except the Father, and no one knows the Father except the Son and

---

47. *ST* 1.1.3, co.

anyone to whom the Son chooses to reveal him" (Matt 11:27). "No one comprehends the thoughts of God except the Spirit of God. Now we have received not the spirit of the world, but the Spirit who is from God, that we might understand the things freely given us by God" (1 Cor 2:11–12).

This is why dogmatics, on the present understanding at least,[48] does not follow the method, common to so many sciences, of reasoning from the totality of created effects back to their principles and causes, both created and uncreated. The method of dogmatic theology is to begin with God, the self-subsistent Trinity, and to trace the works of God "from him and through him and to him" as their principle and end, and that because that is how God has revealed himself and all things in relation to himself in his Word (Gen 1:1; Prov 8; John 1:1–18; Rom 11:33–36; 1 Cor 8:6; Col 1:15–20; Heb 1:1–4). Thus, according to Thomas Aquinas, sacred doctrine is "wisdom above all human wisdom," in part because it "treats of God viewed as the highest cause—not only so far as he can be known through creatures just as philosophers knew him . . . but also so far as he is known to himself alone and revealed to others."[49] Dogmatic theology's method is "analysis by principles" rather than "analysis by elements."[50]

Dogmatic theology's view of God "from God" (i.e., from the perspective of divine revelation) contributes to its "scientific" character. Drawing upon an Aristotelian conception of wisdom, Jason Baehr defines *sophia* as the "deep explanatory understanding of epistemologically significant subject matters."[51] What constitutes wisdom as scientific, on such a conception, is not simply its cognition of this or that feature of reality but also its ability to indicate the *reasons or causes* for this or that feature of reality and to grasp the *relationships* between this or that feature of reality.[52] Materially stated, theology, as a species of contemplative wisdom, is "scientific" because it considers all things *in terms of their relationships to one another and, ultimately, in terms of their relationship to God, their efficient, exemplary, and final cause.* Formally stated, theology is scientific because it considers all things *in view of their meaning and purpose as interpreted by the divine counsel insofar as the divine*

---

48. Once again, the Reformed tradition presents a variety of views on this issue. See Muller, *PRRD*, 1:207–8.

49. *ST* 1.1.6, co.; Junius, *Treatise on True Theology*, 102; *Synopsis Purioris*, 1.10.

50. Kenneth L. Schmitz, "Analysis by Principles and Analysis by Elements," in *The Texture of Being: Essays in First Philosophy* (Washington, DC: Catholic University of America Press, 2007), ch. 2; John Webster, *Domain of the Word*, vii.

51. Jason Baehr, "Theoretical Wisdom and Contemporary Epistemology," in *Virtues and Their Vices*, ed. Kevin Timpe and Craig A. Boyd (Oxford: Oxford University Press, 2014), 310.

52. Baehr, "Theoretical Wisdom and Contemporary Epistemology," 311–312. Compare with Charles Hodge, *Systematic Theology* (repr.; Grand Rapids: Eerdmans, 1997), 1:2.

counsel has been unveiled to us in Holy Scripture. Theology has been granted "deep"—though by no means exhaustive—"explanatory understanding" of God and all things relative to God because God has made "known to us the mystery of his will, according to his purpose, which he set forth in Christ as a plan for the fullness of time, to unite all things in him, things in heaven and things on earth" (Eph 1:9–10). We have been granted a share in "the depths of God" (1 Cor 2:10) because we have been granted a share in "the mind of Christ" (1 Cor 2:16).

Does a scientific conception of dogmatics threaten to turn dogmatics into a Spinozan *more geometrico demonstrata*, where every item within the system follows from its first principles by means of a "rigid logic"?[53] No. As Polyander explains, theology is scientific because "it is the knowledge of things that are necessary, either without relation to any other being, as for example of God and his attributes, or of things that are necessary on the presupposition of God's will, such as knowledge of his worship and works."[54] In other words, in knowing the triune God, theology knows an object that exists by "absolute necessity." God exists *by nature* (Exod 3:14; John 5:26). In knowing the works of God, however, theology knows objects that exist by virtue of a "hypothetical necessity." The works of God exist *only as a consequence of God's free and generous will*, which "loves" creation into existence: "in order that it should be, and in order that it should abide."[55] In studying God, theology considers the eternally perfect, complete, and necessary act of being, knowledge, and love that is God's blessed triune life. In studying the manifold works of God, however, theology does not attempt to deduce the works of God from God or from one another. Instead, it attends to the "dramatic" necessity that accompanies the contingencies of creatures and creaturely events under the wise and loving providence of the blessed Trinity, their author and end.[56]

To the preceding points we may add another. As dogmatic theology is a view of God from God, it is also a view of God *in the presence of God*. The point is worth emphasizing, given our stress upon the scientific character of dogmatic theology: Dogmatics does not contemplate God and all things in

53. Colin Gunton, *Intellect and Action: Elucidations on Christian Theology and the Life of Faith* (Edinburgh: T&T Clark, 2000), 28.

54. *Synopsis Purioris*, 1.10.

55. Augustine, *The Literal Meaning of Genesis*, 1:8, 14 in *On Genesis*, trans. Edmund Hill (Hyde Park, NY: New City, 2002), 173. On the metaphysics assumed here, see Richard A. Muller, *Divine Will and Human Choice: Freedom, Contingency, and Necessity in Early Modern Reformed Thought* (Grand Rapids: Baker Academic, 2017).

56. Robert Jenson, *Systematic Theology* (New York: Oxford University Press, 1997), 1:64.

relation to God from a God's eye point of view. When it comes to God's own knowledge of himself and all things (i.e., archetypal theology), Junius says, "we should not seek to trace it out but rather to stand in awe."[57]

Our theology (i.e., ectypal theology), *our* dogmatics, contemplates its twofold object from a humbler vantage point: "*with* all the saints" (Eph 3:18), *as* a servant of the Lord, *as* a priest in God's holy temple. In this regard, "To profess theology is to do holy work. It is a priestly ministration in the house of the Lord. It is itself a service of worship, a consecration of mind and heart to the honour of His name."[58]

THESIS 4: As a view of God from God in the presence of God, dogmatic theology takes a "systematic" shape in commending the fruits of its contemplation.

Given its pilgrim state *under* God and *short* of the beatific vision, dogmatic theology must beware the dangers of what the late John Webster calls "excessive systematic pretension." Nevertheless, as that Reformed Thomist would also remind us, the limitations "placed upon systematic intelligence" in our pilgrim state are but *restrictions*, not *prohibitions*. Webster continues: "Little theological profit is yielded by the reduction of systematic thought to false consciousness. Theological self-deprecation along these lines appears modest, but the underlying assumption—that there are no systematic intellectual virtues, only intellectual vices—betrays lazy trust in indeterminacy to deliver the mind from folly."[59]

What shape, then, might a modest system of dogmatic theology take? We can only lament, with the loss of John himself, the loss of John's contribution to the genre of systematic theology. However, taking as its starting point Paul's declaration of astonished, contemplative wonder in Romans 11:33–36, and instructed by John's sketches and intimations on the subject here and there, a system of theology might fittingly be constructed in the following manner.

Following a brief introduction to the nature, object, principles, practitioners, and ends of dogmatic theology,[60] a system of theology might treat, first, "the depth of the riches" of the triune God in his unfathomable being (Rom 11:33). Treating God "in himself" before treating God in his relationship to us is not a particularly welcome move in contemporary

---

57. Junius, *Treatise on True Theology*, 111.
58. From Herman Bavinck's inaugural address as Professor of Systematic Theology, Free University of Amsterdam.
59. John Webster, "Principles of Systematic Theology," in *Domain of the Word*, 145.
60. On which, see John Webster, "What Makes Theology Theological?"

theology. In the first volume of his systematic theology, *Theology for Liberal Protestants*, Douglas Ottati treats the doctrine of God as the third major topic, having treated, first, the cosmos, and, second, the human being. His intention is to avoid speaking "of God or the divine nature as it is or may be 'in itself'" and to speak only of God "in relationship with the world as creation and ourselves as creatures." The first proposition he introduces on the doctrine of God states that "theological language is peculiar because God is not an object alongside other objects—and is not knowable as other objects are knowable."[61] Such a proposition is, of course, both true and admirable. However, given Ottati's commitment to treating God exclusively in relation to creatures, he struggles to deliver on the promise of his leading proposition when it comes to theological exposition. "God is not an object alongside other objects that we can measure, distinguish, and define with precision," Ottati states. "Instead, the divine is a reality that we sense *in and through* our interrelationships and encounters with other things."[62] While it is certainly true that, for pilgrim theology at least, our access to God always comes through creaturely media and our sensation thereof, this explanation hardly constitutes an adequate statement of divine transcendence of creaturely categories. Something at once more substantial and more concrete by way of dogmatic description is required.

Treating God "in himself" before treating God in relation to creatures is essential to the extent that theology's contemplation of God aims to be contemplation of his revealed name YHWH. The infinite fullness of the Father, the Son, and the Holy Spirit in their eternal relations of communication, knowledge, and love is not a fullness that God receives from anyone or anything else: "who has given a gift to him that he might be repaid?" (Rom 11:35). The answer is: no one. He is who he is (Exod 3:14; Rev 1:8). "Blessed be his glorious name" (Ps 72:19).

Moreover, treating God "in himself" before treating God in relation to creatures allows theology to properly characterize God's relation to creatures as a "mixed relation," real on the side of the creature but not on the side of God.[63] Far from portraying God as aloof and disengaged from his creatures, such a relation characterizes God's relationship to his creatures as one of absolute benevolence, where God is "absolute giver"

---

61. Douglas F. Ottati, *Theology for Liberal Protestants: God the Creator* (Grand Rapids: Eerdmans, 2013), 313.
62. Ibid., 314.
63. Robert Sokolowski, *The God of Faith and Reason: Foundations of Christian Theology* (Washington, DC: Catholic University of America Press, 1995); Webster, *God without Measure*, 1:115–16.

and the creature is "absolute receiver."[64] God, the blessed Trinity, does not relate to creatures in order to add anything to his perfect life but in order to manifest the fullness of his glory and goodness to and upon the creature and in so doing to bring the creature into its appointed perfection. "Talk of the eternal fullness of God's triune life—theological interest in the hypostatic relations of Father, Son and Spirit that constitute and suffice for the divine life, without addition—secures the divine manifestation without acquisition, and with it the marvellously disinterested interest that God takes in us."[65]

Again following the lead of Paul's doxology in Romans 11, a system of theology might treat, second, the works of God, "all things" that are "from" and "through" and "to" the blessed Trinity (Rom 11.36). The gospel identifies God not only as "the blessed God" (1 Tim 1:11) but also as "the King of the ages" (1 Tim 1:17). Accordingly, a system of theology must trace "the economy of God" (ἡ οἰκονομίαν θεου, 1 Tim 1:4) as it unfolds in the works of nature, grace, and glory. Each of these three works of God is *distinct* from the others,[66] their interrelationship not being one of an unfolding world process but of God's "plan for the fullness of time" (Eph 1:10). Nevertheless, each of God's three works is *related* to the others within God's counsel and purpose: in God's good pleasure, God's good work of creation, ruined by sin, is restored and perfected through God's works of grace and glory. *Gratia non tollit naturum, sed perficit.*[67]

Third, with respect to each individual topic within a potential system of theology, there is the need to connect each topic not only to other topics, relating, for example, sin to grace and justification to good works. There is also the need to connect each individual topic, by means of causal analysis, to God as its efficient, exemplary, impulsive, and final cause. This is not due to an occasionalist impulse that would deny the integrity of God's various creatures in their diverse natures, activities, and ends. It is due to the fact that, strictly speaking, the natures, activities, and ends of God's various creatures only exist in relation to God, their supreme author and end, and therefore that each of God's various creatures can only be understood *with theological intelligence* in relation to God their supreme author and end. It is one thing, for example, to trace biblical teaching about the church as temple

---

64. Charles P. Arand, "Luther on the Creed," *Lutheran Quarterly* 20 (2006): 4.

65. Donald Wood, "Maker of Heaven and Earth," 389.

66. Ian A. McFarland, *From Nothing: A Theology of Creation* (Louisville: Westminster John Knox, 2014), 159–60.

67. *Synopsis Purioris*, 11.11.

along a redemptive-historical trajectory and quite another to relate the church as temple to its triune maker (Eph 2:19–22) and goal (Eph 3:20–21). Only in the latter case do we obtain a truly *theological* understanding of the church as the temple of God.

In following this method or "way through" its various topics, a system of dogmatic theology proves itself true to its name as "theology." Dogmatics, expounded as such, "describes for us God, always God, from beginning to end—God in his being, God in his creation, God against sin, God in Christ, God breaking down all resistance through the Holy Spirit and guiding the whole of creation back to the objective he decreed for it: the glory of his name." Such a system of theology also proves that, far from being "a dull and arid science," dogmatics "is a theodicy, a doxology to all God's virtues and perfections, a hymn of adoration and thanksgiving, a 'glory to God in the highest' (Luke 2:14)."[68]

CONCLUSION

In the preceding argument, I have attempted to commend a conception of dogmatic theology as a "mixed" discipline, partly theoretical, partly practical, focusing on the generative basis of such a conception in Holy Scripture, drawing out some of its major implications, and addressing some of the objections posed against it in classical and contemporary theology. I have also suggested how a contemplative understanding of dogmatics might inform a "system" of theology as an elaboration of the knowledge of God and all things relative to God. In drawing the argument to a conclusion, I want to return to the question of how such a conception might relate to the broader theological and academic curriculum.

While the primarily historical, literary, and practical emphases of the disciplines of biblical theology and missional theology can eclipse, and in many cases have eclipsed, the theoretical and contemplative dimensions of Christian teaching, the same need not be said for the discipline of dogmatics, with its mix of theoretical and practical emphases. Dogmatic theology can function as an inclusive rather than an exclusive discipline in relation to other disciplines. Because of its attention to the supreme object of Christian knowledge and obedience, the triune God, and because of its concern to order all things in relation to him, dogmatics has the capacity for providing a framework that can both organize and preserve the integrity

---

68. Bavinck, *Reformed Dogmatics*, 1:112.

of other disciplines devoted to the various hermeneutical, historical, and literary aspects of exegesis, and to the various moral, pastoral, liturgical, apologetic, and missional aspects of Christian ministry, not to mention other enterprises of human learning, for these disciplines too are finally ordered to the glory of the triune God and to our well-being in him. To the extent that the church and various institutions of higher learning are ready and able to acknowledge this, there may yet be an opportunity for dogmatic theology as systematic theology to take its place, once again, as queen of the sciences: for the good of the world and for the flourishing of human beings in beholding and reflecting the glory of our blessed and triune God. "To him be glory forever" (Rom 11.36).

CHAPTER 3

CHRISTIAN DOCTRINE AS ONTOLOGICAL COMMITMENT TO A NARRATIVE

SAMEER YADAV

CHRISTIAN DOGMATICS AND METADOGMATICS

Suppose that you are savoring a fine German sausage and ask yourself "how is this sausage made?" To satisfy your curiosity, you decide to observe what German sausage-makers actually do in order to produce tokens of tasty meat—so you shadow some representative group of sausage-makers and note both their stated and practiced aims and methods for identifying German sausages, producing them, and commending them to sausage enthusiasts such as yourself. But having done this, you find that among your representative group of German sausage-makers there are very different and in fact incompatible approaches to the practice of German sausage-making.

Further inquiring about these disagreements, you come to discover that whereas some such disagreements are merely controversies about whose preferred practices best achieve some commonly recognized norms for making the best sausages, other disagreements seem deeper. Sometimes sausage-makers justify their preferred practices not in terms of which best conform to shared norms of German sausage-making, but rather in terms of different and competing norms of German sausage-making. In these instances, you find sausage-makers disagreeing about what genuinely counts as an authentic German sausage, who has the proper credentials to identify,

70

produce, and commend German sausages, and the best methods for doing so. Deep divides in the practice of German sausage-making turn out to be grounded in competing *theories* of the norms of German sausage-making. So in your quest to understand the task of sausage-making, you find that some disagreements are *meta*-sausage-making disagreements—disagreements about the nature and content of the norms of German sausage-making, the standards of correctness for making German sausage.

When we savor the religious teachings constitutive of a Christian confession—perhaps including the Trinity, the incarnation, or the atonement—we can likewise wonder just how the *dogmatic* sausage is made, so to speak. We might follow the lead of our sausage enthusiast and attempt to satisfy our curiosity by shadowing some representative sample of theologians that Christians have taken to be responsible for the task of formulating Christian doctrines and commending them for Christian belief. Were we to do so like the sausage enthusiast, we would find that the diversity and conflicts in the practice of Christian dogmatics parallels the diversity and conflicts in the practice of German sausage-making: the doctrinal aims of various theologians seem ordered to different and sometimes incompatible ends by way of different and sometimes incompatible methodological approaches. Moreover, as in the case of sausage-making, so too here, much of the conflict and diversity we find in the practice of Christian dogmatics is grounded in deep theoretical disagreements about the norms of Christian dogmatics—metadogmatic disagreements about what Christian doctrines are and what they're for, about which or what criteria any proposed doctrine must meet in order to count as authentically Christian, about who has the proper credentials to identify, produce, and commend Christian doctrines, and about which methods are best for so doing.

The task of articulating and defending a metadogmatics was an especially important feature of North American theology in the 1980s and '90s, largely in connection with the so called "postliberalism" of the Yale school associated especially with the works of George Lindbeck and Hans Frei.[1] In *The Nature of Doctrine,* Lindbeck attempted to explain the diversity

---

1. There is some debate as to whether there really is or was any coherent social, institutional, or conceptual basis for marking out postliberalism as a unified theological movement. In *Trial of the Witnesses: The Rise and Decline of Postliberal Theology* (Oxford: Wiley-Blackwell, 2006), for example, Paul DeHart attempts to distance Frei from Lindbeck and argues that the lumping of their projects under the auspices of "postliberalism" is mistaken. John Allan Knight, however, has provided a convincing rebuttal to that thesis by demonstrating the deeply shared commitments in the philosophy of language that undergird both of their theological projects. See Knight, *Liberalism vs. Postliberalism: The Great Divide in Twentieth-Century Theology* (New York: Oxford University Press, 2013).

SAMEER YADAV

of practice in Christian dogmatics in terms of theologians' commitments to one of three distinct theories of what "doctrines" are.[2] On one theory, doctrines are informative propositions, on another they are expressions of experience, and on a third they are cultural-linguistic rules, and the differences we find in the modern and contemporary practice of the dogmatic task depend on which of these three metadogmatic theories the theologian holds. When Christian theologians are formulating and commending Christian doctrines, Lindbeck claims, they accordingly construe their task in one of three ways: their job is (1) to formulate some informative propositions that describe some objective realities in the same sort of way we find in the sciences, (2) to construct some symbols that express some inner feelings, attitudes, or existential orientations, or (3) to describe some regulative rules that govern a subset of cultural and linguistic practices.[3]

Hans Frei's posthumously published *Types of Christian Theology* similarly aims to explain the diversity of methods in Christian dogmatics in terms of five types of orientation toward the relative uniqueness of Christian confession.[4] If one takes a view of Christian doctrines as expressions of more generic truths, then theologians should attempt to understand and evaluate those expressions in terms of the methods of the general human, social, and physical sciences. But if the subject-matter of Christian doctrines falls outside of the domain of those disciplines as utterly unique, then it will only be intelligible and evaluable in terms of the community's internal language and the practices of its adherents.[5] Christian dogmatics governed by the metadogmatic commitments of a purely community-internal self-description is a form of "witness," while Christian dogmatics governed by the metadogmatic commitments of purely community-external description is a form of critical "reduction."

But in addition to these purely community-internal and community-external theories of doctrine, one might recognize more or less of an admixture of generic and unique content, best served by more or less methodological correlation with non-Christian academic disciplines. Thus next to pure reduction of the sort Frei finds in Gordon Kaufman (his "Type I"), he also recognizes in David Tracy and Wolfhart Pannenberg a form of

---

2. George A. Lindbeck, *The Nature of Doctrine: Religion and Theology in a Postliberal Age* (Philadelphia: Westminster, 1984), 15–19.
3. Ibid., 18.
4. Hans Frei, *Types of Christian Theology*, ed. George Hunsinger and William C. Placher (New Haven, CT: Yale University Press, 1992).
5. Ibid., 2.

72

reductive criticism more open to the uniqueness of Christian witness as a distinctive exemplification of its genera (Type II). In Schleiermacher's translation of Christian doctrine in terms of religious feeling Frei finds an equipoise between reduction and witness (Type III). He takes Karl Barth's dogmatics to be an attempt to give a theology of witness open to external scrutiny as a kind of critical self-description (Type IV). Finally, he takes D. Z. Phillips's appropriation of Wittgenstein to illustrate dogmatics ordered entirely to internal self-description (Type V).[6] So (presumably) whatever sort of form we suppose doctrine to take (whether propositional, experiential, or cultural-linguistic), Frei claims that our theory about its relative uniqueness will determine the aim of the dogmatic task along the spectrum of witness and reduction as well as the best methods for achieving that aim.

In the few decades since Lindbeck and Frei first attempted to survey the metadogmatic landscape, their proposed taxonomies of the available theories of the dogmatic task have undergone two sorts of developments: the critical revision of one or more of the theories in their taxonomy,[7] or else the proposal of some novel metadogmatic theory that does not clearly fall within the scope of Lindbeck's models or Frei's types.[8] What I propose in this paper is not to add my criticisms or revisions, nor to propose another alternative proposal to set alongside all the others on the list. Instead, I want

---

6. Ibid., 28–55.

7. To cite just a few examples: see Kathryn Tanner's criticism of Lindbeck's reliance on Geertz for a theory of culture, and her revision in the direction of a more "hybrid" picture of Christian cultural identity in her *Theories of Culture: A New Agenda for Theology* (Minneapolis: Fortress, 1997). See also Christine Helmer's recent retrieval of Schleiermacher's conception of doctrine as a complicated interplay between experience and language in *Theology and the End of Doctrine* (Louisville: Westminster John Knox, 2014). Helmer, in my view, offers a more expansive vision of what Lindbeck calls an "experiential-expressivist" model of doctrine as over against a cultural-linguistic one. One way to read Francesca Murphy's criticisms of the "narrative theology" that she identifies with postliberalism in *God Is Not a Story: Realism Revisited* (New York: Oxford University Press, 2007) is as an extended plea for a recovery of what Lindbeck mostly dismisses as a "propositional" model of doctrine, insofar as it emphasizes the metaphysical dimension of doctrinal exploration as aimed at objective realities. DeHart, *Trial of the Witnesses*, revises received readings of Frei to offer a retrieval of his constructive project. Michael Rea proposes some interesting ways of appropriating Frei to classify the methodology of analytic theology regarding the divine attributes. See "Die Eigenschaften Gottes als Thema der analytischen Theologie," trans. Martin Blay, Daniela Kaschke, and Thomas Schärtl, in *Eigenschaften Gottes: Ein Gespräch zwischen systematischer Theologie und analytischer Philosophie*, ed. Thomas Marschler and Thomas Schärtl (Münster: Aschendorff, 2016), 49–68.

8. Medi Ann Volpe, for example, has argued that Lindbeck's taxonomy leaves out traditional views of the development of doctrine as aimed at the moral and spiritual formation of the theologian. See *Rethinking Christian Identity: Doctrine and Discipleship* (Oxford: Wiley-Blackwell, 2013), 13–25. Knight, *Liberalism vs. Postliberalism*, criticizes the whole of both liberal and postliberal theology as grounded in competing accounts of meaning and reference which are now largely defunct in the analytic philosophy of language, and calls for theology to proceed in dependence upon more recent theories of meaning and reference (principally those in the paradigm of Kripke). Lindbeck's taxonomy also arguably excludes contemporary theology informed by more recent theological turns in the phenomenological tradition as influenced by e.g., Jean-Luc Marion.

to note the kind of metadogmatic theorizing represented in this literature and then to offer a metadogmatic theory of a categorically different sort.

The observation is that we can distinguish between two different kinds of metadogmatic theory, each of which serves a different sort of aim. If our interest is to adjudicate the differences in dogmatic practice by appealing to a theory of the norms of dogmatic practice, there are two different kinds of norms that might interest us. On the one hand, we might be after a theory of the norms that tell us what counts as engaging in the dogmatic task *properly*, in doing it well rather than badly. On the other hand we might be after a theory of the norms that tell us what counts as engaging in the dogmatic task *simpliciter*—norms that someone has to satisfy in order to count as engaging the task of dogmatics at all, whether well or badly.

Let's go back to sausages. Consider professed German sausage-makers Horst and Ludger. On Horst's theory, to count as an authentic German sausage, the sausage must be made in Germany from German animals. Ludger disagrees—as long as the relevant processes are observed, the provenance of the sausage doesn't matter. However, neither Horst nor Ludger deny that the other one is actually a German sausage-maker engaged in the task of German sausage-making. It's just that each holds a theory of the norms of *good* sausage-making according to which the other is not a *good* sausage-maker. But we can also imagine Horst holding a much stronger view about his norm of provenance. He might think that satisfying the norm is not only necessary for making German sausage *well*, but that satisfying it is necessary for making German sausage *period*. Ludger, in that case, whatever he may think he's doing, is not in the business of German sausage-making at all.

How then should we classify the metadogmatic theories outlined by Lindbeck, Frei, and those who have responded to them in proposing their various revised and alternative theories? Are these all theories about what it takes to engage in the dogmatic task well, or theories about what it takes to count as engaging in it at all? It seems clear enough to me that they are interested in the former rather than the latter. Lindbeck advocates for a rule-theory of doctrine over a propositional or experiential-expressivist theory, but he nevertheless recognizes that those whom he takes to be guided by the wrong theories in their formulations of Christian doctrine nevertheless count as engaging in the task of Christian dogmatics.[9] Similarly, Frei's is critical

---

9. Lindbeck's defense of a cultural-linguistic theory of doctrine concludes by characterizing that theory not as ruling out alternative approaches to doctrine by definition, but rather as involved in a performative contest with them whose outcome remains as yet undetermined. See *Nature of Doctrine*, 134–35.

of the metadogmatic norms guiding theological method in Types I, II, and V, and he contends instead for the more "witness" based methodologies of critical self-description in his Types III and IV. But this does not lead him to conclude that after all there are only two types of Christian theology, and that the others are merely theology *manqué*, not truly instances of Christian theology at all.[10] The current landscape of disputes about the proper norms that ought to govern Christian dogmatics have likewise continued to maintain this same focus. Insofar as they exhibit a sustained willingness to count the fellow-disputants in their metadogmatic debates as participants in the task of Christian dogmatics, we ought to interpret their theorizing about the norms for formulating and commending Christian doctrine as attempts to convince those disputants to engage in that task *properly*, not attempts to get them to see that they are in fact not engaging in it at all.[11]

If this is so, then it has the surprising consequence that much of the most influential metadogmatic theorizing in the past thirty-odd years has had comparatively little to say about how we ought to theorize the shared norms of the dogmatic task that define the field of disagreement about the norms of doing that task well or badly. We may have achieved a good deal of clarity about the vast and growing terrain of competing conceptions about how Christian dogmatics ought and ought not to be done. But the variety and diversity of those conceptions as well as the apparent depth of their conflicts has had the effect of making it difficult to see how it could be that those guided by such different norms might be engaged in the same basic kind of work. It is thus likely to be controversial whether there is any commonly shared framework of the Christian dogmatic task within which we can interpret the disputes about its proper execution. And if we are inclined to think that there is such a shared framework, it will be a matter of metadogmatic controversy just how we ought to analyze it.

In the remainder of this paper, therefore, my aim will be to offer the beginnings of just such a metadogmatic theory. What I propose is that, whether the disputants about the proper execution of the dogmatic task recognize it or not, they are all likewise engaged in that task, whether well or badly, insofar as they are all engaged in the task of making explicit some sense in which Christians are ontologically committed to a Christian

---

10. Frei's preferred conception of theology is merely the one that he "likes best." See Frei, *Types of Christian Theology*, 13.

11. Thus, when Helmer criticizes, e.g., a cultural-linguistic conception of the doctrinal task, she is attempting to question the priorities and limits of a certain way of doing theology, she is not attempting to define them out of the dogmatics business. See Helmer, *The End of Doctrine*, 14–20.

narrative of creation and redemption. To formulate and commend Christian doctrine, I claim, is at a minimum, to formulate and commend ontological commitment to a narrative. On my theory, therefore, the disputes stemming from Lindbeck about the nature of doctrinal content should be interpreted as disputes about the nature of the content expressed by a Christian narrative of creation and redemption. The disputes stemming from Frei about the aims and methods best suited to the formulation of Christian doctrine should be interpreted as disputes about the aims and best methods for articulating a Christian's ontological commitments to the content of a Christian narrative.

ONTOLOGICAL COMMITMENT TO A NARRATIVE

The proper subject matter for the kind of doctrinal reflection that constitutes the dogmatic task on my theory is a narrative, a Christian story of creation and redemption through Christ. One abbreviated version of the story might go like this:

The one God who created all things made humans in the divine image, but in virtue of their sin humans have tragically fallen from their created purpose of bearing that divine image. But God in love and mercy set about restoring and redeeming humankind from their fallen condition and restoring proper relationships between God, self, and creation. This redemption was first mediated through the life of Israel and then through the fulfillment of Israel's promises in the arrival of their promised Messiah, Jesus of Nazareth. In the self-giving love of Jesus's life, death, and resurrection from the dead, God the Son came to dwell with humankind and remedy the alienation and death brought by human sin. Upon Christ's ascension, God's Spirit continues to mediate Christ's redemption to the world through the redeemed community of the church, which continues to serve God's redemptive purposes in the world while awaiting a final consummation of those purposes at the end of the present age.[12]

---

12. For an argument of the identity-constituting nature of narratives, as well as a slightly different summary of a Christian narrative, see Christian Smith, *Moral, Believing Animals: Human Personhood and Culture* (New York: Oxford University Press, 2003). For a more explicitly metadogmatic argument about the function of a *scriptural* story in constituting a Christian religious identity, see David Kelsey, *The Uses of Scripture in Recent Theology* (Minneapolis: Fortress, 1975); Hans Frei, *The Eclipse of Biblical Narrative* (New Haven, CT: Yale University Press, 1980); Nicholas Wolterstorff, "Living within a Text," in *Faith and Narrative,* ed. Keith Yandell (New York: Oxford University Press, 2001), 202–216; Sameer Yadav, "Scripture as Signpost," in *Sensing Things Divine*, ed. Frederick D. Aquino and Paul L. Gavrilyuk (New York: Oxford University Press, forthcoming). My conception of the role of a Christian narrative derives from the role given to Scripture in these works of Protestant theology, but with an expanded slot for that role which might be filled by other potential sources of doctrinal authority for Christian communities.

A salvation-historical narrative framework of this sort could be further adumbrated or else expanded in many different ways. It may require revision to include additional elements or omit others. It may exhibit the wrong narrative shape in the relevant agents and actions or themes it tracks. Clearly there is no one commonly accepted way that Christian theologians have told the Christian story about God's creating and saving work. Christian theologians routinely disagree on all the details of the above-mentioned sort. Still, one would be hard pressed to find a theologian whose engagement in the task of formulating or commending Christian doctrine was not in some way giving a descriptive or explanatory gloss on what it is that Christians mean or ought to mean when they appeal to some such story as constitutive of their religious identities. Indeed, the idea of Christian doctrinal reflection that is in no way a reflection on the meaning, reference, significance of a Christian story of God's creation and redemption through Christ has a vaguely incoherent or self-contradictory ring to it. The reason for this, I submit, is that the task of Christian dogmatics just is the task of determining the meaning, reference, or significance of some such story.

This is not to say, however, that the dogmatic task as such requires the theologian to take up an affirming stance toward all or any part of that story as it literally stands. Identifying the relevant story as a basis of Christian teaching is not tantamount to identifying what it teaches.[13] Nor is it defining of Christian dogmatics to place any necessary and sufficient conditions on what kind of agential or textual, discursive, or social processes a narrative or any part of that narrative must have in order to make it a proper object of doctrinal reflection. It is safe to say that the relevant story will usually have among its paradigmatic sources the Christian Bible along with the textual and interpretive traditions of its production and use as Scripture in the church.[14] But the relevant story or part of the story that serves as the

---

13. Rudolf Bultmann's dogmatic work furnishes us with a good example of this distinction, insofar as his demythologizing project depends upon first recognizing the importance of what it is that Christians receive in the deposit of their tradition, before turning to query it for what God might and might not be revealing by way of that deposit. For an excellent exegesis of the nature and significance of that project, see David Congdon, *The Mission of Demythologizing: Rudolf Bultmann's Dialectical Theology* (Minneapolis: Fortress, 2015).

14. Appealing to a Christian narrative therefore does not necessarily privilege narrative theology as it is often conceived, or narrative criticism of Scripture, or even the "post-critical" retrievals of premodern practices of theological interpretation more generally. Instead, it is a minimalistic claim that *however* one negotiates the normative significance of the authoritative sources of doctrine that are defining of a Christian identity, that significance will ultimately take the form of a description of some story about God's relation to the world and its significance for the unfolding of human life here and now. The fact remains that Christian adherence to some such story underdetermines any particular metaphysical, epistemological, and moral construal of that story. We can expect

basis for doctrinal reflection may also derive from ecclesial traditions or official teachings beyond and outside the Bible, etc.[15]

In other words, while it is a defining feature of the Christian dogmatic task that it is a form of reflection on a Christian story of creation and redemption, those engaged in that task nevertheless can and do disagree about the proper sources of that story, the proper processes by way of which it has come to be an important mark of Christian identity, or the kind of internal shape or coherence it must have, etc. All of these more particular determinations about what constitutes a Christian story of creation and redemption are manifestly matters of dogmatic (and metadogmatic) dispute, but they are disputes about what sort of credentials a story ought to have to merit becoming the object of the dogmatic task. Grounding that task in a story with the wrong credentials doesn't preclude one from genuinely engaging in the task, only from doing so well, much like building an edifice with bad materials doesn't preclude one's activity from counting as an act of building an edifice. Likewise, the common need to identify a relevant narrative of creation and redemption to serve as the object of doctrinal reflection can explain the wide range of disputes we find about the proper sources of Christian doctrine.

Aside from the source of a Christian story, another important indeterminacy in my account worth noting has to do with what it is *about* a Christian narrative that supplies the relevant information for formulating Christian teachings. So, suppose you endorse Lindbeck's taxonomy on the nature of doctrinal content (along with whatever subsequent revisions you take it to require). Interpreted on my metadogmatic theory, you would thus hold that whereas some look to the relevant Christian story of creation and redemption to derive the propositional or cognitive content it conveys about some objective religious realities, others look to that story as a norm for expressing the content of a Christian religious experience, and others find in it the regulative rules that govern a Christian form of life. In each case, some suitably identified story of creation and redemption is serving as the

---

that the identification of the appropriate story to which Christians ought to adhere and the proper metaphysical, epistemological, and moral construal of that story will be matters of dispute.

15. Thus, I take this account to be compatible with various versions of Christian confession, which would include Roman Catholic accounts of the dogmatic task of the sort we find in, say, Paul J. Griffiths's *The Practice of Catholic Theology: A Modest Proposal* (Washington, DC: Catholic University of America, 2016). I am simply too ignorant of the dogmatic task as practiced by, say Mormons or Jehovah's Witnesses to judge whether they can be counted as satisfying this criterion for being engaged in the task of Christian dogmatics, but I suspect that they can, with most of the contention of many mainstream Christian theologians being whether it is possible to execute the Christian dogmatic task properly within the constraints that Mormons or Jehovah's Witness theologians place upon the sources of dogmatics.

basis for "doctrine" variously understood. Christian doctrines, therefore, are expressions of whatever the relevant sort of content is that a narrative of creation and redemption conveys as Christian teaching. Disputes about how to properly characterize the relevant sort of content conveyed by a Christian narrative can explain the wide range of competing metadogmatic theories we find about the nature of doctrine.

We have thus far identified some commonly shared metadogmatic norms about the narrative source of Christian dogmatics and its role as an evidence base for the doctrinal outputs of dogmatics, but not the nature of the dogmatic task itself. What sort of reflection is doctrinal reflection? What is the aim that defines one's orientation to the relevant sort of doctrinal content of a Christian story as an instance of engaging in the dogmatic task? I take the defining aim of Christian dogmatics—one that is shared across its various competing metadogmatic construals—to be that of determining for Christians what it is to which their story *ontologically commits* them. While philosophers have understood the notion of ontological commitment in various ways, I follow Bradley Rettler in taking it to mean that when the content of a sentence implicitly or explicitly represents things as being a certain way, and one affirms that sentence, then one is thereby committed to there actually being something (or some things) that makes that sentence true.[16]

For example, if in uttering some sentence I affirm or imply that there are tables, then I have thereby ontologically committed myself to there being something that makes it correct to affirm that there are tables, even if I don't know what it is about the world that explains, accounts for, or makes it the case that there are tables. So maybe what makes it correct to say that tables exist is that there exist some subsets of atoms arranged table-wise, or maybe what makes it correct is some much larger state of affairs, like the current state of the world, or perhaps some phenomenologists are right and what makes it true to say that there are tables is just the appearance of tables to us in a certain way. Simply by affirming that there are tables, I don't ontologically commit myself to whatever *specific* truthmaker is responsible for ensuring that I have spoken correctly. Rather, I only ontologically commit myself to the more general belief that *something* (or *some things*) is so responsible.[17] But whereas it is not necessary for us to know what the specific truthmakers are for the content of the sentences we affirm, it is the metaphysician (or physicist, or

---

16. See Rettler, "The General Truthmaker View of Ontological Commitment," *Philosophical Studies* 173 (2016): 1405–25.
17. This is my own slightly revised way of putting the summary he gives. See Rettler, "The General Truthmaker View," 1405.

phenomenologist) who ought to be "in the business of investigating what the truthmakers are/must be/could be for various sentences."[18]

On my analysis, the relevant sentences for the theologian are sentences belonging to a Christian narrative of creation and redemption, and the relevant sort of content affirmed by those sentences is determined by some antecedent theory of doctrinal content of the sort explored by Lindbeck. So if some feature of a Christian story includes a sentence such as "God was in Christ reconciling the world to himself" (2 Cor 5:19 NASB), and if the doctrinal content expressed by that sentence is a proposition that represents God's being in Christ reconciling the world to himself as an objective reality, then Christians are (or ought to be) ontologically committed to there being something (or some things) that makes (or make) it the case that God was in Christ reconciling the world to himself. If, on the other hand, the doctrinal content expressed by that sentence is the content of an inner feeling, attitude, or existential orientation, then Christians are (or ought to be) ontologically committed to there being something (or some things) that makes (or make) it the case that there are such inner feelings, attitudes, or existential orientations. Or if the sentence instead expresses the doctrinal content of a rule regulative of Christian practices of reconciliation, then Christians are (or ought to be) ontologically committed to there being something (or some things) that makes (or make) it the case that there are such rules that regulate their practices of reconciliation.

But just as it is the metaphysician's (or whomever's) job to investigate just what the truthmakers are for various sorts of sentences, what defines the task of Christian dogmatics is just to investigate what the specific truthmakers are, must be, or could be for the sentences constitutive of a Christian story of creation and redemption. Christian doctrinal formulations, however else they might be understood, are always at bottom just attempts to do two things: (1) to make explicit the Christian's ontological commitments and (2) to identify their specific truthmakers. Suppose, for example, that the relevant Christian story that provides the content for the dogmatic task includes (or can be made to include by the right sort of doctrinal theorizing) sentences about God as Trinity: Father, Son, and Holy Spirit.[19] In that

---

18. Ibid., 1421.
19. Of course, whether Trinity-talk belongs to the story that serves as the object and evidence-base for doctrinal reflection or whether we must earn the right to include such talk in our story by way of dogmatic work (i.e., by deriving it as a doctrinal formulation from some prior narrative that makes no reference to it) depends on one's metadogmatic views about the proper sources of doctrinal reflection.

case, we should take Christians to be ontologically committed to whatever makes it the case that God is triune.

On Christine Helmer's version of what we might call an experiential-expressivist view of doctrinal content, for example, such Trinity-talk would express the doctrinal content of there being some transformative experience of a reality whose pressures on our use of words and concepts merits our articulation of that experience in terms of Trinitarian language.[20] Christians are thus in her view ontologically committed to there being something (or some things) that makes (or make) it the case that there are transformative experiences of a reality whose pressures on our use of words and concepts merits our articulation of that experience in terms of Trinitarian language. An explication of the doctrine of the Trinity consists in articulating just what it is that makes it the case that there are such experiences, in terms of an exploration of the possible metaphysical, historical, cultural grounds that could explain such an experience.[21] Those theologians adopting a different metadogmatic view of the sort of doctrinal content expressed by Trinity-talk, however, will identify the ontological commitments of such talk differently, and that will no doubt send them searching after altogether different sorts of specific truthmakers to further explicate whatever it is that they take the doctrine of the Trinity to express.[22]

This theory of doctrinal explication as the explication of ontological commitment to a narrative leaves open the question of how to theorize the appropriate methods of investigation best suited for that task. It only requires that we interpret the range of possible approaches to the task of doctrinal formulation and commendation as various proposed approaches to specifying the truthmakers for the doctrinal content of a Christian narrative. So recall Frei's taxonomy of the five types of theology, from those that most completely reduce the content of Christian doctrine to claims explicable by the humanistic, social, and natural sciences, to those that treat that content as most completely irreducible to explication in any terms other than that of the internal self-description of a Christian community. On my analysis, all five of Frei's types on this spectrum are predicated on different theories of the epistemic availability of the specific truthmakers for the doctrinal content to which Christians are ontologically committed. But

---

20. Helmer, *The End of Doctrine*, 112–13.
21. Ibid., 169.
22. For example, Bruce Marshall has argued that the very concept of truth has a Trinitarian shape, and that not only orthodox beliefs about the Trinity, but all truths are made true by a Trinitarian reality. See Marshall, *Trinity and Truth* (New York: Cambridge University Press, 2000), 242–82.

we can interpret all five types as sharing the same basic aim of specifying what the relevant truthmakers are for their preferred notions of Christian doctrinal content and determining their methods for doing so by assessing the epistemic constraints that content imposes on us. For example, suppose, with Helmer, that we take Christians to be ontologically committed to experiences of a reality that merits our Trinity-talk.

But suppose, contrary to Helmer's view (as I read her), that the truth-maker of that experience is only identifiable by way of the experience itself, and further that the relevant experience is *sui generis*, irreducible to any other sort of experience to which I might compare it. In that case, we can imagine an experiential-expressivist taking up something like a self-descriptive witness view of a sort that belongs somewhere near Type V of Frei's taxonomy, while Helmer's own view might belong closer to a Type II or III. The methodological difference between the two, however, is explicable in terms of their different judgments about the epistemic availability of the relevant doctrinal content (in this case, an experience).

A final shared norm that I take to be a defining feature of the task of Christian dogmatics is that of the possibility of orthodoxy and heresy. Given the vastly different metadogmatic standards for determining what counts as good and bad doctrine, it might seem implausible to suppose that there is any shared conception of orthodoxy or heresy at work in defining the task of Christian dogmatics per se. But I suspect that the idea of specifying a truthmaker for our ontological commitments makes something in the neighborhood of those notions available to us. Two of the claims I've made thus far are especially relevant. First, I've claimed that a Christian narrative of creation and redemption is or includes a narrative that is in some way constitutive of a Christian identity. If a Christian denies or refuses to affirm a sentence that is constitutive of a Christian identity, then that Christian thereby denies or refuses a Christian identity. Suppose, for example, that Christians are ontologically committed to the claim that Christ is morally perfect or impeccable, and further that affirming the moral impeccability of Christ expressed by the Christian story is essential to a Christian iden-tity. In that case, for a professing Christian to claim that Christ is in fact immoral is to thereby deny something essential to a Christian identity. Such a denial, we might say, is a *heresy*, whereas its contrary, the affirmation of Christ's impeccability, is an *orthodoxy*. On the other hand, if there are sentences of the Christian story that we can judge to be nonfundamental or inessential for constituting a Christian identity, then while Christians may be ontologically committed to them, denying them may have various sorts of consequences for their Christian identity, but it does not amount to a denial or refusal of that identity.[23]

But, secondly, I've also claimed that it is the business of Christian dogmatics to investigate what the truthmakers *are*, *must be*, or *could be* for the doctrinal content expressed by the sentences of such a narrative. So if a Christian theologian succeeds in identifying something that *must be the case* in order for the doctrinal content expressed by a sentence to be true, and the sentence expressing that content is constitutive of a Christian identity, then it follows that one can deny a Christian identity not only by rejecting the content expressed by the relevant sentence, but also by denying what *must be the case* in order for that content to be true. So, for example, suppose that while Christian narrative ontologically commits us to Christ's impeccability as a matter of orthodoxy, it does not explicitly commit us to any particular claims about Christ's sexuality. Now further suppose that it must be the case that being impeccable is incompatible with being disposed to committing sexual assault. It would thereby follow that Christians are ontologically committed as a matter of orthodoxy to the view that Christ was not disposed to committing sexual assault.

To take another example, suppose that a Christian story constitutive of a Christian identity ontologically commits Christians to holding that there is a single entity identifiable as God, while identifying that entity with three distinctly divine persons, Father, Son, and Holy Spirit. And now further suppose that the necessary truthmaker for that ontological commitment is something that fits the traditional, Nicene formulation of the Trinity. It follows that Christians are thereby ontologically committed to the traditional formulation of the Trinity in the Nicene Creed. Identifying what *could be* or what is *actually* but *needn't be* the case to make a Christian's ontological commitments true, however, might be an important matter for the dogmatic task, but they will not be matters of orthodoxy or heresy. Whenever Christians deny or disagree about either something inessential to the story or about something that merely could be but is not necessarily a truthmaker for something essential to that story, they do not flout any norms of orthodoxy and as such cannot court heresy. To be orthodox is to be ontologically committed to whatever doctrinal content is expressed by the identity-constituting features of a Christian narrative as well as

---

23. Rowan Williams spells out this internal relation between orthodoxy/heresy and the gradual evolving of a normative Christian identity or self-understanding in *Arius: Heresy and Tradition*, (Grand Rapids: Eerdmans, 2001), 22–25.

being committed to the necessary truthmakers of that content.[24] To be a heretic, conversely, is just to deny or refuse the ontological commitments of orthodoxy.

My proposed theory of the Christian dogmatic task can therefore be summed up this way: to engage in the task of Christian dogmatics is to explicate the Christian's ontological commitments to the doctrinal content expressed by a narrative of creation and redemption, to identify the specific truthmakers for that content, and to appropriate the methods best suited to the epistemic availability of those truthmakers. Insofar as the dogmatic task involves making judgments of orthodoxy and heresy, those judgments are made on the basis of affirming or denying what is deemed to be either essential to a narrative constituting Christian identity or else a necessary truthmaker of one's ontological commitment to the doctrinal content of such a narrative.

META-METADOGMATICS? TOWARD AN ECUMENICAL METATHEOLOGY

I have been thinking about a way of defining the Christian dogmatic task as a kind of metadogmatic theory: it is the most general and commonly shared norm that guides the task of Christian dogmatics as it is variously practiced.[25] As such, I have argued that the theory can accommodate the wide and deep metadogmatic disagreements about what counts as a good and faithful execution of the dogmatic task. But it also occurs to me that the theory plays a similar structural role with respect to these divergent metadogmatic theories that those theories themselves play with respect to the practice of dogmatics. That is, whereas dogmatics attempts to explicate the substance of Christian confession and commend its teachings to Christians, and metadogmatics attempts to explicate the norms that guide the task of dogmatics, what I have proposed can rightly be read as an attempt to explicate the norm that guides the task of metadogmatics, the common standard of correctness that guides theologians when they are

---

24. Note that claiming some truthmakers are necessary for the doctrinal content expressed by a story to be true is not the same as claiming that the truthmaker necessarily *exists,* only that the truth of the doctrinal content expressed by the story necessarily depends on its existing whether it exists necessarily or not.

25. Much of what I've said thus far has been in a descriptive mode, as an analysis of what I take to be the formal backdrop that in fact governs what theologians are doing, whether they recognize it or not. But insofar as my theory is a controversial one or faces rivals, I would also want to argue that this is what the task of Christian dogmatics *ought* to be.

trying to explicate the norms that ought to guide the task of dogmatics. So perhaps my theory is best seen not as a metadogmatic theory but instead a meta-metadogmatic theory.

I'm not sure much is at stake in the terminological issue. But I do wish to avoid giving the false impression that the order of determination for these three distinct levels of theorizing is a strictly top-down affair. On that picture, first we should fix the more general underlying norms of doctrinal theorizing, then we can be guided by those to determine the more specific norms of doctrinal theorizing, until at last (if we aren't too tired by then) we may finally get around to actually engaging the task of deriving particular doctrinal formulations about, say, the meaning, reference or significance of the incarnation.

On the contrary, the direction of our theorizing may well (and often does) include a bottom-up rather than top-down type of doctrinal theorizing. It may well be the case that, for example, the way we understand Christian teaching about the incarnation has significant implications for what we think we ought to be doing when we formulate and commend doctrines, or for what we take to be a common feature defining of all Christian dogmatics. Nor do I wish to suggest that we can resolve lower-level controversies simply by appealing to higher-level theories. For one thing, the higher-level theories leave open what sort of theories best satisfy their norms. For another, we should expect that our meta- (and meta-meta-) dogmatic theories are or could become every bit as controversial as our first-order dogmatic views about the incarnation, for example. But if all this is so, then what's the use of offering such a theory?

What initially sent us looking for a theory of the defining norms of Christian dogmatics that all of its practitioners share was just our noticing how deep and wide the metadogmatic disagreements are between them, whether those disagreements conform to the taxonomies suggested by Lindbeck and Frei or not. Ironically, what originally motivated Lindbeck's work on the nature of doctrine was an interest in ecumenical dialogue. He hoped that by advocating for a cultural-linguistic theory, he could find a basis for recognizing common rules that regulate a Christian form of life despite the deep differences in the propositional or experiential commitments that divide Christians. But the reception history of Lindbeck in North American theology has mostly resulted in fomenting a corresponding sense of division amongst theologians. The state of post-postliberal theology has encouraged a kind of tribalism amongst theologians operating under distinct paradigms of the dogmatic task with their own literatures and conversation partners, and without much engagement with alternative paradigms.[26] It's almost like the taxonomies and their revisions function like a noncompete clause, or an injunction to "stay in your own lane."

The purpose of articulating a more expansive theory of the task of Christian dogmatics that can place all of these competing paradigms on the same field of discourse is thus very much in the spirit of Lindbeck. If our attention can be turned from our preferred theories of doctrinal sources, content, method, and the role of doctrines in defining Christian belonging, and if we can instead fix our gaze on the common desiderata that all our rival theories are trying to secure, then perhaps our gaze will meet, and our preferred theories will confront questions that they are not often enough made to answer.

So, for example, analytic theologians might become more open to engaging the metadogmatic theories of postcolonial, black, or feminist theologians who identify colonial, white supremacist, or patriarchal corruptions of their preferred evidence base, content, methods, or standards of communal belonging. Likewise, recognizing that the deep structure of their theorizing involves a form of ontological commitment, liberationist theologians might become more open to the methods of working out such commitments offered by a theological use of contemporary analytic philosophy. If a mutual recognition of our shared interests in the dogmatic task made engagements of that sort possible, then I suppose that the task of Christian dogmatics would be better for it.

---

26. If you doubt this, then simply attend the next American Academy of Religion meeting, mark your schedule to attend papers covering the same general theological topics in the Theology and Continental Philosophy Group, the Postcolonial Theology Group, the Analytic Theology Group, and the Systematic Theology Group. Then make a note of the shared theological norms, argument strategies, aims, and bibliographical sources across those papers. My prediction is that you will come up with very few, if any, such shared norms, strategies, or sources.

CHAPTER 4

"KNOWLEDGE PUFFS UP, BUT LOVE BUILDS UP": THE APOSTLE PAUL AND THE TASK OF DOGMATICS

CHRIS TILLING

> *Revelation is a way of indicating the communicative force of God's saving, fellowship-creating presence. . . . The knowledge of God in his revelation is no mere cognitive affair: it is to know God and therefore to love and fear the God who appoints us to fellowship with himself, and not merely to entertain God as a mental object, however exalted. . . . The idiom of revelation is as much moral and relational as it is cognitional.* JOHN WEBSTER[1]

INTRODUCTION

An essay on the "task of dogmatics" is not usually something a New Testament scholar would be invited to write. Surely this is a subject best left to the systematic theologians among us, whose job it is to explicate theological themes, their purposes and interrelationship. New Testament

---

1. Webster, *Holy Scripture: A Dogmatic Sketch,* Current Issues in Theology 1 (Cambridge: Cambridge University Press, 2003), 16. Much of what follows is a Pauline articulation of crucial aspects of Webster's dogmatic work on Scripture, from which I have learnt much.

specialists, on the other hand, are supposed to be concerned with historical matters, with the social, cultural, and religious particularity of this or that text, with the grammatical and lexical questions surrounding the translation of given sentences, and so on. Dogmatics requires a different skill set, different interlocutors, *different books.* What is more, the thought that a New Testament specialist, like myself, might have something to add to a conversation about dogmatics might be frowned upon by other members within my own guild. New Testament scholars are meant to proceed on the basis of public (if not objective) methods which are neutral with regards to faith commitments articulated in terms of dogmas. I am delighted to write this essay, however, for on the contrary I believe that one of the most pressing needs for biblical studies is to relearn theological literacy, to open doors of communication with dogmaticians, and I hope that the following will facilitate these kinds of conversations. First and to this end, I focus on the apostle Paul with half an eye on questions relating to the task of dogmatics. Second, I will highlight a key moment in the theological tradition that has captured this Pauline set of concerns. Third, these two sections will enable us critically to engage some modern trends in systematic theology, trends that arguably need to reexamine Paul's insights.

THE TASK OF DOGMATICS IN PAUL'S THEOLOGICAL IDIOM

To explicate what one could call the task of dogmatics within Paul's theological idiom, I turn to a rather curious and complex argument in the middle of his second longest letter, 1 Corinthians. This passage is usually mined, simply, for the low-hanging fruit of 1 Corinthians 8:6, which has been called a christological redefinition of Jewish monotheism.[2] But this verse is part of an explicitly epistemological argument, which we must address in order to clarify matters relating to purpose and the language of "task."

The situation concerns certain Corinthian Christ-followers who want to enjoy food offered to idols in the temple precincts. This was not just about enjoying a more varied menu, but offered opportunities for striking up business deals and pursuing financial contacts. Wanting to justify participation in these idol-honouring feasts, for to be absent would be a bad business move, certain Corinthian Christians offered theological rationale.

---

2. See, e.g., N.T. Wright, *The Climax of the Covenant: Christ and the Law in Pauline Theology* (Edinburgh: T&T Clark, 1991), 121.

Schrage reconstructs their position as follows: "We have the authority to eat meat offered to idols because we all have knowledge and know there are no idols in the world and there is no God apart from one."[3]

As Volker Gäckle has maintained in a deeply learned study on the "strong" and the "weak" in Corinth and Rome, these Corinthians are to be characterized as intellectual snobs (on the basis of their own words embedded within Paul's argumentation). An "aristocratic consciousness shines through," Gäckle argues in comment on 1 Corinthians 8:1, "one grounded on *an intellectualized knowledge of the world and God*."[4] These Christians looked upon the "weak" as those with a "cognitive-rational deficit," hence the posture of their grasp of knowledge is to be understood in terms of intellectualized, rationalistic discourse.[5]

As Paul explains beginning in 8:7, their position, and the consequently justified practices, were causing harm to other Christians. It seems that other church members saw these "knowledgeable" Christians going into the idol temple to eat food offered to the various gods, and were then led to go and join them. But these "weak" Christians, not knowing what the Corinthian knowledgeable knew, could only participate in such feasts in a way that meant unambiguous idol worship. In so doing, these weak brothers were "destroyed."[6] So the theological justifications of the "knowledgeable" became "a stumbling block to the weak" to such an extent that their existence as Christians was jeopardized (1 Cor 8:9).

But before Paul explains the problem of the Corinthian position in terms of its impact on other Christian brothers and sisters, he first makes an *epistemological* argument. This appears at the beginning of this section, in 8:1–7, and we will spend some time grappling with this now, for it speaks into our questions about the task of dogmatics.

Although this passage contains numerous puzzles that I cannot address today, I hope to steer a course around many of the choppy waters by leaning on conclusions that I and others have already drawn elsewhere. In particular, I will assume (with the majority), rather than defend, the presence

---

3. Wolfgang Schrage, *Der erste Brief an die Korinther* (Zürich: Benziger, 1995), 2:221; trans. mine. Original: "Wir haben die Vollmacht, Götzenopferfleisch zu essen, den wir haben alle γνῶσις und wissen, daß as keinen Götzen in der Welt und keinen Gott gibt außer dem einen."

4. Volker Gäckle, *Die Starken und die Schwachen in Korinth und in Rom: Zu Herkunft und Funktion der Antithese in 1 Kor 8,1–11,1 und Röm 14,1–15,13* (Tübingen: Mohr Siebeck, 2005), 190, trans. and italics mine. Original: "Wie fast alle korinthischen Zitate und Begriffe lässt auch dieses Zizat ein aristokratisches Bewusstsein durchsheinen, das auf eine intellektuelle Welt-und Gotteserkenntnis gründet."

5. Gäckle, *Starken*, 191, trans. mine. Original: "kognitive-rationale Defizit."

6. Paul uses strong language here (ἀπόλλυμι) to indicate the "destruction" these weaker brothers experience. Unless otherwise noted, Scripture translations are my own.

of citations of Paul's Corinthian interlocutors in 1 Corinthians 8, and I will assume, rather than defend, that these citations include only "all of us possess knowledge" (8:1), "no idol in the world really exists," and "there is no God but one" (8:4).[7]

Let us turn to the text.

---

1 CORINTHIANS 8:1–7

C = Corinthians; P = Paul

Περὶ δὲ τῶν εἰδωλοθύτων (8:1–3)

[1] Now concerning food offered to idols:

(C_1) we know that "all of us possess knowledge."

(P_1) Knowledge puffs up, but love builds up. [2] Anyone who claims to know something does not yet have the necessary knowledge (δει γνωναι); [3] but anyone who loves God is known by him.

Περὶ τῆς βρώσεως οὖν τῶν εἰδωλοθύτων (8:4–6)

[4] Hence, as to the eating of food offered to idols:

(C_2) we know that (1) "no idol in the world really exists," and (2) that "there is no God but one."

(P_2) [5] Indeed, even though there may be so-called (λεγόμενοι) gods in heaven or on earth as in fact there are many gods and many lords

---

7. I will also assume that the earliest reading of 8:3 contained the phrase τὸν θεόνand ὑπ' αὐτοῦ, together with the vast majority of textual traditions (See Chris Tilling, *Paul's Divine Christology* [Grand Rapids: Eerdmans, 2015], 79–81.), making 8:3 read "anyone who loves God is known by him." And I also will assume the attributive reading of the repeated pronoun οὐδὲν . . . οὐδεὶς in 8:4, making the translation "no idol in the world (exists) and (there is) no God but one." For discussion of these issues, I refer to the superb commentary of Anthony C. Thiselton, *The First Epistle to the Corinthians. A Commentary on the Greek Text* (Grand Rapids: Eerdmans, 2000) and Erik Waaler, *The Shema and the First Commandment in First Corinthians: An Intertextual Approach to Paul's Re-Reading of Deuteronomy* (Tübingen: Mohr Siebeck, 2008). German language scholarship, on these issues at least, tends to be one or two steps ahead of the rest. Important works include Johannes Woyke, "Das Bekenntnis zum einzig allwirksamen Gott und Herrn und die Dämonisierung von Fremdkulten: Monolatrischer und polylatrischer Monotheismus in 1. Korinther 8 und 10," in *Gruppenreligionen im römischen Reich: Sozialformen, Grenzziehungen und Leistungen*, ed. J Rüpke (Tübingen: Mohr Siebeck, 2007), 87–112; and relevant sections in Johannes Woyke, *Götter, "Götzen," Götterbilder: Aspekte einer paulinischen "Theologie der Religionen"* (Berlin: De Gruyter, 2005); Eckhard J. Schnabel, *Der erste Brief des Paulus an die Korinther* (Wuppertal: Brockhaus, 2006); Schrage, *Korinther*. Further confusion can be avoided by remembering that Paul is dealing with different situations in this argument: with food explicitly dedicated to an idol and eaten in the temple precincts in one case, with food which may or may not have been offered to an idol and eaten in a private house in another, and so on. Furthermore, Paul argues pastorally and wants to *convince* his addressees, in 1 Cor 8, not simply command. He wants to engage with their own position and win them over.

⁶ yet for us there is one God, the Father, from whom are all things and for whom we exist, and one Lord, Jesus Christ, through whom are all things and through whom we exist.

⁷ It is not everyone, however, who has this knowledge.

———

Crucially, 1 Corinthians 8:1–3 provides the hermeneutical and epistemological key for Paul's forthcoming argument. He begins by stating the broad issue: "now concerning food offered to idols" (περὶ δὲ τῶν εἰδωλοθύτων). Paul then immediately creates a contrast that structures much of what follows, marked by C_1 and P_1:

(C_1) "we know that 'all of us possess knowledge'" (as the Corinthian 'knowledgeable' say)

So Paul responds,

(P_1) "Knowledge puffs up, but love builds up. Anyone who claims to know something does not yet have the necessary knowing (δεῖ γνῶναι); but anyone who loves God is known by him."

Two points merit attention. First, whereas the Corinthian "strong"—or better, "knowledgeable"—claim to have knowledge as a possession (γνῶσιν ἔχομεν), Paul is clear that this kind of knowledge puffs up; it is knowledge that only *claims* "to know something." But note that Paul is not simply anti–intellectual, for he speaks of "necessary knowing (δεῖ γνῶναι)" in his contrasting claim. It is a particular way of knowing that Paul contradicts.

Second, over and against the type of knowing that claims to have knowledge as its possession, Paul articulates what could be called a relational,[8]

---

8. Of course, "relational" is a slippery word, use of which can create problems. See N. T. Wright, "The Letter to the Romans. Introduction, Commentary, and Reflections," in *The New Interpreter's Bible*, ed. L. E. Keck et al. (Nashville: Abington, 2002), 446; Stephen R. Holmes, "Classical Trinity: Evangelical Perspective," in *Two Views on the Doctrine of the Trinity*, ed. Jason S. Sexton (Grand Rapids: Zondervan, 2014), 28, 37–39. To be clear, I use relational in the sense colored by Paul's own argumentation. So, at a theoretical level I do not necessarily mean by "relational" more than "the way in which one person or thing is related to another" (Judy Pearsall and William R. Trumble, eds, *The Oxford English Reference Dictionary* [Oxford: Oxford University Press, 1995], 1216). But in terms of descriptions of Paul, the word tends to indicate interpersonal relationality rather than impersonal relations of, say, "origin." I am attempting faithfully to name that participatory and interpersonal dynamic in Paul's own discourse. This means that objections that point merely to the various ways "relational" can be used, as if this thereby makes deployment

covenantal way of knowing: one spoken in terms of the knowledge God has of us and, reciprocally, one expressed in terms of our love of God. This case understands the clauses in 8:2 and 8:3 to interpret one another. The repetition of the verb γινώσκω suggests that the "necessary knowing" in 8:2 is expounded as loving God and being known by him in 8:3. To "be known by God" connotes *God's special, covenantal relationship with his chosen people*.[9] As Amos 3:2 says, "You only have I known (ἔγνων) of all the families of the earth."[10] Eric Waaler, therefore, concludes his study with the claim that Paul's language here of loving God and being known by him "describes the personal relationship between the believer and God."[11] As Jewish scholar Jon Levenson recently argued in his delightful study on the love of God, "If we are to employ the term 'monotheism', long used to describe Judaism, the only meaning the term can have within the specific context of covenant is in reference to this rigorous exclusivity of relationship."[12] This is why Paul couples the language of being known by God, which connotes God's covenantal relationship with his people, with talk of loving God. Within Paul's idiom, covenantal knowledge of and love for God necessarily go hand in hand.

In sum, then, Paul's "necessary knowing" is a knowledge of God understood in terms of covenant, relationship, and love for God. Thus, it is not a possession, contra the claim of the Corinthian "knowledgeable." Instead, it is God's knowledge of his people. And this provides the epistemological and hermeneutical key for the rest of Paul's argument.

Indeed, Paul is explicit that the opening three verses should be understood as framing his continued argument,[13] and this takes place as 8:4–6 repeats and elaborates the contrast established in 8:1–3. First, Paul cites the *content* of the Corinthian "knowledge" in 8:4, and it involves two propositions:

---

of the word necessarily redundant, should be seen as nothing but a cheap attempt to side-step issues originating from scriptural resources.

9. For an articulation of the thematic associations relating to the phrase "known by God," see Brian Rosner, "Known by God: The Meaning and Value of a Neglected Biblical Concept," *The Tyndale Bulletin* 59, no. 2 (2008): 207–30; and Brian S. Rosner, *Known by God: A Biblical Theology of Personal Identity* (Grand Rapids: Zondervan, 2017).

10. See also Deut 9:24; 34:10; Exod 33:17, etc. and the discussion in Schnabel, *Korinther*, 442–3, esp. n60. Indeed, his entire discussion relating to 1 Cor 8 is exemplary.

11. Waaler, *Shema*, 351.

12. Jon D. Levenson, *The Love of God: Divine Gift, Human Gratitude, and Mutual Faithfulness in Judaism* (Princeton: Princeton University Press, 2016), 11.

13. He marks a shift from 8:1–3 to 8:4ff. by using the coordinating conjunction, "therefore" (οὖν). Something *follows* as a consequence of his reasoning in 8:1–3. What is more, Paul *repeats the opening phrase* that introduced the whole section (περὶ δὲ τῶν εἰδωλοθύτων), making it now more specific, a subset of what he has already discussed. It is unsurprising, then, even if it remains insufficiently acknowledged by NT scholarship, that the C/P contrast established in 8:1–3 is repeated in 8:4–6.

(C$_2$) we know that (1) "no idol in the world really exists," and that (2) "there is no God but one."

This is the knowledge used to justify their attendance at feasts in idol temples. After all, if there is no idol and no God but one, why worry about those nonexistent gods? "Let's go and enjoy the idol food because we know better."

Paul responds to claims (1) and (2) in what follows: P$_2$, beginning in 8:5, is a qualified concession to claim (1) in C$_2$ that no idol really exists. Paul's point appears to be that they don't exist *as real divine beings*. Hence, he writes, in 8:5 in a tone of agreement ("indeed" translating εἴπερ), that there are "so-called" (λεγόμενοι) gods, and only as such exist, that is, only as nongods are there many gods and lords.

But it is likely that this is already what Schnabel has called a "differentiated understanding" of the claims of the Corinthian "knowledgeable."[14] This is why I suggest that the correction of the Corinthian position begins in 8:5.[15] It continues in 8:6: "but for us there is one God, the Father, from whom are all things and for whom we exist, and one Lord, Jesus Christ, through whom are all things and through whom we exist." Corresponding with the mentioned love for God in 8:2 (in P$_1$), Paul reuses the words of the *shema* in 8:6, as is now well known, and does so by dividing the Lord and the God of the *shema* between God and Jesus.[16] But this is to be expected if one remembers the way the argument was set up in 8:1–3. In a context which expresses a Corinthian knowledge of the one God, Paul corrects this by pointing to the love-for-God-orientated nature of true knowing. And the clearest articulation of such relational knowing of the one God in the Scriptures of Israel is, of course, the *shema*. "Hear, O Israel: YHWH our God, YHWH is one. You shall love YHWH your God with all your heart, and with all your soul, and with all your might (Deut 6:4–5)." As McConville argues, Deuteronomy "always thinks of God's oneness in relational terms,

---

14. Schnabel, *Korinther*, 445, translation mine. Original: "differenziertere Sicht der Wirklichkeit . . . als die korinthischen Christen."

15. Paul is not saying simply that "no idol in the world exists" as there *are* many gods and lords (when understood as λεγόμενοι, "so-called," gods). Indeed, it almost seems that Paul wanted to start correcting claim (1) of C$_2$ more extensively, but then swerved back onto course to stick more closely with the C/P contrast set up in 8:1–3, and he does so by turning immediately to claim (2) in C$_2$. This at least would explain some of the bumpy grammar in these verses.

16. See now Crispin Fletcher-Louis, *Jesus Monotheism*, vol. 1, *Christological Origins: The Emerging Consensus and Beyond* (Eugene, OR: Cascade, 2015), 39–55, which seeks to apply a numerical analysis of 8:6 to affirm the claim, against detractors like James McGrath in *The Only True God: Early Christian Monotheism in Its Jewish Context* (Urbana: University of Illinois Press, 2009) that Paul truly endorses a christological monotheism.

that is, in the context of his relationship with Israel."[17] Likewise, as Moberly argues, the Deuteronomic *shema* language of oneness, *'ekhad*, expresses that "YHWH is the one and only *for Israel*,"[18] and so goes on to speak of the command to "love the LORD your God with all your heart, and with all your soul, and with all your might" in the next verse (Deut 6:5). So Paul can press his point now, highlighting what is inherent in the *shema*, by packing 8:6 with relational terms: "but *for us*," "*for* and *from* whom *we* exist," "Father," and "Lord." In contradistinction to the Corinthian knowledge that "there is no God but one," Paul emphasises the relational. Though presenting propositional truth in 8:4, the Corinthians would fail entirely if the issue remained abstract, if they didn't grasp matters relationally.[19] It is this relational, participatory knowledge that not all have (8:7).

It is time to sum up our argument so far. What we see in 1 Corinthians 8:1–7 is a discussion relating to ways of engaging with theological propositions. Although what the Corinthians stated was true enough at a pure, naked, propositional level, it was judged negatively by Paul. Their knowledge puffed up and was a false claim to know something. The startling upshot is that *the confession of true propositions can, when this relational context is subdued, nullify the presence of any knowledge at all.* So Paul is not anti-intellectual, but rather aims for a knowing he calls "necessary," one rooted in the covenantal and relational reality of being known by God.

It follows that good readings of Paul don't simply look at the edifice of Paul's theology from a distance and admire the whole as if it were something "over there." As we have seen, we best read Paul by approaching up close and personal, climbing through a window to see the whole from *within*. In this chapter, I am attempting to facilitate just this, with 1 Corinthians 8:1–7 providing an entrance point. From this vantage point, I will now briefly cast our eyes more widely to behold the way in which these claims about Paul sit next to other major themes. Without wanting to discourse on Paul's epistemology as a whole, it suffices to offer our analysis of 1 Corinthians 8 a broader grammar in two points for reasons that will become clear in the next sections.

First, if one tracks with the rest of Paul's argument about idol food, up to 1 Corinthians 11:1, it becomes clear that this love-towards-God-knowing

---

17. J. Gordon McConville, *Grace in the End: A Study in Deuteronomic Theology* (Grand Rapids: Zondervan, 1993), 124.

18. R. W. L. Moberly, *Old Testament Theology: Reading the Hebrew Bible as Christian Scripture* (Grand Rapids: Baker Academic, 2013), 26.

19. On relational, see n8 above. I will elucidate what is meant by "abstract" on p. 96.

is expressed in terms of love for others. It is a relational knowing that is embodied in real life and relationships, as well as in the rejection of idolatry.[20] We also see in the rest of the argument that it is a knowing expressed, as I have argued elsewhere, most consistently in terms of loyalty to and relationship with the risen Lord over against idolatry. This Christ-relation is Paul's divine Christology.[21] It is a way of knowing that isn't prior to but indeed *is* discipleship.[22] It is, to use Mary Healy's turn of phrase, knowledge expressed as relationship.[23]

Second, and looking more broadly across Paul's letters, we see repeated the theme that, for Paul, the knowledge of God is not something one strictly possesses. It is better to speak of God's knowledge of us. Likewise, just a few chapters later in 1 Corinthians, Paul admits that "now I know only in part" and "I will know fully, even as I have been fully known" only when seeing face to face (πρόσωπον πρὸς πρόσωπον, 13:12). This πρόσωπον language indicates the desired eschatological encounter with the living Lord, which Paul speaks of in numerous other places.[24] "For while we are at home in the body," as he puts it in 2 Corinthians, "we are away from the Lord" and so "we walk by faith, not by sight" (2 Cor 5:6–7). Knowledge, then, is eschatologically determined and christologically permeated, all parsed according to the grammar of faith, hope, and love.[25]

This should not be taken to imply that Paul's epistemology is embarrassed by the notion that sentences can be truth-bearers. Paul himself makes plenty of sentences involving "claims that things are such and such and so not their contradictories,"[26] to use the language of Colin Gunton.[27]

---

20. I make this case in Tilling, *Paul's Divine Christology*, ch. 5.

21. Indeed, this points the way to recognition of both Paul's divine Christology and his Trinitarian faith, one expressed in his own theological idiom. See Tilling, *Paul's Divine Christology*; Tilling, *Paul the Trinitarian* (forthcoming, 2018).

22. See also the language of the "renewal of minds" in Rom 12, and related issues such as the presentation of our bodies as living sacrifices (12:1), discerning God's will (12:2), and the recognition of the body and its many members (12:4–8).

23. See Mary Healy, "Knowledge of the Mystery: A Study of Pauline Epistemology," in *The Bible and Epistemology*, ed. Mary Healy and Robin Parry (Milton Keynes: Paternoster, 2007), 134–57.

24. See, e.g., 1 Thess 4:17–18; 5:10–11; Phil 1:23.

25. Likewise, as we see explicitly in Galatians 4, knowledge of God correlates with liberation from the elements of the world and from beings that by nature are not gods, both of which enslave (4:1–3, 8). Paul speaks of a knowledge bound up with being adopted by God (4:5–6; see also Rom 8:15), with *coming to be known by God* (Gal 4:9), with repentance from the weak and poor elements of the world, and so on. Paul's God-talk repeatedly turns to relational themes, to discipleship. Such are the kind of concerns which correlate with the knowledge of God, for Paul.

26. I speak of "sentences" rather than "propositions" here, aware of the distinction between them in philosophical discourse relating to truth (see, e.g., E. J. Lowe, "Truth," in *The Oxford Companion to Philosophy*, 2nd ed., ed. Ted Honderich [Oxford: Oxford University Press, 2005], 2197).

27. Colin E. Gunton, *A Brief Theology of Revelation* (London: T&T Clark, 1995), 13.

Without wanting to enter the complex arena of debates concerning theories of truth, it seems safe at least to think Paul resists the reduction of the truth of a sentence about God to its correspondence with facts about God. For Paul, the knowledge of God is not possessed, mastered, and treated as formula external to the graced knower, but is a part of that subject's life and interpersonal relations. To what extent this means Paul can be seen to instantiate a pragmatic or subjective theory of truth at this point is one I cannot address in this essay. What we can say simply is that to be known by God involves, for Paul, speech embedded in lives of worship and in the rejection of idolatry; knowledge is expressed in sentences which gain their meaning in terms of that muddy network of ground-level relationships in which disciples live.[28]

"Abstract," a word I have deployed already at various points, can now be specified more closely. An "abstraction," in Pauline hue, indicates a concept that is deployed and understood as if discipleship was not essential to the appropriation of its meaning and the reception of its articulation, existing merely as a transcendent thought or idea, claiming its theological veracity only in terms of its correspondence with naked facts. It follows from this that it names the kind of rhetoric in which one claims to represent a universal truth by means of a concept, irrespective of the particularity of the life of the graced knower or the historical events that have served to communicate that truth to us.[29]

Armed with these realisations, we are poised to comment on the task of dogmatics in contemporary theological discourse.

PAUL, THE TASK OF DOGMATICS, AND "BARTHIAN" THEOLOGY

The spirit of Pauline God-talk seems to have found particularly vigorous representation and extension in modern theological trends influenced by Karl Barth.[30] Tracing these similarities with and developments beyond Paul will help us engage with rather different fashions more critically.

Now even a superficial reading of Barth can see how he resisted abstract

---

28. As we shall see, it does not follow that theologians cannot analyze the rational or logical coherence of various propositions or sentences.

29. When understood christologically, these two levels of particularity are directly related, for we exist as agents in the time God has made for us in the life, death, and resurrection of Jesus Christ. That is, historical and existential particularity join together in Jesus Christ. We shall note this briefly in our discussion related to Barth, in what follows.

30. Regarding "Barthian," I will not pretend to be able to educate theologians on the debates

or general language in the theological enterprise, and that this involved a simultaneous emphasis on the personal nature of revelation. So Barth means, by revelation, "a concrete relation to concrete men," something that is, as Kevin Diller describes, "fundamentally personal."[31] God is not known from a distance, nor in general terms, for Barth, but in the actuality of our personal transformation.[32]

For Barth, the criterion and possibility of dogmatics, namely the Word, is described in *CD* I/1 in personal terms. But because revelation happens— God does not merely try to reveal himself—we can speak of the Word of God as a "success-Word." So the human response is included in the Word of God such that revelation is not simply "over there," but includes "the entire correspondence on man's side to the divine act of revelation" which is "just as seriously the content of the biblical witness to revelation as is the objective reality of revelation" (*CD* I/2, 206). This means that the personal Word becomes a relational or a participatory one. Similarly, in 1 Thessalonians 2:13, Paul gives thanks because "when you received the word of God that you heard from us, you accepted it not as a human word but as what it really is, God's word, which is also at work in you believers" (NRSV). Barth famously gives this reasoning a strong christological under-girding, which means that we can speak of the particularity of theological rhetoric both in terms of human faith and repentance, and in terms of its concrete reference to the man Jesus Christ. Indeed, these are two sides of the same coin, for Christ is the time in which we live as agents—Christ is God's time for us.[33]

It indeed follows from all this that theological description will always be provisional, and never "an end in itself," to cite Alan Torrance.[34] As Kevin Diller puts it in commentary on Barth, "individual propositional expressions in human language do not have the power to contain the Truth." Second-order reflections can only be "derivative of and dependent on the actual knowing relation."[35] As such the task of theological knowledge is understood

---

surrounding labels here, and whether one should rather speak of "dialectical theology," "neo-orthodoxy," or "Barthianism." Each has its strengths and weaknesses, as far as I see it.

31. Kevin Diller, *Theology's Epistemological Dilemma: How Karl Barth and Alvin Plantinga Provide a Unified Response* (Downers Grove, IL: IVP Academic, 2014), 51, 53.

32. See Diller, *Theology's Epistemological Dilemma*, 61.

33. See now James J. Cassidy, *God's Time for Us: Barth's Reconciliation of Eternity and Time in Jesus Christ* (Bellingham, WA: Lexham, 2016).

34. Alan J. Torrance, *Persons in Communion: An Essay on Trinitarian Description and Human Partici-pation, with Special Reference to Volume One of Karl Barth's Church Dogmatics* (Edinburgh: T&T Clark, 1996), 44.

35. Diller, *Theology's Epistemological Dilemma*, 86.

in terms of that wider relational, christological, and eschatological grammar of faith, obedience, and repentance that we saw exemplified in Paul.

Much of what animates Barth here could as well be direct commentary on 1 Corinthians 8:1–7. And Barth manages this precisely as he engages the topic of theological epistemology situated within a different conceptual milieu. Hence "Barthian" theology wrestled with the issue of the knowledge of God in a context that foregrounded questions such as the conditions, possibility, and validation of the knowledge of God—in other words, all the issues that have been unavoidable since Kant's separation of the *Ding an sich* from the realm of rational knowledge.[36] Such issues were not driving Paul's agenda at all, but Barth has preserved the Pauline grammar to address and subvert these different sets of issues, and in so doing necessarily extends and looks beyond Paul. The task of dogmatics could hardly be exemplified more constructively.

PAUL AND ABSTRACTION IN SONDEREGGER AND HOLMES

However, although all of this is heartening for a New Testament scholar such as myself, I have noticed different trends in theological circles in the last decade. Quite simply, they do not give weight to the lessons explored so profoundly in Barth's corpus. Put sharply, I suggest that insecure and abstract γνῶσις is again being taken to condition the reality of God in our God-talk, derailing the task of dogmatics from its relational and participatory tracks.

Let me immediately make clear that in what follows I do not wish to take aim at metaphysics, speculation, or philosophically minded theological rhetoric per se, any more than Paul rejected the intellect as such. Likewise, Barth did not reject philosophy per se; rather, he rejected the way it could operate in theological discourse as a putative (and illegitimate) foundation.[37] Instead, my target is abstract thinking that is then taken to *condition* God-talk, that is, constructions that are used to *govern* what can and must be said about God.

The two examples of this, which I turn to examine now, are outstanding scholars both of whom have been brilliant keynote speakers at the very event

---

36. On this, see the seminal works of Bruce L. McCormack, *Karl Barth's Critically Realistic Dialectical Theology: Its Genesis and Development, 1909–1936* (Oxford: Oxford University Press, 1995); Bruce L. McCormack, *Orthodox and Modern: Studies in the Theology of Karl Barth* (Grand Rapids: Baker Academic, 2008); as well as the discussion concerning Bultmann in Congdon, *The Mission of Demythologizing*, ch. 4.

37. See Diller's brilliant exposition of the matter in the chapter on "Barth's Engagement with Philosophy: A Theo-Foundational Epistemology," in *Theology's Epistemological Dilemma*, 66–93.

behind this book, the LA Theology Conference. I am speaking of Steve Holmes and Katherine Sonderegger. So please let me begin by stating in clearest terms that I do not wish to suggest that either of their theological projects are wholly problematic! Indeed, I have learnt from and enjoy both important scholars. Sonderegger's chapter in this very book is, indeed, one of the finest dogmatic expositions of Scripture I have ever read! I simply want to critique aspects of their otherwise learned scholarly contributions, to further some important conversations that need to take place.

First, to Sonderegger. If the apostle Paul claims that the knowledge of God is bound up in loving God and others within the ambit of God's covenantal knowledge of his own, and as such cannot be a possession or abstraction, then I see a different direction in Sonderegger's work, at least in the first couple of chapters of her *Systematic Theology*. There I see the imposition of nonrelational, abstract knowledge that is then taken to govern her engagement with Scripture and the content of some key theological claims.

In these first couple of chapters she presses the distinction between the who and what of God, and between (scriptural) narrative and metaphysics. Although Sonderegger claims that Scripture does not present us with detailed metaphysics, such questions can and must still be asked (here we agree!). She cites Barth's claim that we "must learn to see beyond Paul,"[38] as legitimation of this kind of engagement with Scripture, to look beyond the "genre" of Scripture to its subject matter, which she takes to indicate the (metaphysical) oneness of God.[39]

Although she is aware that Scripture does not present this oneness as a "'metaphysical analysis' of Divine Nature,"[40] we "must go further" because "in the end, Holy Scripture reveals to us what kind of Being God is: Divine Oneness, we must say, is a metaphysical predicate,"[41] and only recognition of this aspect of engaging Scripture can amount to a "proper theological reading."[42]

The problem Sonderegger identifies is that in the world of Barth and others, such metaphysical oneness is threatened by the narrative focus on divine threeness. She notes the resistance of others to begin with a "'naked'

---

38. Katherine Sonderegger, *Systematic Theology*, vol. 1, *The Doctrine of God* (Minneapolis: Fortress, 2015), 11.

39. She claims that "we discern in Scripture its proper heart and subject matter: the Oneness of God," a "Divine Oneness" she explains on the next page "is a metaphysical predicate" (Sonderegger, *Systematic Theology*, 1:14, 15).

40. Ibid., 1:14.

41. Ibid., 1:15.

42. Ibid., 1:16.

doctrine of God—a God considered apart from or prior to Trinity."[43] Instead, Sonderegger appeals to the oneness of God as the first step in her task, one which "is recommended principally by Holy Scripture itself."[44] Indeed, as such, Sonderegger claims that her *Systematic Theology* is "biblical theology."[45]

This leads to her exegesis of Deuteronomy 4:10–14, which speaks of the way God hid his form from Moses. For Sonderegger, this bespeaks God's invisibility and thus dovetails with the metaphysics of the "Divine Nature as One."[46] She concludes that "the True God of Judaism and the church is marked off from the false by invisibility: the nature of the One God is to have no image, form, or likeness."[47]

But my concern with all of this, and it is not an insignificant one, is that Sonderegger begins her *Systematics* by deploying a *governing* metaphysically abstract concept. I speak of "abstraction" here given the way Sonderegger coordinates oneness with invisibility, and because of her description of it as a metaphysical predicate, which speaks of the "Whatness" of God.

In contrast to this, Pauline knowing has a double particularity, both by being bound to the name Jesus Christ and to the relational or participatory nature of necessary knowing.[48] Indeed, although he does not directly correct the Corinthian language of "oneness," he puts it on the wrong side of his contrasts because it was framed wrongly. Oneness, parsed in Sonderegger's terms, appears to be just brute theological fact. Discipleship, the knower's love for God, and love for others are not a *necessary* part of this dynamic, and that is troubling for readers of Paul. After all, Sonderegger is explicit that her task is to discourse on oneness as a concept *before* engaging the Trinity. If the Trinity involves the articulation of the grammar of God's saving *relationship* with humans, it follows that "oneness" is construed apart from and before God's knowledge of us. So Paul, responding to the brute fact of the Corinthian knowledgeable, explicitly articulated his God-talk in relational terms, which was, after all, to capture the spirit of the *shema* itself.

So does Sonderegger's emphasis on conceptual abstraction in the core claims in her first chapters correspond well with Paul's necessary knowing? For the apostle, knowing does not take place when its (necessary) theological propositions merely discuss what is "over there" irrespective of the

---

43. Ibid., 1:7.
44. Ibid., 1:9.
45. Ibid., vol. 1, xv.
46. Ibid., 1:19.
47. Ibid., 1:20–21.
48. See 91n8, where I dialogue with Paul about what "abstraction" might mean.

placement of these propositions in the grammar of love for God and others. My worry is that despite the wonderfully devotional *style* of Sonderegger's rhetoric, the *content* of her theological claims can too easily land on the wrong side of Paul's contrasts in 1 Corinthians 8.

Of course, Sonderegger does this because she sees the theological task bound to her construal of metaphysics. But perhaps this underestimates the eschatological and therefore provisional nature of abstract dogmatic terms. It seems to me that she absolutises an abstract concept and calls this the subject matter of Scripture, which not only pays too little attention in expression to the relational but also puts too much weight on that abstraction. It is creaking under the eschatological pressure Paul's language of knowing in part expresses—until we see face-to-face. So I am certainly not suggesting that God is not one or that theology cannot articulate this as central to its project—of course not. It is, rather, to cast doubt on *how* these issues are articulated, by means of both the kinds of themes which coordinate them and the function they perform (here the abstract concept of oneness *governs* her God-talk).

All of this has exegetical ramifications. In the first place, I think Sonderegger underestimates the metaphysical content of Scripture itself, so making space to push through another. Scripture's own metaphysic of oneness insists that recognition of God as one cannot be separated from loving commitment to God. In a chapter entitled "So Love Yahweh, Your God: 'Monotheism' as Devoted Love," Hebrew Bible scholar Nathan MacDonald notes that while in modern intellectualised definitions "'monotheism' is a truth to be comprehended," in Deuteronomy, it is "a relationship in which to be committed."[49] This oneness of God, MacDonald reminds us in a way that dovetails neatly with our comments about Paul's theological epistemology, *"cannot be abstracted from the relationship between YHWH and Israel."* Scripture speaks "about the nature of YHWH, [offering] *an ontological statement, so to speak*, but a statement that cannot be divorced from [God's] personal claim on Israel."[50] Indeed. Here we see aspects of Scripture's metaphysic and ontology.

But has not this scriptural idiom, which respects the historical particularity of these texts precisely on the issue of God's oneness, been subdued by the imposition of only one kind of metaphysically orientated concept of oneness? Almost every attempt of a theologian to pull a metaphysical construct over Scripture is the flip side of underestimating the metaphysical

---

49. Nathan MacDonald, *Deuteronomy and the Meaning of "Monotheism"* (Tübingen: Mohr Siebeck, 2003), 97.
50. Ibid., 207; emphasis added.

dynamics proffered in Scripture itself. It is just that Scripture's metaphysic, with its profoundly relational epistemology (and ontology, as we are begin ning to see), is often not recognised, so it is ignored and a vacuum is created. Inevitably, Scripture is then dealt with only in a piecemeal manner.[51]

Is not this why Sonderegger can claim, in her exegesis, that God's oneness is most obviously linked to the theme of invisibility? Not only are these two concepts voiced less than one might imagine in Scripture, they are not explicitly correlated in these terms anywhere in the canon. What is more, in claiming that invisibility is what marks off God from what is false runs into the problems of accounting for the fact that God *does* have an image and a likeness: humans.[52] (To be properly *theological* by avoiding generalisations, arguably we must speak first of Christ as the image of God. But that is a subject for another day.)

Thus, and in the second place, Sonderegger's project is in danger of imposing certain metaphysically driven dogmatics onto the text. Whereas Barth managed to respect the grammar of Pauline concerns, and precisely so look beyond Paul, here I see, in Sonderegger, the text being forced onto a procrustean bed, even though it may be an "exalted" one, to cite Webster in my epigraph. The upshot is that this is not, I suggest, a biblical theology that entirely does justice to the adjective "biblical."

Further, this is why I must question the confidence that her method constitutes a proper theological reading. Metaphysics will have a part to play, but ultimately, a theological reading, if it is going to include necessary theological knowing, will directly involve *discipleship*. It follows that our (I think necessary) metaphysics must also continually seek to be discipled by the living Lord.[53]

Perhaps most importantly, and this flows from my previous points, I worry Sonderegger is awry to claim that the subject matter of Scripture is divine nature as One, when understood in her particular metaphysical terms. The subject matter of Scripture is not a human doctrine or expression but the *reality of the living God*, and this One known as such *in the knowing relation*.[54]

---

51. I would argue that precisely the same issues are in play in accounts of the Trinity that seek to make a particular metaphysical construal of divine simplicity the controlling ontology (whether it is called ontological humility or not). This is done in tandem with (popular but I think false) claims that the New Testament only contains the "seeds" or "inchoate grammar" of the doctrine of the Trinity, that was then only first grasped centuries later. On this, see my forthcoming, *Paul the Trinitarian*.

52. On this, see Fletcher-Louis's provocative thesis that Adam is the true image-idol of God (see the relevant sections in Fletcher-Louis, *Jesus Monotheism*, e.g., 1:285).

53. Robert Jenson is exemplary, if controversial, in this respect. See, e.g., Robert W. Jenson, *Theology as Revisionary Metaphysics: Essays on God and Creation* (Eugene, OR: Cascade, 1997).

54. It seems to me that Sonderegger's chapter in the present volume resonates much more closely

Of course, I must immediately add that, speaking for Sonderegger's whole project, she is asking fresh and important questions and that in doing so her *Systematics* adopts the kind of devotional rhetoric that encourages a delighted posture of worship. We have much to learn from her in this. On this count, we see her otherwise profound grasp of Pauline concerns. If only this found more direct expression in the content of her theological claims in these opening chapters.

Second, I turn to a particular aspect of Stephen Holmes's argumentation relating to the doctrine of the Trinity. Again, I am only picking up on a single strand of Holmes's proposals, much as I did with Sonderegger. But I pull this thread in Holmes's works because I suspect it is tied together with an underlying philosophical posture, which I will address shortly. This is to say that I do not address Jonathan Edwards directly, upon whom Holmes leans in this argument, because of the relationship between Holmes's endorsement of these views and wider trends in contemporary theological discourse, which I take Holmes to represent.

In a lively book in which two views on the Trinity were debated by four scholars, each were asked to answer the "so what?" question, to articulate the *use* of the doctrine. Now the doctrine of the Trinity has been pressed into the service of all manner of agendas, so Holmes is clear: "The doctrine of the Trinity is necessarily and precisely useless, and that point must never be surrendered." The doctrine is an account of the divine life and "knowledge of the divine life is necessarily our highest end." Following Jonathan Edwards, Holmes presses the point, and here I must cite him at length:

> It is of the essence of a highest end that it has no use. A highest end is of value in itself, not an instrumental step to some other end. If the doctrine of the Trinity is taken . . . to be an anticipation, partial and hesitant, but still an anticipation, of this eschatological vision, then it can have no instrumental use. If the doctrine has any use, it is in clarifying errors about its own articulation. . . . Fundamentally, however, the doctrine serves no end.[55]

Some may sense tension here with my account of the knowledge of God in relation to Paul and "Barthian" theology. For I have been happy to argue that knowledge of God that is not discipleship—not a lived, concrete relation with God and others—is not theological knowledge at all, but a mere puffing up. For Holmes, however, the doctrine of the Trinity must be "useless."

---

with Pauline concerns at this point.
    55. Holmes, "Classical Trinity," 47–48.

Now of course, Holmes presents the doctrine of the Trinity as a mode of worship, which is to be noted. So my concern is not a large one. I worry, simply, that Holmes may have allowed an abstract conceptuality to condition his God-talk, much like we see in Sonderegger. Here it is the ordering of theological topics according to a means-end schema. And I propose that adherence to this logic, while seemingly reasonable, is not without problems.

Although all theological rhetoric *can* be subjected to such classification, it may not always be appropriate and so create more problems. For starters, and as is well-known, ethical actions can be organised and evaluated according to a means-end schema, as teleological positions insist. But it does not always seem appropriate. Some means, such as murdering innocents or torture, seem wrong whatever ends supposedly justify them. Hence there are deontological accounts of ethics. The point is that a means-end schema does not always seem obviously correct for all actions, so why should it be used as a formal structuring principle articulating the doctrine of God?

The means-end schema also seems to assume a metaphysic in which a distinction between actions (as means) on the one hand and states of affairs (as ends) on the other is fundamental. So the beatific vision, which Holmes refers to in his argument, is an accomplished state and all means are understood in terms of usefulness, as "instrumental steps." But must theology commit to this philosophy? Perhaps this resonates well with wider philosophical/theological commitments in Holmes's work. After all, if an account of God's goodness is at home in philosophical accounts of divine simplicity—which Holmes promotes with great learning—this does suggest an account of perfection that implies stasis. Hence the end can be more easily associated with a "state of affairs" as opposed to actions, which tend to be instrumentalised. The figure of Aristotle is not far away, for whom relation, location, and action are accidental to a thing's essence.

In other words, while I appreciate the notion that doctrine, for Holmes, seems to be articulated as a worshipful beholding of the life of God, my concern is that matters are framed too statically. And this philosophy does seem less comfortable in the world in which the liveliness of the God of Abraham, Isaac, and Jacob is central. Indeed, does not the Christian theologian have resources for thinking of the highest end in active terms, as worship rendered in acts of service? As Paul says, "Present your *bodies as a living sacrifice*, holy and acceptable to God, which is your *spiritual worship*" (Rom 12:1).

Furthermore, Paul tends to portray Christ as both means and end, which further problematizes these distinctions. On the one hand, and as we have already seen, Paul can speak of Christ as the instrument through whom we live (1 Cor 8:6). We also boast through him (Rom 5:11), are delivered by God through him (Rom 7:25), are conquerors through him (Rom 8:37), and "every tongue acknowledges that Jesus Christ is Lord" for its own end? No! "To the glory of God the Father" (Phil 2:11).

And yet elsewhere, and less frequently acknowledged even by New Testament scholars, Paul can also speak of Christ in terms of his ultimate end. In Philippians 1:20, Paul is only concerned that "Christ will be exalted now as always in my body, whether by life or by death." He then adds "for to me, living is Christ" (1:21). Indeed, Paul regards "everything as loss because of the surpassing value of knowing Christ Jesus my Lord" (3:7–8). Or again, in 1 Thessalonians 4:17–18 and 5:10–11, both passages speak of being with Christ as the greatest hope, and so on. Christ is both means and end. Why, then, seek to fit an account of the life of God into a means-end schema? The means-end schema can be useful to clarify thought, but it should not condition the nature of God-talk. This is why, despite agreement that the doctrine of the Trinity attempts to worshipfully articulate the eschatological vision of the divine life, I hesitate to speak of the doctrine of God in terms of being useful *or* useless, as a means *or* an end.

CONCLUSION

To conclude, Paul had a controversy with the Corinthian "knowledge-able," one which, I have argued, our construals of the task of dogmatics can take on board. If, with Gäckle, we maintain that the propositions of these Corinthians were "grounded on an intellectualised knowledge of the world and God," then Paul responded by insisting on both the participatory and provisional nature of necessary knowing. Even affirmation of true propositions does not necessarily constitute knowledge for Paul. This is to say that the intellectualised knowledge of some Corinthians wrongly claimed that their knowledge was sufficient, a knowledge possessed external to that network of relationships with God and his people that constitute the coordinating axes of the knowledge God has of us.

"Barthian" theology resonates profoundly with much of this, both in its understanding of theological propositions as always "derivative of and dependent on the actual knowing relation" (so Diller), as well as in the manner in which it locates theological knowledge in the wider grammar of faith, obedience, and repentance. This offered "Barthian" theology a sense for the dangers of loose conceptuality, abstracted from discipleship and from the particularity of the name Jesus Christ.

But other more recent trends, I worry, are starting to lose this Barthian sensibility, and so are allowing various abstract conceptualities to condition their God-talk. Again, my target is not philosophical categories per se, but the role they play in *governing* God-talk. And in Sonderegger, I suggest that we see an abstract concept of oneness, one associated with a static "Whatness," deployed with significant hermeneutical force. But pressed through Scripture, this marginalises Scripture's account of God's oneness in terms of its own network of related themes. So MacDonald argues that Deuteronomy's explication of oneness *"cannot be abstracted from the relationship between YHWH and Israel,"* and this dovetails precisely with the participatory account of "necessary knowing" that one sees in Paul. An account of oneness that appears merely as sheer fact does not put one firmly enough on the right side of Paul's contrasts in 1 Corinthians 8 and ultimately leads to a misconstrual of the very subject matter of Scripture.

Although Holmes understands the doctrine of the Trinity to involve a worshipful beholding of the divine life, his suggestions were also controlled by the imposition of a means-end logic that established the meaning of God-talk. While containing some pedagogical use, Holmes's move nevertheless distracts from facilitating scriptural nuance. Indeed, I worry that the means-end logic is undergirded by wider philosophical commitments about stasis and perfection that seem discordant with Paul's understanding of necessary knowing. Both examples, I suggest, impose abstractions on Scripture, pulling through mere scriptural threads, rather than allow, in that cruciform and two-way hermeneutical movement, the matrix of interrelated scriptural themes to find voice. If this continues unchallenged, I predict that the gap between dogmatics and biblical studies will widen even further.

Instead, if we are going to articulate the task of dogmatics in conversation with the apostle Paul, as I have argued, it will mean questioning all accounts that allow abstract conceptuality to determine the nature of theological knowledge; otherwise, we evacuate theology of the kind of necessary knowing Paul articulates in 1 Corinthians 8. To do anything else would be to agree with the Corinthian knowledgeable against Paul, and imply that there is a knowledge of God that is not necessarily bound up with the life of discipleship. But such knowledge puffs up. *Love* builds up, for anyone who loves God is known by him.[56]

56. A special thanks to Andrew Torrance, Jeremy Begbie, Lincoln Harvey, and Darren Sumner for critical feedback on earlier drafts of this paper. They saved me from even more mistakes.

CHAPTER 5

PERMANENT VALIDITY AND CONTEXTUAL RELATIVITY OF DOCTRINAL STATEMENTS

HENRI BLOCHER

This is why I am going continually to remind you of these things [most precious promises, virtues added to faith, confirming calling and election], though indeed you have knowledge and are solidly established in the present truth (en tē parousē alētheia).

2 PETER 1:12[1]

MYSTERY AND *MIST* ARE NOT COGNATES! Our weak eyes cannot gaze too long at the high mysteries of the Trinity, the incarnation, or God's love, just as they cannot the sun at midday: too much light and no mist at all! Some mist, however, inevitably reduces our perception of many of the objects of revelation, as long as our earthly pilgrimage lasts. Only, too much mist is not necessary.

Now, mist unduly thick (sometimes fog and smog) hovers on the way one tries to articulate the permanent validity of propositions (in a broad,

---

1. My own translation, as will be the case, regularly in what follows, when quotations are drawn from non-English sources.

nontechnical sense, e.g., statements, assertions, theses, the central content of speech-acts, etc.) with their being bound to and affected by particular contexts. The French philosopher Paul Ricœur signaled the difficulty: "How can we speak of the *truth* of an explanation if significations are contextual?"[2] "Contextual" implies specific times and places. Many, it appears, feel uneasy as they face the question: How should our theology combine "truth" and the participle normally translated "present" (*parousē*), as 2 Peter 1:12 freely does?

I hope to thin the mist, as an evangelical theologian (standing under Scripture), not as an anthropologist or as a linguist (I claim no expertise in their fields) but as a theologian looking for clarifications.

The issue, as I see it, has been most sensitive on three fronts:

Roman Catholic theology has had to wrestle with the development of dogma. Could it show the legitimacy of apparent changes in the course of time? For centuries, it prided itself of the *semper eadem* note of the church ("always the same"). It applied confidently the so-called "canon *lerinense*," (that is, of Saint Vincent de Lérins): the catholic faith is what was believed of all, always and everywhere. (Actually, this was a veiled attack on Augustine's radicality.) Catholic polemics used the canon against the "variations" of the Protestant churches, as in the learned and painstaking volumes from Bossuet's pen (more than 1,000 pages).[3] But the new sense and valuation of temporality in the second modernity—becoming preferred to being—and the rise of critical historiography have led to a reversal. John H. Newman pioneered a new treatment. The ability to bring forth new fruit became the sign of life. This outlook gained the ascendancy, and Vatican II was seen as its victory. Yet the claim has been maintained that continuity had been safeguarded. The permanent validity of the main magisterial pronouncements has been upheld, both in official discourse and by most influential theologians.

Tensions there have been, and the evolution has been rather slow, even in recent decades. Compare two Vatican documents entitled *Mysterium*: Paul VI's *Encyclical Mysterium fidei* (1965) stipulates in §24, concerning dogmatic

---

2. Paul Ricœur, *La Métaphore vive* (Paris: Seuil, 1975) 121, while discussing Monroe Beardsley's views in *Aesthetics* (New York: Harcourt, Brace & World, 1968); emphasis added. I will refer several times to Ricœur, a benefit of my having been close to him at times, and a way to nuance the representation many have made of this thought.

3. Jacques-Bénigne Bossuet, *Histoire des variations des Eglises protestantes*, 2 vols. (Paris: Garnier, [1921]), first published in 1688. According to the unsigned article on Bossuet in the 1961 edition of the *Encyclopædia Britannica*, III:931c, Leibniz replied: "We prefer a Church eternally variable and for ever moving forwards"—a typically modern choice.

formulas, that "they express concepts which are not tied to a certain form of culture," and are therefore "understandable by men of all ages and places." On the contrary the 1973 declaration *Mysterium Ecclesiae* underlines that "they may bear the mark of the conceptions of their time." Bernard Sesboüé, to whom we owe the quotation, comments, "This affirmation introduces a new element . . . what is being expressed may include 'marks,' i.e., obsolete elements bound to mutable conceptions."[4] Sesboüé and his famous predecessor and fellow-Jesuit Karl Rahner, whose acute perception of historical conditionings is well-known, stand as major Catholic witnesses of theological work on our topic.

Missiology, Roman Catholic but also evangelical, has grown more and more appreciative of the diversity of cultures. Missionaries have tried to escape the charge of cultural imperialism and ethnocentricity, levelled at former missionary styles. Contextualization has become the rallying cry ("inculturation" among Catholics).

Not without controversy, many evangelicals were concerned that permanent validity could be jeopardized. Charles Kraft's bold proposals aroused a great stir. Matthew Cook, a representative missiologist today, still complains that "dynamic equivalence" in Kraft's manner "demands dropping the text down into its equivalent cultural function."[5] "Dynamic equivalence" alludes to *translation* theory. Not seldom, and with good reason for doing so, the focus has been on the translation model. A tongue or idiom characterizes a cultural context, and, since William Carey, translating the Bible has been recognized as the first task to be accomplished by evangelical missionaries! With so pregnant a model, linguistic science and even philosophical views of language have been invited to share in theological debates.

The third front is broader: ideological, philosophical—the front of the contemporary "culture war" in our Western democracies. *Late modernity* shows a majority distrust of "grand narratives" (the phrase coined by Jean-François Lyotard) and wishes to deconstruct universal claims. (I say "late modernity," sometimes "modernity-post," to ward off the false suggestion

---

4. Sesboüé, *Le Magistère à l'épreuve: Autorité, vérité et liberté dans l'Eglise* (Paris: Desclée De Brouwer, 2001), 189 (text), 191 (comment). The part I have omitted in Sesboüé's sentence is most surprising: "[The declaration] does not only say that the truth affirmed is not independent of the *Weltanschauung* of an epoch . . ." When one reads the declaration, one sees that it remains anxious to maintain that the truth is *not dependent* on such a *Weltanschauung*. I suspect a *lapsus calami* on the part of the prestigious scholar Sesboüé (a Freudian slip?). The declaration only grants "marks," but it is already a significant concession.

5. Cook, "Unchanging 'truth' in Contextual Exegesis," *Evangelical Review of Theology* 31, no. 3 (July 2007): 203.

of a radical and wholesale discontinuity with modernity.) Perhaps the trend is starting to ebb, but it is still being felt. Situatedness, practically synonymous with "contextual relativity," is the strident slogan. "If modern theology sought a universal view from nowhere," Kevin Vanhoozer writes, "the first principle of postmodern theology is 'location, location, location.' The situatedness of the theologian trumps his or her supposedly neutral methodology."[6] Since it renounces universal moorings, it can hardly prevent an "ethnification of theology."[7]

One meets all degrees of radicality. Extreme (lucid?) forms flatly deny any permanent validity to doctrinal statements. Milder forms face the problem on our table.

TWO PILLARS

It is mpossible to ignore the strong cases one can make for both assertions— that propositions remain valid forever if ever valid and yet that they are relative to their contexts. They stand as two solid pillars, erected on rational and *biblical* grounds.

PERMANENT VALIDITY

Truth remains truth: such has been the Christian and human conviction through millennia. Even today, it may pass for "common sense." We see it operative in the reactions of the very prophets and priests of its denial. Though far from conservative, but sober and honest, Paul Ricœur could confess: "Truth, finally, cannot be multiple without denying itself. The True and the One are interchangeable notions."[8]

The boomerang argument against skepticism and relativism—you are sawing the branch on which you are seated—has received no answer. Neither has the "no way logically to stop" criticism. Abraham Kuyper, for instance, complained that skepticism "undoes all sense of solidity. Once you begin to slide down that slope, there is no stopping."[9]

---

6. Vanhoozer, "Systematic Theology," in *Dictionary for Theological Interpretation of the Bible*, ed. Kevin Vanhoozer et al. (Grand Rapids: Baker Academic, 2005), 775b.

7. Kevin Vanhoozer, "Theological Method, Part 2. A Theodramatic Proposal," in *Global Dictionary of Theology*, ed. William A. Dyrness & Veli-Matti Kärkkâinen (Downers Grove, IL: InterVarsity, 2008), 895a.

8. Ricœur, "Histoire et praxis," in *Histoire et vérité*, 2nd ed. (Paris: Seuil, 1955), 193. I remember him saying the same in a lecture in 1962.

9. Kuyper, "Modernism: A Fata Morgana in the Christian Domain," in *Abraham Kuyper: A Centennial Reader*, ed. James D. Bratt (Grand Rapids: Eerdmans, 1998), 122.

And there is the scent of sophistry one smells in the dialectic of more than one relativist defense. Hear what special pleading Alexandre Kojève—no mean thinker, the father of the Hegelian revival in France in the mid-twentieth century—offered to prove the Hegelian tenet that *truth itself changes with time*: "Let us suppose," he wrote, "that a poet, in the Middle Ages, had written in a poem: 'At this moment, a man is flying above the ocean.' Undoubtedly, it was an error, and it remained an error for centuries. But if now we read again that sentence, chances are that we read a truth, for it is almost certain that at this moment an airman is flying above the Atlantic."[10] We are not far from the way Eubulides, the Megarian philosopher, claimed he could destroy all certainty: "Don't you know the man under the blanket? No, I can't see him! Then, you confess that you don't know your own brother [Orestes]!"

Yet a serious question arises worth pondering: why are skeptics so *little* moved by rebuttals?[11]

Not only common sense, but "canon sense"![12] Scripture *massively* witnesses to the blessed immutability of God and the permanent validity of his Word. The Lord is the rock, in sharp contrast with the fickle nonentities invented and worshipped by the nations. He is the Rock of Ages, *tsur 'ola-mim* (Isa 26:4), who changes not. While stars, which the ancient admired as divine powers for their perfect regularity, do exhibit variation (*parallagē*), he never does (Jas 1:17). As he does not "repent" as mortals do, as he cannot deny himself and cannot lie, his words remain valid. "Validity" applies both to the true and to the good, to norms that rule thinking and doing, faith and practice; validity corresponds to the nuance of Aramaic *qesheh*, truth. The Hebrew word *'emeth* approaches the meaning "stability." One could speak of a conceptual contiguity, or even union, between truth and permanence, everlasting permanence. Psalm 119:160 mirrors the understanding, as does Jesus's statement that his words shall never pass away.

Could anyone explain away such an emphasis as a residue of an orientation

---

10. Kojève, *Introduction à la lecture de Hegel: Leçons sur la* Phénoménologie de l'Esprit *professées de 1933 à 1939 à l'Ecole des Hautes Etudes,* ed. Raymond Queneau (Paris: Gallimard, 1979), 464. On p.462, Kojève quotes a similar, though simpler, example, and would-be proof, from Hegel himself, in the first chapter of his *Phaenomenologie.*

11. Jonathan Culler, *On Deconstruction: Theory and Criticism after Structuralism* (Ithaca, NY: Cornell University Press, 1982), 149, answers: sawing the branch is not foolhardy for Nietzsche, Freud, Heidegger and Derrida; for them there is no ground to hit. This is not only a witty comment; it goes deep into the matter. (I would not include Freud and hesitate about Heidegger.) I borrow the reference from Vern S. Poythress, *In the Beginning Was the Word: Language in a God-Centered Approach* (Wheaton, IL: Crossway, 2009), 379n19.

12. An apt phrase and antithesis coined by Vanhoozer, "Theological Method," 896b.

towards archaic timeless time, of the downgrading of motion and the mutation at mythical stages, or later, of Platonic influence? Not likely. It is part and parcel of the future-oriented and historical faith of both Old and New Testaments. God is the God of hope *because* his promise remains permanently valid. And this belief is not only expressed, it is put to practice: the New Testament use of the Old would be totally enervated if permanent validity were denied. No evangelical reader could find fault in Karl Rahner's nonambiguous statement: "Revealed truth remains the same, remains 'true', i.e., it reaches the object [*die Sache trifft*] and is of binding authority in all ages."[13]

CONTEXTUAL RELATIVITY

The second "pillar," similarly, would not be easy to pull down. Common sense has also recognized the importance of context. (I basically use "context" in the way that now predominates, for historical, social, cultural, situations; some say "co-text" for what was previously meant by the term.) Experience has bitterly taught humankind that you can secure the condemnation of any person if you take that person's words *out of context*. One may discuss the validity of a proposition only within the parameters of the situation in which it was put forward; they determine what is being said.

This conviction has been heightened, amplified, and sometimes radicalized with the rise of the "social sciences" (*Geisteswissenschaften, sciences humaines*). Emphasis has been put on the role of symbolic systems in shaping the mind-set of all in a given people group. Such systems are peculiar to communities and shape their identities; they are diverse as the communities are diverse; insiders learn them and interiorize them with language, so that they function, to a great extent, *unconsciously*. They beget the "natural" way of looking at things, of speaking and behaving. "Culturalism" has seen each culture as an independent whole, incommensurate with others—despite dismissal by foremost experts (Marcel Gauchet),[14] it is still influential.

Language represents a major dimension of culture.

The arbitrary character of signs, especially lexical units, which Ferdinand

---

13. Rahner, "Zur Frage der Dogmenentwicklung," *Schriften zur Theologie* (Einsiedeln: Benzinger, 1954), 1:53.

14. Gauchet, answering a journalist, *Le Nouvel Observateur* 1508 (Sept. 30, 1993), 1: "These ideas are now called into question everywhere. We observe, in renovated forms, the themes of innate traits, human nature, universality, coming back to the fore." Culturalism, however, dies hard—its roots are more ideological than scientific. Cf. the title of the book by Stephan Bevans & Roger Schroeder, *Constants in Contexts: A Theology of Mission for Today* (Maryknoll, NY: Orbis, 2004).

de Saussure, the founder of modern linguistics, highlighted,[15] supports the idea of cultures as discrete entities. If the same word means two different things in two languages—"Can I?" if mistaken for a French expression, *canaille*, will be understood "rascal"—and the same thing is referred to by totally different words (e.g., "dog" and *chien*), then the suggestion is that each language, a key determination of context, is a self-contained system. Any statement using this language is enclosed in the system and therefore tied to context.

Does "canon sense" rule out what common sense seems to accept? By no means. Scripture is heedful of cultural and historical diversity. It makes room for linguistic plurality: it is even unique in this! The theme is central in the Babel story, and the intention of the Genesis 11 narrative is complex. On the one hand, those recent interpretations which read into the text their own glorification of dispersion and difference must be firmly resisted: too much ideology! The play on the name *Bàvèl* with the root *bll*, "confound," flings an ironic dart at Babel (Babylon), the archenemy through the whole Bible: it shows that the LORD's action implies judgment. On the other hand, one can discern in that judgment a merciful protection against a *worse* evil, against the dehumanizing success of a totalitarian empire.[16] Hence the retrieval—the redemption—of linguistic plurality in the gift of Pentecost, and the celebration of Revelation 5:9 (7:9).

Scripture knows of contextual relativity. Changes, in time, of divinely authorized norms and practices is clearly taught and accepted. The Christian freedom regarding the external (fleshly) institutions of the Old Covenant—also enjoyed by believers of Jewish descent—is most spectacular. General statements such as Colossians 2:17 (they must be seen as shadows now fleeting) and Hebrews 9:10 (such ordinances were only to be observed until a time of reformation) underline their relativity to their location in history (*Heilsgeschichte*). Already in the Old Testament, one can see how the rules concerning sacrifices or marriage in the patriarchal age are no longer in force after Moses.

When Peter unfolds the considerations that warrant his exegesis and

---

15. Cf. Ferdinand de Saussure, *Cours de linguistique générale*, ed. Tullio De Mauro (Paris: Payot, 1982), xi: the editor illustrates the thesis with an example drawn, presumably, from Saussure's lectures: I VITELLI DEI ROMANI SONO BELLI. This same sequence of signs can be read in Italian "The calves of the Romans are fine" and in Latin "Go, Vitellius [a well-known general] to the sound of the Roman God's war."

16. Several similarities between Gen 11 and Gen 3 suggest a parallel between that protective judgment and that of Gen 3:22; the Tree of Life is forbidden because everlasting persistence in sin would be a worse evil.

application—a rare thing in the New Testament, where they remain often implicit—he strikingly sets forth elements from David's historical context to validate his interpretation of Psalm 16 (Acts 2:29ff.).

ATTEMPTS AT CONNECTION

Both "pillars" stand. We do well to hearken to the Ecclesiastic voice at this juncture: "It is good to grasp the one and not let go of the other" (Eccl 7:18). And yet, appropriate schemes that would connect the two with each other are not so easy to find!

Perhaps the most common, quasi-spontaneous offer is the distinction of kernel and husk or, a little more refined (with a cultural component), of *body* (or a synonym) and *garb*. What is permanently valid is found under a superficial appearance; this appearance, being contextually determined or adapted, retains little or no value in itself.

This scheme is severely criticized today. Although Matthew Cook can find several examples of competent scholars—still recently—making use of it,[17] it falls under heavy fire. It downgrades culture, it is claimed, which becomes a mere epiphenomenon. It falsely suggests that permanent truth can be expressed independently of culture, whereas the interpreter's formulation is just as much cultural as the original one (the scheme is secretly rooted in imperialism). It relies on vague metaphors, with no explanatory power.

One can notice, however, how persistently the aforementioned metaphors show themselves! Matthew Cook can write, "Any bifurcation of the supracultural minimalist kernel (proposition) and the cultural (read 'disposable') husk discards too much of the text at hand," and can use the equivalent metaphor himself a few pages later: "There is no point where the naked supracultural proposition(s) are viewed in themselves. They are always clothed by some culture."[18] Benno van den Toren, with a critical intention, asks: "Can We See the Naked Theological Truth?"[19] Such a

---

17. Cook, "Unchanging 'truth,'" 200–1 (see also Buswell, Duvall, George Guthrie, etc.).
18. *Ibid.*, respectively 200 and 204.
19. The title of Benno van den Toren's contribution, ch. 5, to Matthew Cook, Rob Haskell, Ruth Julian, and Natee Tanchanpongs, eds., *Local Theology for the Global Church: Principles for an Evangelical Approach to Contextualization* (Pasadena, CA: William Carey Library, 2010). I was unable to gain access to this book and had to use a French translation enriched by two valuable chapters, Hannes Wiher, *L'Eglise mondiale et les théologies contextuelles: Une approche évangélique de la contextualisation* (Nuremberg/Charols/Ecublens: V.T.R./Excelsis/Alliance Missionnaire Evangélique, 2015). Except for H. Wiher's contributions I was constrained, when quoting from the book, awkwardly to make a translation back from the French translation. In the case of van den Toren's chapter, the French version is his own, and had been published as "Y a-t-il un noyau supra-culturel de l'Evangile humainement accessible?" in *Hokhma*, no. 99 (2011): 41–66, from which article I will quote.

master in the choice of words as J. I. Packer uses "to enshrine" for the particular tradition (and its "embodiment"), "to mesh" for the gospel with it, and "to unshell and repack" for the interpreter[20]—each one a similar metaphor. Other instances would not be so hard to find.[21]

This warns us against triumphalism and may hint at that some stubborn element of truth lying hidden somewhere under such (admittedly too facile) figures of husk, garb, or wrapping.

A second and typically modern choice finds permanent validity in the original writer's "thrust," while the contents of his beliefs and teachings are being relativized. Under the word "thrust" one is to think of existential decision, of patterns of subjective involvement. So argues an able and influential essay by Daniel von Allmen, whom D. A. Carson, with admirable acumen, takes to task.[22]

Sifting the still valuable "thrust" from the now obsolete contents of teaching leads interpreters, one may fear, into the temptation of arbitrariness; yet we grant that the question is relevant. What is essential and to be retained in a legacy: subjective attitudes, existential moves, or objective contents of teaching? When a "rebel" (Luther?) has founded a new institution, is one's true faithfulness to rebellion or to institution (Lutheranism)? Choosing the former alternative is typically modern not only because of the romantic premium put on rebellion, but also because it confers supreme value on the individual's move, the *exercise of freedom*.

Choosing here between the alternatives cannot be severed from the primary and ultimate choice each person makes, for time and eternity, *coram Deo*. The decision proceeds from the very commitment of faith. It is a point of personal confession. My faith (I commit myself; here I stand) is worth nothing apart from its object, which/who transcends it. My faith is worth nothing as an existential determination; it reaches out to salvation because of the saving truth of its object. This is reflected in the acknowledged privilege of contents.[23]

---

20. J. I. Packer, *Collected Shorter Writings*, vol. 2, *Serving the People of God* (Carlisle: Paternoster, 1998), 221, 228.

21. E.g., Albert Lang, "Unfehlbarkeit der Kirche," in *Lexikon für Theologie und Kirche* (Freiburg: Herder, 1965) 10:487, uses *Gewand* for linguistic and conceptual determinations which official texts owe to their times. Paul Ricœur (*Sur la traduction* [Paris: Bayard, 2004], 68) ascribes to "the first Husserl" the unfortunate "prejudice" that "considers expression (*Ausdruck*) as a *clothing* that does not belong to the body."

22. D. A. Carson, "Church and Mission: Reflections on Contextualization and the Third Horizon," in *The Church in the Bible and in the World: An International Study* (Exeter/Grand Rapids: Paternoster/ Baker, 1987), 222–53, for his presentation and critique of Daniel von Allmen, "The Birth of Theology: Contextualization as the dynamic element in the formation of New Testament theology," *International Review of Missions* 64 (1975): 37–52. (Carson also uses the metaphor "in the garb of culture," 249–50).

23. This is not to deprive the "existential" determination of its importance; it must be authentic

The most attractive model is that of *translation*. It can boast of an early use by so distinguished a scholar as Lamin Sanneh.[24] It has biblical precedent. It benefits from a wealth of experience and from the fruit of theoretical pursuits.

Despite clear-cut linguistic diversity, translation functions. Paul Ricœur rightly emphasized the fact that "translation exists."[25] George Steiner underestimates it: his refinement and his prodigious literary culture (in the old sense!) make him disregard, and despise, to some extent, the ordinary use of language, and they lead him to write: "*L'intraducibilità* is the life of speech."[26] Yet, he must admit: "We *do* translate."[27]

To Ricœur, this remains a paradox, since there is no "third language" to mediate between the original statement and its translation.[28] (The discussion whether one can extract a "supracultural core" out of diverse cultures runs on parallel lines: this core corresponds to an expression of content or meaning which would not depend on any given idiom.)[29] I dare suggest that Ricœur tends to exaggerate the difficulty since he does not take into full account the insertion of human speech in the real interaction of persons among themselves and in the world. The "third term" is found in the

---

if the power of saving truth is to affect *me*. Søren Kierkegaard's comparison, as he seeks to define (religious) truth as subjectivity and to locate truth in the *how* rather than in the *what*, between the self-complacent Lutheran who recites the creed as a matter of socially accepted behavior and the pagan man who prays his idol with the passion of the infinite—the latter, not the former, prays God in truth (Kierkegaard, *Concluding Unscientific Postscript to the* Philosophical Fragments, pt. 2, ch. 2), should not mislead us. It can only be accepted as a provocation (Kierkegaard's deeper intention, I believe, for he did subscribe to the creed). Biblically, *neither* of the two men is "in the truth." Without subjective faith, the objective truth avails nothing, and remains a stranger to the person. But "passion of the infinite" (which infinite?) is not acceptable to God if it is not awakened and directed by the revelation of the *true* Infinite.

24. Lamin Sanneh, *Translating the Message: The Missionary Impact on Culture* (Maryknoll, NY: Orbis, 1989).

25. Ricœur, *Sur la traduction*, 56, whatever the reasons to cry: "untranslatable" (53–54). Already in Ricœur, *L'Homme faillible*, in *Philosophie de la volonté*, vol. 2, *Finitude et culpabilité* (Paris: Aubier-Montaigne, 1960), 77, he had written: "There is no human sign radically impossible to understand, no tongue radically impossible to translate from, no work of art to which my taste cannot extend."

26. Steiner, *After Babel: Aspects of Language and Translation* (New York/London: Oxford University Press, 1975), 224.

27. Ibid., 250. On the same page he adds, "The defence of translation has the immense advantage of abundant, vulgar fact"—we can catch a glimpse of his aristocratic disdain—and he goes on: "Translation *is* 'impossible' concedes Ortega y Gasset in his *Miseria y esplendor de la traducción*. But so is all absolute concordance between thought and speech. Somehow the 'impossible' is overcome at every moment in human affairs."

28. Ricœur, *Sur la traduction*, 14 (cf. 39, 60).

29. Cook, "Unchanging 'truth,'" 201, argues against dreaming of such a supracultural core. He finds support in D. A. Carson, "Church and Mission," 248. He does not notice, however, Carson's cautious qualifications: "in the sense demanded by Kraft" (248); "from the perspective of human perception and formulation" (249). Benno van den Toren affirms both a humanly accessible supracultural kernel of the gospel and *no formulation* of it which would be always and everywhere valid ("Y a-t-il," 65).

cognitive and practical participation in reality through language. A greater dose of epistemological realism and a stronger emphasis on the referential dimension opens up the way to a solution of the "paradox." Theologically, I would add: not only "in the world" but, whether acknowledged or denied, before and even in God, the absolutely real. All humans stand *coram Deo*; they live, and move, and are in him (Act 17:28). This ontological all-embracing context should not be forgotten when one inquires about the possibility of translation!

Common presentations have seldom sounded such underlying conditions. The question of application to other components of contexts than language, and of criteria to be used, has generally been left in the shade. That weakness limits the helpfulness of the translation model.

Roman Catholic theologians and official documents are prone to use *incarnation* as the model for "inculturation." Characteristically, the Fourth Latin-American Episcopal Conference declared in its Santo-Domingo meeting (October 1992): "The analogy between the incarnation and the Christian presence in the social, cultural and historical context of peoples leads us to the theological perspective of the incarnation. The incarnation is a dynamic process which goes from the Gospel to the heart of each people and community, through the mediation of language and of accessible symbols received by the Church."[30] Not a few evangelicals follow suit.[31] Have they pondered the stakes enough?

Suggestive analogies do catch our attention. Becoming "flesh" for the eternal Son-*Logos* implied being located in a particular context, with particular identity markers: he became first-century Palestinian Jewish flesh, with Aramaic (surely Hebrew and probably some Greek) as his linguistic medium. This central truth of the gospel surely bears upon our subject.

Yet Scripture does not know of an "incarnation principle." Incarnation is a unique event, in many respects unthinkable. How can one being possess two natures? A "nature" is everything one is and can be described as being (the *principium quo*, while the "person," in the case of personal existence, is the *principium quod*, as medieval masters used to say). There is one nature per person. It is obvious. Only deity can rise above the constraints of that

---

30. Quoted by Efoé-Julien Penoukou, "Inculturation," in *Dictionnaire critique de théologie*, ed. Jean-Yves Lacoste (Paris: Presses Universitaires de France, 1998), 567.

31. Cf. Dean S. Gilliland's title, "The Incarnation as Matrix for Appropriate Theologies," according to Hannes Wiher, *L'Eglise mondiale*, 11 (cf. 284), who also quotes, 38, Dean Flemming's definition of contextualization as "the dynamic and encompassing process through which the Gospel is incarnated in a concrete situation, both historical and cultural."

definition. Only deity, and the unique relationship of deity to humanity, make possible what is impossible: for one person to be in two natures which remain distinct! It happened, and could happen, only once.

We should keep on the alert when cheap rhetoric trivializes this uniqueness (I remember gratefully John Webster issuing such a warning at the April 2004 Wheaton College Theological Conference).

The French missiologist Jean-François Zorn reminds us that extending incarnation to the whole world has been a Roman Catholic tendency which Protestants, standing on biblical ground, had to oppose.[32] In recent decades, representative Catholic theologians have softened, de-emphasized, and sometimes veiled the classical theme of the incarnation-continuing-in-the-church. As far as I can see, it has remained structurally determinative.[33] If heirs of the Reformation maintain that it jeopardizes the New Testament *ephapax*, "once for all," and unduly divinizes the community of Christ's disciples, then they should beware of ways of speaking that suggest such a teaching; praiseworthy ecumenical goodwill and courtesy must not disarm discernment.

Caution, therefore, advises against making incarnation the paradigm of contextualization and against making it a key conceptual instrument when one seeks to combine the permanent validity of doctrinal statements with their contextual relativity.

A FEW OBSERVATIONS: TIMELY OR UNTIMELY (?)

Proposed models fail to satisfy entirely, though it would be unwise to discard them—especially the "translation" one. Some observations may help us strengthen what has been offered so far, refine our grasp of the issues, purify, perhaps, our approach from useless or misleading presuppositions.

Beware of tropes! When some phrases or ways of expressing a matter become very common, critical vigilance easily dwindles. If they belong to figurative speech (tropes), one runs the risk of forgetting that character and of drawing mistaken consequences from them (as if they could be taken literally).

One often hears or reads, "We live in an entirely different world from the world of Abraham," or David, or Calvin—even of Carl F. H. Henry for some. That consideration buttresses the call to contextualization:

---

32. Zorn, "La contextualisation: un concept théologique?" *Revue d'Histoire et de Philosophie Religieuses* 77, no. 3 (1997): 179–82.

33. One should remember that a major Vatican II document, the dogmatic constitution *Lumen gentium* makes room for the thesis. The church blends a human and a divine element: *Ideo ob non mediocrem analogiam incarnati Verbi mysterio assimilatur* (§ 8). Continuity obtains: the promised restoration *incepit in Christo, provehitur in missione Spiritus Sancti et per eum pergit in Ecclesia* (§ 48). The divine mystery of salvation (with incarnation just mentioned) *revelatur et continuatur in Ecclesia* (§ 52).

propositions that were valid in Abraham's, David's, Carl Henry's times urgently need recasting today. Now, the proposition about different worlds can be accepted as *hyperbole*. But *literally* it is by no means true to fact. We do live in the same world as Abraham did! When traveling in the Middle East, we cross the same valleys as he did, we drink from the same sources, we gaze upon the same stars, we breathe the same air as he did.[34] The same physical laws ruled the world millennia ago—and they must have some effect on ways of thinking themselves.[35]

Potent factors foster a misrepresentation of the actual case; they twist the picture out of proportion. Some factors are psychological, bound to modalities of human perception. One black spot on the white sheet catches our whole attention. What is common and regular is trite, uninteresting. It goes without saying—without being duly taken into account. Some factors are ideological. "Difference" has arisen on top of contemporary values, and universal claims are immediately suspect of imperialistic intentions.

What's the outcome? Common representations of human diversity ignore or minimize the constants and universals of the human condition. They are basic, and they regulate the human condition everywhere, but they escape notice. Leading anthropologists, as we mentioned earlier, have redressed the balance. Noted philosopher Charles Taylor offers a fine example of sounder procedure: "alternative possibilities" in various cultures are to be understood "in relation to some human constants at work in all."[36] And yet these commonalities remain commonly ignored. The truncated picture retains its hold on the general public and on the work of many thinkers. Common sense is to react. One should not, even, affirm constants and universals as a "supracultural" core. They are not above cultures (as if "culture" were to be *reduced* to difference), but the basis of all cultures, a main part in all cultures!

Since language is such an important part of the cultural context, one may recall Chomsky's generative grammar and its affirmation of underlying universal structures. Ricœur, a little reluctantly, grants the partial success

---

34. I remember reading that a statistical treatment of the exchanges and circulation of the atoms of the earth's atmosphere (with flora and fauna) established that we have in our lungs at least one atom which was, at a time, in the lungs of all previous inhabitants of the planets (who lived, at least, for a few decades). If this is true, it means: in Abraham's lungs—and also in Jesus's!

35. Geneva psychologist Jean Piaget argued that human interaction with the laws of space shapes the genesis of intelligence; his views have been disputed—even if this is not the only factor, it is most probably one at play.

36. Taylor, "Understanding and Ethnocentricity," in *Philosophy and the Human Sciences* (Cambridge: Cambridge University Press, 1985), 125, as quoted by William A. Dyrness, "Crosscultural Theology," in *Global Dictionary of Theology*, 216b. Hannes Wiher, *L'Eglise mondiale*, 28, offers a beautiful summary of the argument.

of Chomsky's endeavor.[37] The French linguist Jacques Lerot boldly asserts, "Most concepts are the same or nearly the same in different idioms."[38] In his masterly synthesis on language, Vern S. Poythress upholds the universal perspective, though I wish he had highlighted it even more insistently.[39]

We may add a further methodological consideration. In this *abnormal* world, with the damages caused by sin and sin's sequels, exceptions are not enough to refute universality. Clearly, we may count on a substantial measure of human commonalities to help us hold together universal validity and contextual particularity—not a desperate task.

"Canon sense" brings a full confirmation. Scripture happily proclaims the unity of the whole human family. It emphasizes its one origin (Acts 17:26). It interprets the empirical sinfulness of all in terms of this origin and union "in Adam." It sees all the various times of history under the Lord's unifying sovereignty. One God—God of non-Jews as well as the God of Jews (Rom 3:29)—one world, one *anthrōpos*.

Within the Bible, translation does not raise any problem of principle. It is naturally introduced in Nehemiah 8:7ff., the origin of targum in Jewish tradition. The idea of a normative human "nature" surfaces a few times (the most striking instance is provided by Rom 1:26ff.).

Beware of metaphors. Metaphors are powerful among tropes, and some have exercised a major influence on majority thinking. Hans-Georg

---

37. Ricœur, *Sur la traduction*, 31.

38. Lerot, *Précis de linguistique générale* (Paris: Editions de Minuit, 1993), 82, as quoted by Sylvain Romerowski, *Les Sciences du langage et l'étude de la Bible* (Charols: Excelsis, 2011), 317.

39. I dare differ on a very minor point. In his zeal against reductionism, Poythress espouses Kenneth Pike's "tagmemics" (*In the Beginning Was the Word*, 266, 337n22). He adopts Pike's "emic" and "etic" categories, names which are derived from the words Phonetics (science of spoken sounds in their physical and physiological characteristics) and Phonemics (science of "phonemes," linguistically significant phonological units that compose words). He explains: "Phonetics takes an outsider's or foreigner's point of view," like a tape recorder, whereas in Phonemics, linguists "study sound from the insider's point of view, by asking which sounds are perceived as making a difference" (151n3). He then affirms, "The particular genres in a particular culture are 'emic' categories, in the terminology of chapter 19. The commonalities shared by different cultures are 'etic'" (196n3). I doubt the usefulness, and even the propriety, of the outsider/insider pair to differentiate between the phonetic and the phonemic levels; rather, Phonetics deal with sounds as phenomena of nature, and Phonemics as linguistic elements, that is, as *bearers of meaning*. This distinction is open to all, insiders and outsiders (only these do not reach the linguistic level, as long as they are ignorant of the language—as they do not know *tèn dunamin tès phônès*, as Paul says, 1 Cor 14:11, the meaning of the linguistic sign, as they cannot receive sounds as phonemes). One may encounter *phonetic* traits that are *peculiar* to a given people group. This is why adults are so often unable to pronounce the words of a foreign tongue though they know it well (there even seems to be differences in voice-texture). Conversely, *phonemes* only vary within limits and their diversity cannot be separated from universal conditions of human linguistic communication. "Genres" are rooted in these, "commonalities." Poythress himself notes, with reference to Robert E. Longacre, that "narrative discourse in a broad sense is a linguistic universal, characteristic of all human language" (195n1; this rings truer to me than assigning Vladimir Propp to the *emic* particular category and Algirdas J. Greimas to *etic* universality, 201n13).

Gadamer's *horizons* have been granted the status of key categories. Has this been sufficiently guarded? Do horizons merge, melt, or fuse? Are there really *two* horizons with author and reader? Should not our "horizon" be what is revealed of God's all-embracing design?

The Greek neutral participle *horizon* means that which limits, a boundary. There is no access to what lies beyond the horizon. Does this apply to the human spirit in historical, social, and cultural "contexts"? Benno van den Toren, an apostle of contextualization, maintains, "All human thought is *rooted* in a particular cultural context but it is not necessarily *imprisoned* in that context."[40] Ricœur follows Descartes in his own way as he discerns some *infinity* in man's "intention of truth."[41] Emmanuel Levinas, also in his own (most original) way, perceives a reference which goes beyond all horizon: "Having a meaning is taking a position respecting an absolute."[42] It could be described as Karl Rahner's central conviction: "Human speech is, in advance, open onto the infinity of God (both naturally by virtue of its *potentia obœdentialis* and supranaturally by virtue of its being enunciated by the Spirit and raised to a higher level by the Spirit [in Scripture])."[43] Vern Poythress offers an exact wording: "Human beings have the ability to stand back from their immediate situation and look at larger wholes. They can even think about the whole of history,"[44] and "We can in a sense 'transcend' the immediacy of our local situation and our small-scale use of language."[45] If the human heart was made for truth, for the fellowship of the God of Truth, with "eternity" engraved in its very constitution (Eccl 3:11), then we are warranted in affirming a kind of transcendence beyond all earthly horizons.[46] This undermines the logic which sees contextual relativity and permanent, universal validity as mutually exclusive.

The metaphor of *perspective* must be handled with care. The younger

---

40. Van den Toren, "Y a-t-il," 56.

41. Ricœur, *L'Homme faillible*, 52–54.

42. Levinas, *Totalité et infini. Essai sur l'extériorité* (Paris: Librairie générale française-Kluwer Academic, 1990 [La Haye: Martinus Nijhoff, 1961, 1971]), 99.

43. Rahner, "Überlegungen zur Dogmenentwicklung," *Schriften zur Theologie* (Einsiedeln: Benzinger, 1962), 4:23.

44. Poythress, *In the Beginning Was the Word*, 89 (cf. 170). He adds, "In this ability, they imitate God, who has complete knowledge of himself and of all of history."

45. *Ibid.* Cf. his "Canon and Speech-Act: Limitations of Speech-Act Theory with Implications for a Putative Theory of Canonical Speech-Acts," *WTJ* 70 (2008): 354: one cannot escape relativism "unless there is a transcendent adjudication of truth." (I use my notes from this first publication; the essay is also included in the book *In the Beginning*; the critique of speech-act theory is aimed at simplistic applications, and Poythress acknowledges that John Searle keeps clear of them.)

46. Emmanuel Mounier (a founder of "Personalism"), *Introduction aux existentialismes* (Paris: Gallimard, 1962) 46, 180ff., suggested a distinction between *transproscendence* (transcending beyond oneself) and *transascendence* (towards God).

Edward Schillebeeckx wielded it as a tool to sap the permanent validity of dogmatic statements.[47] We can only see things from a particular perspective, and perspective depends on location, which is not the same for all—how could we require others to see things as we do? Here again, Ricœur was able to show himself (at least in 1960) remarkably sensitive to the claims of truth: "When I stand back, I do not institute a higher viewpoint, but I aim at truth without a point of view,"[48] and even more pointedly, "How could I know a perspective, in the very act of perceiving, if *somehow* I did not escape from my perspective?"[49] One can argue that what we think and say (see?) from our limited point of view escapes relativism because it is grafted on the archetypal knowledge of him who has been described as "a sphere whose center is everywhere and whose circumference nowhere" (already quoted by Thomas Bradwardine).[50]

A rather persuasive appeal is made by the "postmodern" (modernity-post) party to yet another feature of the conditions of knowledge: the interrelatedness of everything. It apparently precludes the possession of any cognitive stability, and therefore rules out permanent validity. Poythress aptly replies that the remedy is found in the linkage of our knowledge to the knowledge of God, who masters all relationships.[51] This is fulfilled in redemption (fellowship restored) but based in creation, and remains basic for humanity. The privilege of being God's image, the "metaphysical" framework it implies, is not simply annihilated as creation subsists in a corrupt and disrupted state. Owing to that creational dependency—which is not abolished when people deny it and sin against it—human knowledge is stable enough. Though partial and contingently conditioned, it still aims at truth.

I would add that the truth of relation does not cancel the converse truth of singular identity. We must acknowledge the "granular" constitution of our world: the insight of the Greek atomists. Rain falls in drops, sand aggregates grains, reality is made of particles—I first met this observation in Pierre Teilhard de Chardin.[52] Creatures do not dissolve into waves inter-

47. Schillebeeckx, *Theologische Peilingen*, vol. 1, *Openbaring en Theologie* (Bilthoven: Nelissen, 1962), known to me through the French translation by Paul Bourgy, *Approches théologiques I. Révélation et théologie* (Bruxelles/Paris: Cep/Office du livre, 1965).

48. Ricœur, *L'Homme faillible*, 49.

49. Ibid., 44.

50. Bradwardine, *De causa Dei* 1.5, p. 180 (*Deus est sphaera infinita cuius centrum est ubique et circumferentia nusquam*), referring to the *Book of 24 Philosophers*, as quoted by Alexandre Koyré, *Etudes d'histoire de la pensée philosophique* (Paris: Gallimard, 1981), 92n1; Blaise Pascal, *Pensées*, 231 in Brunschvicg, 420 in Lafuma, which added "a point moving at infinite speed."

51. Poythress, *In the Beginning Was the Word*, 246, 330.

52. Teilhard de Chardin, *Le Phénomène humain* (Paris: Seuil, 1955), 34ff., 53, 82ff., cf. 97.

secting. God causes creatures with a distinct existence to stand before him with a stable *enough* identity. He shows that it is so by giving *names*. The supreme expression of this "law" of creation concerns the creature of God's election and covenant. This creature is granted distinctive existence as an individual person—whom the Lord addresses, "I know thee *by thy name*."

In language, one may recognize a similar distinction of *words*. Against a tendency of structuralists, a tongue (Saussure's *langue*) cannot be reduced to network, to systematic relationships. Ricœur was rightly led to affirm a "hard core" of meaning in lexical units.[53]

The area of my observations, ultimately, is the arena of the old mêlée of the *same* and the *other*, of being and becoming, of the legacies of Parmenides and Heraclitus, avatars of the one and the many. When one reads Karl Rahner, for instance, one is struck by his covert Heraclitean preference; when he characterizes history, he always implies a flux that ever brings up novelty, change ever changing.[54] He never critically scrutinizes this assumption. He never listens to the antagonistic accent of Ecclesiastes: nothing new under the sun!

If they are treated as *principles* in the strong sense (absolutely primary) there is no hope of reconciliation. Actually, a lucid reflection realizes that one cannot *think* them together. A compromise such as Plato's realm of ideas (as in the *Sophistès*) cannot be ratified. Only the foundation in God and his plan or design makes possible holding them together. I find Ricœur's confession that he cannot account for the unity of history, once he has discarded the biblical "Plot of plots," a most moving moment of his entire career.[55] We trust the Word of the Sovereign Lord, whose Trinitarian being grounds both unity and plurality and frees us from the antinomy of pagan (apostate) thought.

Under the blessing of the revelation of God's design, we may explore a little further what is meant by "contextual relativity."

Every speech-act is indeed located in time and space, and this *may* limit its intended import. It usually implies tacit references to elements of the situation and assumptions shared with the addressee. It often implicitly answers a prior question. It is free to select some aspects only of the matter

---

53. Ricœur, *La Métaphore vive*, 144 (143f). "Hard core" in English in Ricœur's French text.
54. Rahner, "Zur Frage der Dogmenentwicklung," 1:55; Rahner, "Überlegungen zur Dogmenentwicklung," 4:37, no repetition; Rahner, "Zur Geschichtlichkeit der Theologie," *Schriften zur Theologie* (Einsiedeln: Benzinger, 1967), 8:89, "constant movement and flux."
55. Ricœur, *Temps et récit III. Le temps raconté* (Paris: Seuil, 1985), 372n1, for his rejection of a biblical theology of history, embracing all partial plots ("the bare fact that we have four Gospels" is enough, he claims, to forbid it!); 374ff. and 391 for the failure to account for unity and to solve the *aporia* of time (Ricœur transmutes his failure into a sober stance of modesty).

at hand. It chooses a language, with particular connotations. If the Benjamin Lee Whorf hypothesis about a specific worldview bound to a given idiom cannot be sustained (Ricœur, who also stresses, after Charles S. Peirce, the wonderful flexibility of language, discards with welcome clarity the hypothesis[56]), worldview is involved in utterance.

On the receiver side, similar contextual conditions operate—hence the suspicion that the proposition *as appropriated* is no longer the same as the proposition as uttered.

This is not dramatically devastating for "permanent validity" if we consider (as was suggested) what is common to both situations, de facto translatability, and the "transcendence" of the human spirit. As Schleiermacher discerned, a common sensitivity (*Empfänglichkeit*) begets a marvelous sympathy between author and reader. Many do experience what Poythress describes, a figure of humility woven in the life of mind and soul: "The reader gives up the exclusive concentration on his own ideas, in order that another person's ideas may prosper and momentarily have preeminence in the reader's mind."[57] Transfer (the meaning of "translation"!) happily happens despite the losses it implies. Losses there are—they can be serenely borne if one remembers that language lives by approximation (I will soon come back to the point).

I observe (and *this is decisive* in my opinion, and strategic in contemporary debates) that contextual relativity so described affects the *meaning* of the proposition or illocutionary act rather than its *truth* or ethical goodness. Truth/rightness/validity is acknowledged or denied, in a second move, through a judgment passed on the meaning once the meaning has been ascertained.

If one then claims that *criteria*—indeed, there is no judgment without criteria—are entirely relative to the social, cultural, and historical context and that they are part of the "local" worldview as local, then he/she *imprisons* the person in their situation, an option we may confidently reject. Conditioning is obvious. The decisive word is "entirely." If one maintains this "entirely," permanent validity dissolves. There is no stopping on the slippery slope, and why should one debate anymore? I am afraid Ricœur himself, who was able to pen the fine statements quoted above, falls a prey to relativism when he suggests that no thinker can break free from

56. Ricœur, *Sur la traduction*, 27ff, 45. What I have read of Edward Sapir dissuades me from imputing to him the Whorfian hypothesis (which has romanticist roots, with Wilhelm von Humboldt).

57. Poythress, *In the Beginning Was the Word*, 177.

the *croyable disponible*, "what is available for belief," in his or her time.[58] We do measure how formidable the effort to rise above the "plausibility structures" of one's epoch must be, and our imagination reels when we realize our dependence on education, on peer-opinion, on information as "formatted" by media. But some men and women *do* shake off the chains (common grace also is at work), and an ultimate ability to resist the pressure must remain if accountability and truth-intention are to be preserved. The locus of decision can only be the deeper commitment of faith.

One more remark on a common way of reasoning about contextualization should be critically assessed. Culture, commonly considered as context, is taken to be a well-circumscribed and homogeneous whole; it defines the people's identity and utmost "respect" is due. However, this representation is woefully inadequate. A culture is rather an evolving conglomerate with qualitatively different, and often antagonistic components. It negotiates its continuity, in every generation, with outside influences. Material factors disturb precarious equilibriums.[59] The relationship of permanent validity to the various components of a culture cannot be the same!

A pleasant alliteration runs through the elements to be considered in a culture: conduct, code, creed, and cult.[60] I select *code* (in a different acceptation of the term) and *creed* as the most relevant categories for our purposes. "Code" not only includes all semiotics systems and language, but also all the other regular correspondences between signifiers and signified (they are sometimes called languages in an analogical sense), all sets of symbols, and all meaningful gestures and attitudes such as the movements of the head to say "yes" or "no." In its local peculiarity, code is arbitrary to a great extent, and its choices are basically *legitimate*. They do not raise the question of truth and ethical goodness. "Creed," on the contrary, is made up of beliefs and value-judgments, which come under the qualifications of true and false, good or bad, valid or not (they do, Matt 12:36ff.[61]). There is

---

58. Ricœur, "La Critique de la religion et le langage de la foi," *Bulletin du Centre Protestant d'Etudes* [Geneva] 16, no. 4–5 (June 1964): 14, cf. 21, and 12: the atheistic suspicion of religion developed by Marx, Nietzsche and Freud "now belong to all possible faith." The same conviction in other words (I don't remember the same phrase) occurs elsewhere in Ricœur's works, e.g., *Le Conflit des interprétations. Essais d'herméneutique* (Paris: Seuil, 1969) 294, 383. (He agrees with Bultmann.)

59. I summarized a few points in my "Invoquer la culture," *Théologie Évangélique* 2, no. 2 (2003): 151–61, which shows how George Devereux influenced my understanding. (Born a Hungarian Jew, he was converted to [rather liberal] Christianity, and had a brilliant twofold career, French and American, as an ethnologist and anthropologist.)

60. Melba Padilla Maggay and William A. Dyrness, "Culture and Society," *Global Dictionary of Theology*, 222b.

61. I do not imply that the judgment of Jesus's warning is *restricted* to the validity of the thing said: it will also surely weigh subjective attitudes, faithfulness to personal calling, etc.

a kinship between the distinction of code and creed and the Saussurian one between *langue* and *parole*,[62] or Noam Chomsky's between "competence" and "performance." Undoubtedly, there is in culture a vast expanse between the two poles of code and creed: the field of customs (one can think of the ways of cooking and table manners), preferences, and some priorities, which may have links with beliefs and ethical principles, but links so loose while human apprehension is so "rough," *grosso modo*, that prudence recommends not to ask about truth and right (let insiders take the initiative!).

Worldviews, on the contrary, are not immune from judgment. Amalgamated with other material, they embody the key beliefs and values, what people under their control think *true* and *right*. Creed indeed! When scholars give the impression that "local" worldviews should function as the norms of inculturation/contextualization, there is matter for concern.[63] Rather, they should undergo transcendent appraisal and reformation.

SKETCHING TENTATIVE CONCLUSIONS

If some patches of unhealthy mist were dispelled, we may perceive, through the mist that remains, what can be concluded regarding our two "pillars" and the connections between them.

May we say something solid and clear-cut regarding the "objective" pole of communication, the original speech-act—whether it reaches us in oral or in written form makes no radical difference? Common sense and, above all, "canon sense" allow us to affirm the permanent validity of propositions: once true or right, always so.

Location, location, however! This applies to the meaning, the meaning

---

62. A long end-note in the edition of the *Cours de linguistique générale*, 423–425 n68, deals with the translation in other tongues of the two key words. In Greek, *glōtta* [*glōssa*] and *logos*; in Latin, *lingua* and *sermo* or *oratio*; in German, *Sprache* and *sprechen*, but some prefer other pairs, *Sprachtum* and *Sprechakt*, *Sprachgebilde* and *Sprechakt*, etc. In English, linguists do not agree; W. Baskin has chosen *language* and *speaking*, with *speech* or *human speech* for the vaguer and intermediate "language" in French.

63. Rahner, "Zur Geschichtlichkeit der Theologie," 89, teaches that the translation of statements of faith must "conform [*konform werden*] to the prior horizon of understanding of the dialogue-partners" (he nuances, however, his surprising choice of the word "conform" [cf. Rom 12:2] at the end of his [long] sentence: the partner's presuppositions have not been adequately reflected upon and their rightness has not been examined). He brands as theology's shortcoming that it "does not take seriously the questions of the time, deep into its heart." The emphasis is here and elsewhere in Rahner's writings on espousing the *Zeitgeist*, though he may mention in passing the critical role that is still called for. Sesboüé, *Le Magistère à l'épreuve*, 289, preaches a twofold faithfulness: to Christ's teaching *and* "to its credibility in our time"—does this entail that we should leave to the side what is unpalatable to our contemporaries, as it disagrees with their worldview? Matthew Cook, according to the French translation of the book he edited, *L'Eglise mondiale*, 139, seems to yield to Whorfian confusion and make worldview part of the linguistic system—fortunately, he qualifies: "to some extent."

which is contextually identified. *If* the assertion or injunction was valid within the parameters of the original situation, which parameters forever define what was said, then it remains true/right/valid as such for thinkers of every age and place. This clarity disposes of the sophistry brought forward by the great Kojève: the statement "a man is flying above the ocean" belongs to its AD 1300 context. Whether explicitly or implicitly it is qualified by the clause "at the moment of utterance," it remains true to this day that in AD 1300 no man was flying; its truth has not changed.

The universal character of validity is grounded in the unity of monotheistic creation and history under God. God's consistency in his words and in his works—he cannot deny himself—the role of the Son-*Logos* in whom all things hold together (Col 1:17, *synestēken*, the verb from which "system" derives), ensure that creatures form a universe. There is no *absolute* otherness in created being. We resist seductive Hegelian dialectics (which turns the negative into a principle, though it is circumscribed by the total becoming it generates) and irrationalistic "bragging," such as San Pietro Damiani's thesis that God can ensure that what happened did not happen (as Hegel also professed)—the medieval cardinal was proud to fight for faith with a donkey's jaw-bone! We confess consistency and, therefore, permanent validity.

On this basis, it is *possible* for a listener/reader/interpreter to overcome the difficulty caused by differences of context. An arduous task, in which failure remains a risk—*traduttore, traditore*—but not an impossible one. Readers/interpreters can *tend* towards that goal. Sympathetic relocation requires both information and an inner attitude of humble welcoming. It can bear fruit.[64]

Ambiguity unfortunately attaches to some statements in the literature. Benno van den Toren, while he valiantly defends that humans can access the supracultural kernel of the gospel, still concludes that "it is impossible to produce a formulation of the kernel of the Gospel always and everywhere valid."[65] Karl Rahner rightly reminds us that "the formula is never the thing itself" but adds that it "remains inadequate in respect to the thing."[66] "Adequacy," I grant, may be used in slippery ways. I would reverse Ricœur's choice of terms. He suggests that translation offers "equivalence" *without*

---

64. To add one witness, Zorn, "La contextualisation," 187, (statement in italics in his text): "We must affirm that theology has a universal dimension which transcends contexts."

65. Van den Toren, "Y a-t-il," 65.

66. Rahner, "Kleines Fragment. 'Über die kollektive Findung der Wahrheit." *Schriften zur Theologie* (Einsiedeln: Benzinger, 1968) 6:107 (p. 106 evokes God's silence).

"adequacy" or "sameness."[67] I would question "equivalence," in the strict sense of the word, but claim that translation provides an "adequate" access to the same meaning.[68]

The last point calls for some elaboration. For strict equivalence, no translation *equals* the original. The transfer is not complete; there is always a deficit. Connotations are lost like echoes, like a halo of shared memories. If some are added by a skillful translator, this is not translation proper. These additions constitute a new text that enriches the original one; it's not a part of it. Adequacy means, however, that whatever is essential in the original word, the contents of the illocutionary act, does "come through."

Several considerations may be offered. The first would be the primacy of meaning in linguistic communication. The loss mostly concerns the emotive efficacy, the aesthetic enjoyment produced, though some translators are able of near-miracles in this regard. Not meaning. Language (speech activity), admittedly, fulfills other functions. But I suggest that they presuppose the communication of meaning: information on realities, expression, injunction, etc. (incidentally those overlap to some extent). I wish Poythress had made the privilege of meaning clearer.[69]

The loss mostly affects poetical and literary texts; I interpret in the light of this fact George Steiner's celebration of *intraducibilià*. Attention for those features which, admittedly, are difficult to translate, receives texts as works more than words. Remember the meaning of *poièma*! Jean-Paul Sartre proved how sharp he could be when he wrote: "Poets are men who refuse to make use of language. . . . They consider the words as things and not as signs."[70] Although the Scriptures contain works of art, they wish to be received first and foremost as the *Word*, and doctrinal statements summarize the meaning-contents as the Word.

A third reason why meaning suffers little in (a good) translation would

---

67. Ricœur, *Sur la traduction*, 14, 60.

68. Poythress, *In the Beginning Was the Word*, 134, uses "adequate vehicle" for language; van den Toren, "Y a-t-il," 65ff., affirms that our contextualized knowledge is "adequate" though not "absolute." I welcome these statements.

69. Poythress, *In the Beginning Was the Word*, 173ff., is led by his Trinitarian method to put on the same level presence, meaning, and control. He sees them as interlocking, but pens the following passage (174): "We *may stop* worrying about the author's meaning. Is the reader a student with assignment? Or is he just an ordinary reader looking for entertainment or stimulating ideas?" The reader may take the text "as a springboard for his imagination." I am reluctant to apply the suggestion to most parts of canonical Scripture. Does it fit the disciple's posture listening to his Lord's words?

70. Sartre, *Qu'est-ce que la littérature?* (Paris: Gallimard, 1985), 17 and 18. What follows the quotation on p. 17 is also perceptive: "Since it is in and through language, conceived of as an instrument of a certain kind, that the search for truth operates, we should not imagine that poets aim at discerning and exhibiting truth."

be because of the *grosso modo* functioning of natural language. "Fuzzy edges" is an apt metaphor for the way we handle concepts and words. Infinite precision is not human, whereas groping for words and more exact understandings, as Poythress powerfully stresses,[71] is human indeed!

If we focus our attention on the "subjective" pole, that of reception and appropriation in other contexts, a *second* move is legitimate and normal. The first move, which we claimed was "not impossible," is an empathetic and informed transfer to the birthplace of the text in order to ascertain its meaning there. Once this is done, one is in a position to ask about the bearing of the proposition in the interpreter's context. Presumably, because of the interrelatedness of all situations in the one world of the one God, it has one. Creatures, being mirrors of the divine perfections, also mirror one another, and the meaning in the original context "reverberates" in others. One can speak of "significance" as distinct from "meaning," of "application" after "understanding." Permanent validity bears *relatively* new fruit.

The enterprise is a venture. It must be done in the light of the biblical worldview. It should seek for cues in the biblical text and argue from analogy. Again, it is *not impossible*. It may imply changing emphases, adding complements, developing seed-thoughts to answer new questions. Whatever our evaluation of arguments set forth by Roman Catholic apologists in Newman's wake (I am not convinced), we may admire their skill and personal honesty. We are to acknowledge for ourselves a broad margin of freedom in the reception of permanently valid propositions—when it is done in new contexts, with an eye to import and application.

The *same* and the *other* hold together by virtue of the divine foundation. It will be rewarding for us finally to meditate on a question which we only touched upon: beyond the unified diversity of creation guaranteed by his design and government, how do permanent validity and ties to changeable contexts relate to God as he is?

The Rock on which the first pillar is erected is nearly obvious. He is the immutable Rock of Ages. On his being, as he is, rest all stability and dependability that can be found—indeed, the validity of true propositions *semper et ubique*. The *'ekhad* of the confession: "Listen, Israel, YHWH our God, YHWH is one" (Deut 6:4),[72] probably implies the qualitative oneness of the divine essence. The classical name for it is *simplicity*, if one accepts

---

71. Poythress, *In the Beginning Was the Word*, 168, and "Canon and Speech-Act Theory," 347.
72. Traditionally, the last letter of the first word, *'*, and the last letter, *d*, of the last word are written in bigger size in Hebrew Bibles; in order to form the word *'ed*, "witness, confession."

the paradox (no cheap escape out of difficulty here) that simplicity may be affirmed together with the complexity of the multicolored riches of the wisdom of God and therefore of his essence. The supreme degree of unity—far above any unity in creatures, unity as fits the Absolute—is the perfection we confess. Saint Augustine was right when he repeated, as he was fond, the God *is* what he *has*. We should purge our worship of those anthropomorphic images of God as are current even among evangelicals, images of petty gods tailored to suit late modern wishes.

Distinction, diversity, is no less primary and ultimate in the Trinitarian confession. Father, Son, and Spirit are, as such, absolutely distinct, more so than any creature from another. They are distinct not in essence, which exists only once as one God, but as subsisting relations (*relatio* is the Latin term which corresponds to the Cappadocian Fathers' *schesis*). (No quaternity, however. It is essential for the divine essence to be possessed by Father, Son, and Holy Spirit. We should never separate them as we try to think along the lines of revelation.) As such, God's being constitutes the root and fountainhead of all diversity in the world.

The Trinitarian model may help us hold together the one and the many when meditating on divine eternity. Neither the merely one pure present (excluding the distinction of past and future) nor the mere infinite succession of the many moments whose union would be problematic. The God who is and who calls himself *'ehyeh* (Exod 3:14) is the God who is, and was, and is to come (an explanatory paraphrase of the Exodus name in Revelation 1:8). The Son, Jesus Christ, is the same yesterday, and today, and forever (Heb 13:8). Paradoxically again, the Rock is not immobile; he is the Living Rock, and Paul can strikingly write that he would accompany his people through the desert wanderings (1 Cor 10:4).[73]

We may thus celebrate the *life* of the eternal God as the source and warranty of meaningful history. The mystery of God, the mystery of all mysteries, emboldens us to confess "present truth."[74]

73. We should not accept too easily the idea that Paul was borrowing from Jewish *haggadah*: the homiletical legend is only attested much later in Jewish tradition.

74. I tried to develop the main theses briefly introduced above in various essays or articles: "Divine Immutability," in *The Power and Weakness of God*, ed. Nigel M. de S. Cameron (Edinburgh: Rutherford House, 1990), 1–22; "Yesterday, Today, Forever: Time, Times, Eternity in Biblical Perspective," *Tyndale Bulletin* 52, no. 2 (2001): 183–202; and "Réinterprétations récentes du dogme trinitaire" followed by "Les appropriations trinitaires," *Hokhma*, no. 104 (2013): 14–55.

CHAPTER 6

HOLY SCRIPTURE AS SACRED GROUND

KATHERINE SONDEREGGER

PERHAPS IT'S TRUE THAT OUR WESTERN CULTURE turns on the reading of a book—but not quite the one we had in mind! Early in his education, Aurelius Augustine opened and read the rhetor Cicero's work, now lost, *Hortensius*; and the world changed that day. In *Hortensius*, Augustine discovered the passionate longing for truth that was to animate all his days, and that gave us the remarkable Augustinian themes of Illumination, of the Transcendentals, and of the intellectual ascent to the True and Lovely Goodness who is God. Here is how Augustine expresses his captivity and his liberty in the light of Cicero's essay: "It altered my outlook on life," he wrote in his *Confessions*, "All my empty dreams suddenly lost their charm and my heart began to throb with a bewildering passion for the wisdom of eternal truth."[1] All of us in this room can recognize that raw tumult of that experience: it breathes the air of conversion. The old has passed away; behold the new has come. Augustine was nineteen when this revolution erupted in his young life. In the first blush of his new identity as philosopher, he returned to another Book, one that his mother Monica prized, the Bible. In those days, Cicero cast everything, even Holy Scripture, in the shade. Here is Augustine on that early reading of the Sacred Text: "To me the Scriptures seemed quite unworthy of comparison with the stately prose of Cicero, because I had too much conceit to accept their simplicity

---

1. Aurelius Augustine, *Confessions*, trans. R. S. Pine-Coffin (Baltimore: Penguin Books, 1961), 3.4 (58–59).

and not enough insight to penetrate their depths. It is surely true that as the child grows these books grow with him. But I was too proud to call myself a child. I was inflated with self-esteem, which made me think myself a great man."[2] Characteristic of Augustine's moral temper is his wrenching honesty that rushes all of us readers headlong down his *Confessions*; he will not give himself a cheap pardon, or an easy, embarrassed shrug at youthful vanities. No, Augustine is always set on a higher, or better, a deeper pathway, and he is relentless in his pursuit of the God who broke and remade him, who found him even as he sought Him, in tears and the singsong chants of little children. Without hesitation, Augustine trains his unflinching light on his own failings: he was too proud, he reports, too caught up in his own ambition and self-satisfaction to read a Book like the Bible. He was not ready to become a child of the Kingdom.

I begin with Augustine here, and the Augustine of the early *Confessions*, the Roman rhetor and Ciceronian, because I think Augustine is willing, even now, to be more forthright, more scandalously honest and searching than are we, centuries after learning from and being shaped by him. Augustine is willing to say that we cannot read the Bible if we lack certain moral traits—humility at the head—and he dares to say what we often cannot bring ourselves to admit: the Bible is a difficult, sometimes offensive Book to read. After years of Christian life, reflection, and worship, Augustine can echo his youthful disdain in a subtle and chastened form: "I discovered something that was at once beyond the understanding of the proud and hidden from the eyes of children. Its gait was humble [what a wonderful line!] but the heights it reached were sublime. It was enfolded in mysteries, and I was not the kind of man who could enter into it, or bow my head to follow where it led."[3] The Bible is a deeply mysterious Book, for Augustine, and it is not to be entered into lightly, and its exposition will require the whole of us, our intellect, our will, and our humble self-offering. It is a Book like no other.

I suppose that this short summary—the Bible is a Book like no other— stands as my strongest conviction about Holy Scripture as Sacred Ground of theology. This unshakeable sense that the Bible confronts us as nothing else will or can; that it belongs to no kind or class; that it brooks no rival yet can speak to all; that it un-makes us as we read it; and that we can never come to the end of it—all this I find drawn up in the brief compass of Scripture's uniqueness. All theology is properly reflection upon the Sacred Page, I say,

---

2. Augustine, *Confessions*, 3.5 (60).
3. Ibid.

as the schoolmen do, and this is so because all Christian thought is to set its anchor deep into this strange soil, the bedrock that is the Bible.

Now, Augustine has awakened the confessional impulse in me, and I must say too—in the midst of confessions about Scripture's difficulties and offense—that in truth I simply love the Bible. I simply love to read it, and I think I always have. My mother and I used to sit cross-legged on the play-room floor and play the game, Bible Land, modelled on that ever-popular board game of my childhood, Candy Land. I loved the Bible verses and the vivid characters and their doings, the town names and the odd landscape, so alien to my own. I suppose my own future as teacher and theologian was signalled there on the simple, winding path of Bible Land and its homey pieties. The much-lamented John Webster—what a loss his death is to us all!—must have loved the Bible with an immediacy and passion that I could only hope for. His dogmatic work on Scripture, most especially on his simple and deep call to *read*, not categorize or explicate or worse, interpret, is I believe a complex, subtle, and healing appeal to the direct, unembarrassed love of Scripture.[4] And I think Calvin, too, may have had a passion for the Bible something like mine and John's, although of course in the idiom of his day—and surely without the comfort of a cozy game of Bible Land! In the *Institutes*, Calvin writes warmly of the self-evident dignity and solemnity and power of Holy Scripture. He seemed to think that no one could pick up this Book, and put it down unimpressed; it spoke with a commanding voice. These were not the *grounds* for the Bible's authority; *Sola Scriptura* does not rest on apologetic or experiential warrants such as these.[5] But Calvin lived in a Christian world, an Ecclesial one, as I did, even so many centuries on after the great Reformers, and it seemed unthinkable to him that the Bible would give offense, or be met with disdain.

But those days, it seems, are gone. In these ways, as in so many others, we all now live in Augustine's world: a diverse, secular, and pagan world with Christian overtones, one in which the Bible once again unfolds an alien world, one we cannot understand, one we do not prefer above all others. Of course this is a great impoverishment! We cannot hope these days to hold a candle to the Bible knowledge and mastery of our ancestors, of novelists and coal miners and school children and shopkeepers of only a few generations ago. One glance at any nineteenth-century novel will

---

4. John Webster, *Holy Scripture: A Dogmatic Sketch* (Cambridge: Cambridge University Press, 2003), esp. ch. 3.

5. For these themes, see *Inst.* 1.1.6–10.

tell us that. But under the *Providentia Dei*, this stubborn ignorance on our part is turned to our good. We now can see the striking and irresistible uniqueness of the Bible as our Christian ancestors did not. The Bible does not fit in any genre or kind, and in just this way serves as the irreplaceable, the unshakeable ground of dogmatics.

Let me express all this in more formal terms. Holy Scripture, I believe, conforms to the odd strictures the English ethicist G. E. Moore applied to the notion of the good: the Bible, like the good, is "simple and unanalyzable," it is "non-naturalized," and it cannot be defined or identified with anything else.[6] It can be recognized, or acknowledged—"intuited" in the Kantian idiom of late Idealist thought—but it cannot be wholly described nor exhausted in any other category. The good, Moore taught us, is philosophically "primitive": it rests at the bottom—or perhaps better, the top—of all else and it gives its own reality to everything else brought into its orbit. Goodness is its own reality, Moore tells us; it is strongly unique. Moore and his contemporary Sidgwick capture an intellectual position that I would like to extend to the place, dignity, and character of Holy Scripture: the Bible is strongly unique, and in just this way, stands at the beginning of all our theological ways. The Bible will be demanding to our intellect and our categories, offensive to us and a stone for stumbling, just because it *does not fit*. It is not a member of a class, not an instance, however exalted, of a larger kind, not an example or exemplar, not the best of all its kindred. No, the Holy Scriptures of the Old and New Testaments are the *kenōsis* of the proud and the *mystērion* of the humble; they are beyond all familiar landscapes, genres, and kinds. Just this is what it means to say that the Bible is not like anything else. It has no rival. It is strongly unique.

Note that little word "strongly." It is possible of course for objects and living things to be unique in a rather ordinary or weaker sense. This is the sense we intend when we note that a novel has characters that do not appear anywhere else; or when we say that we have never seen a landscape as striking and haunting as the mesas around the Central Valley; or when we affirm that each human being is unique, unlike any other, even if a twin, even if deeply known and loved by another. This kind of identity, this form of weaker uniqueness, has been given the term by Scotists, of "haecceitas," "this-ness." Now the medieval scholastic Duns Scotus had a remarkable and subtle notion of individuation, of the degerming property of "this-ness," one that I find persuasive, especially in its claim that in the

---

6. G. E. Moore, *Principia Ethica* (Cambridge: Cambridge University Press, 1903), esp. chs. 1, 6.

end only Almighty God knows our identity, our haecceity truly. Scotus's doctrine of individuation did not prevent him, however, from recognizing kinds and classes, the moderate universals of the medieval thought-world. So, though I think Scotus might be considered an ally of the position I want to develop here—or at least his thought might be opened to be strengthened and radicalized in this way—I think on its own, being *this very one*, being an individual, is not strong enough for the uniqueness I seek to accord to Holy Scripture. No, here lies something stronger.

Let me set out some examples that might capture the elusive idea I have in mind. One of Friedrich Schleiermacher's signal contributions to hermeneutics, the art of interpretation, was to argue that the Bible should be read as an ancient text, read like any other ancient text.[7] Now this is a rich and daring proposal! Note what it does to the understanding of Holy Scripture. First it assigns a class to which the Bible belongs: a text of the ancient world. It might even be narrowed some, to sacred texts of antiquity. It can find its place along the shelf that holds Cicero's *Hortensius*, or the sacred poetry of the Lower Nile, or of Hesiod and his stories of the gods, or of Plato's *Timeaus*. We develop certain tools and patterns of thought to read such texts: a knowledge of ancient Rome or golden age Greece or the late expansion of classical Egyptian culture into the delta of the Nile. We learn languages; we study syntax and vocabulary; we read across the literature of that ancient tongue. This is what our ancestors in the Faith called "lower criticism," and it is the mainstay, to this day, of much beginning instruction in the reading of the Bible. Now I hasten to say here, and will elaborate in a moment, that I certainly do not want to discourage the thought of ancient languages, the practice of studying and mastering Hebrew or Greek or Latin, or the close, attentive study of ancient cultures and their sacred texts. No! To say that the Bible is strongly unique is not to practice a form of obscurantism in which ignorance is pious bliss. My point, rather, is to say that in all this study of the Bible as ancient text we have not yet encountered the Bible as Holy Scripture.

Let me explore some additional examples, more demanding and more wide-spread in our contemporary theological world. Let me take the so-called "higher criticism" as my first example. Now here we assimilate the Holy Bible to a literary or historical text: it is a member of a well-known class, the cultural artifact of an earlier day. We say here that, like Julius

---

7. See, for example, Schleiermacher, *Hermeneutics and Other Criticism*, trans. A. Bowie (Cambridge: Cambridge University Press, 1998).

Caesar's *The Gallic Wars*, we have a history that can be examined critically, held up against canons of historical research, and can be understood in light of the literary and rhetorical conventions of its day. I don't need to tell anyone in this room that the story of *this* development in the reception of the Bible is a remarkably complex and still painful legacy of the modern world and its self-critical study of the past. David Friedrich Strauss's application of the term *mythos* to the Bible was electric in his day, and remains so for many Christians in our era.[8] To say that Genesis or the Gospel of Luke is *mythos* is to say that it does not *refer to* historical events or material objects in a direct and verifiable manner. It is not narrating historical or scientific fact, in this view, and to say that in some way, perhaps as "folk-science" it aims to do so, is to open it to falsification. That the Bible could be *wrong*, that is, that it could contain factual errors, is an out-working of the assimilation of the Bible to the class and world of historical texts. Now I don't want to pretend that I carry some dissolving fluid in my travelling kit that can simply erase or ease or wash away the deep and tangled dilemmas the higher criticism has posed for theology and for faithful Christians. Albert Schweitzer famously called the historical study of the Gospels a "painful school for honesty,"[9] and I think it is probably a pilgrimage or fiery passage that all of us who belong to our time and culture must face and enter into.

But here I simply want to raise a question about this initial move, the originary instinct to locate the Bible among a particular genre, the historical or instructional text. Here I think that more traditional positions, ones I might call Doctrines of Inerrancy, or of Plenary Inspiration, share more in common with modernist traditions than is sometimes recognized. In my eyes, what a strong Inerrantist position affirms, perhaps under the direct and mighty influence of the Holy Spirit, is that this One Book, the Bible, stands as a historical and moral record without error. It is like a history or ethics text; but this time, as a perfect one. The *place* of the Divine Inspiration, the *locus* of the Holy Spirit and the Bible's authority, is raised to the level of the Bible's *content*, to what it reports and records and teaches. The Bible is authoritative, the foundation of theology, in this view, just because it can be trusted to be

8. The original, daring use of 'mythos' can be found in D. F. Strauss's early work, *The Life of Jesus, Critically Examined*, trans. George Eliot (Philadelphia: Fortress, 1972), esp. the introduction.

9. Albert Schweitzer, *The Quest of the Historical Jesus*, trans. W. Montgomery (New York: Macmillan, 1968). An eloquent stylist, Schweitzer summed up his opening chapter, "The Problem" with this elegy: "Those who tried to bring Jesus to life at the call of love found it a cruel task to be honest. The critical study of the Life of Jesus has been for theology a school of honesty. The world had never seen before, and will never see again, a struggle for truth so full of pain and renunciation as that of which the Lives of Jesus of the last hundred years contain the cryptic record" (p. 5).

without error, unlike others of its kind, that sometimes relate the true facts and principles and at times do not. Now I happen to be a fallibilist about the Bible—I believe its matchless authority and beauty and power are compatible with error—but my main argument here is that the controversy over higher criticism is ill-suited for the work it intends to do. I want to remain *neutral*, that is, about Inerrancy and fallibilism, because I think the originary framework is wrong. I want to step behind this framework to a much stronger, much more radical notion of Biblical authority: it rests properly, I believe, on a strong notion of uniqueness. It is not enough to say that the Bible is a member of the class, historical, moral, and sacred texts, but this time a perfect one. It is not enough to say that it gives us a matchless or reliable or even flawless portrait of the people Israel and of our Lord, Jesus Christ. The Holy Scriptures are not that kind of Book—indeed not a kind, at all. It stands utterly alone, sovereign, majestic. It stands at the beginning of all our theological ways simply because there is nothing like it—really nothing at all.

Let me give a final example that I think might illumine another feature of modern reading and reception of the Bible. Is the Bible *revelation*? Does it belong to that kind and class, revelatory texts? Does the Bible constitute the Revealed Word of God that is to be guide and ground of all Christian teaching? Now this conviction seems to me the hallmark of modern accounts of the Bible in contemporary theology. I will use the great name of Karl Barth here but I think his name in truth is legion, and there are many who hold to his views.[10] It is a remarkably powerful account. Here we move the Bible out of the realm of text—that in itself is a startling and radical decision. If we follow Barth we do not deny that the Bible is now a Book, nor do we lose sight of the patient and crucial tasks of editing, translating, and assessing manuscript variants that is all part of the textual legacy of Holy Scripture. But we do hold that the principle identity of the Bible is as revealed word: *Deus dixit*, thus says the Lord! The Bible in Barth's hands is a form of *speech*, Divine Speech, and it addresses, encounters, judges, and guides the sinner along the ways of the Lord. The Bible as Revelation, then, has a temporal character; it inhabits the structure of speech that is a creature of time. God *speaks*, yes. And we live by that living Word. But God has also spoken; there is a proper past, a record, a deposit, and legacy of that speaking, that is the great gift and prize of Israel's ordinances, commandments, and statutes. And the LORD God *will speak*; the future is also His. As the Revealer, the Lord retains the High Office of Prophet, the One who speaks to and for His people. Nothing is ever dead,

---

10. *CD* I/1 §§4–5; I/2 §§19–21.

buried, lost, and irretrievable in the land of the Living God. In just this way, John Webster marvelously developed these Barthian notes by taking account of how Holy Scripture unfolds through the word of Prophet and Apostle, by the community gathered around the Living Word, by the tradents, the scribes, the collators and authors, all of them sharing the life-stream that pours forth from the God of Revelation, all sanctified creatures in His service. So, the written text is taken up into a larger class, the world of Divine Self-disclosure. This is why Barth's Doctrine of Scripture has such remarkable vitality, such impressive dynamism. Nothing inert, nothing wholly given and lifeless here! Instead the Holy Spirit which has given the words to prophet and apostle, laid this speech down deep into the soil of Israel, can seize that revealed word and make it once again the Living Speech, the very Word of God. Barth calls this the Secondary Objectivity of the Word of God: Jesus Christ in His Secondary Identity as Divine Speech. The Bible can *become* this too.

The splendid Barth scholar George Hunsinger calls this the "Chalcedonian relation,"[11] and in this facet of the whole, he is joined by many modern Scripture scholars. The Bible for many of our contemporaries is a kind of two-nature reality: a Divine Word and a human artifact. The Bible must be a member of this Chalcedonian relation in just this sense, that the human or cultural nature must not be mixed or confused with the Divine, nor must they be entirely prised apart, the Divine lost sight of, say, or the creaturely ignored. It is a wonderfully imaginative and attractive proposal. We can see an elegant application of this proposal in the path-breaking Constitution of the Second Vatican Council, *Dei Verbum*.[12] There, the Bishops suggested with a light touch that we might well consider the Bible as a kind of Sacrament, a verbal companion to the Holy Eucharist: it is Body and Blood of Christ, a nourishment and stay for pilgrims, all the while the creaturely properties remain, the taste and feel and weight of a human artifact. Two elements, held in complex relation. But even here, in the midst of several wide-ranging and evocative proposals, the Council Fathers gave this document the title the "Constitution on Divine Revelation," and included a direct and rare citation from Vatican I and its pronounced accent upon proper theological knowledge to head the Constitution as a whole.[13]

In all this, I want to underscore the *epistemic* character of the modern

11. George Hunsinger, *How to Read Karl Barth: The Shape of His Theology* (New York: Oxford University Press, 1991), ch. 7.

12. "Dogmatic Constitution on Divine Revelation" [*Dei Verbum*] in *The Documents of the Vatican II*, ed. Austin P. Flannery (Grand Rapids: Eerdmans, 1975), 6.21.

13. *Documents of Vatican II*, 1.5–6.

interpretation of the Bible. To say that the Bible is *revelation*, even the event of Christ's Lordly speaking, is to train our eyes upon *knowledge*, the Source, the content, and the Means whereby we know the deep things of God. In just this way, it belongs to the modern. Nothing has so preoccupied modern philosophers and theologians than the problem of knowledge: its certainties, its pathways, its verification, its success in referent or judgement or progress in scientific endeavor. To say that dogmatics finds its foundation in revelation, in the event of Divine Speech, is to house theology in the living quarters of epistemology, the art of knowers and the known. Now of course there are metaphysical dimensions or implicatures to any episte-mology; the Chalcedonian relation tells us that. And Barth himself is far too accomplished and complex a theologian to ever reduce a theological locus to any one discipline. But I think all the same the strong magnetic pull of modern conceptuality, and the fascinating rigors of post-Cartesian thought, has drawn the Bible itself within its orbit, and made it a citizen of its domains. As modern people, we are ineluctably drawn to the notion that the Bible tells us something we need to learn, teaches us something we could not find elsewhere, and lifts the veil that covers the nations so that we now know the Living God. To affirm all this is to say that the Bible is Source, perhaps matchless source, of knowledge; it is to affirm that Christians are those who *know* because properly instructed.

Now I want to say a rather odd thing about all these comparison classes and kinds. I do not want to *reject* them, nor deny that they might be fitting, perhaps remarkably illuminating for understanding the Bible. I do indeed think it possible to treat the Bible in all these ways, and even more, that we can learn many things, even very many, valuable things, by doing so. But I think this is so for an odd reason. I believe the Bible can be grouped into many kinds and classes, its strong uniqueness hidden away like a measure of meal in a jar, just because it does not belong to any of the known genres on this earth. The Bible is so strange, that is, so removed from ordinary, earthly objects, that it cannot even be contrasted with them. This is a species of the common "apple and oranges" maxim. In that well-known phrase, we say that we can't really compare the apple with the orange because there is simply not enough to tie them together in order to see them as distinct. (Now, in the annoying way of every-day maxims, it's possible of course to find commonality—they are both fruits! But that's not really the point of the maxim, we know, so we cut that home-spun example some slack.) Let me give another, slightly more elevated, example of this point. Thomas Aquinas tells us very early on in his great *Summa Theologiae* that in order to disagree we must hold certain elements in common—his disputants must believe, on both sides, in God or in Holy Scripture or that there is such a reality as the Church—in order to dispute and argue at all. In this surprising way, to argue is in some ways to simply agree.[14] So, it seems to me that the Bible simply does not hold enough in common with other books or speech or sacred artifact to be compared, to be shown distinct, or to excel over them. The strong uniqueness of the Bible means, in this way, that it can be grouped almost anywhere. It is a "universal donor," in virtue of its unexcelled identity. Just this makes us say, the Bible is Holy, Holy Scripture.

Note here that I am quietly affirming that in some distinctive ways, the Bible is likened only to Almighty God. This is a daring and rather dangerous proposition, so I want to linger a moment on this claim of mine. One of the ways that Holy Scripture is like the Lord God Himself is the manner in which the Bible, like our Majestic God, does not compete with or fight for space in the creaturely realm. This is what the marvelous theologian Kathryn Tanner calls the "non-competitive relation" between God and creature: God cannot be *over against* the creature just because God is so utterly Unique and Sovereign.[15] They would have to have altogether too much in common to differ as competitors for acting or taking up space in the world. This is why God can be present *within* us, *within* our Churches, our Sacraments, our souls. We do not have to drive something away to make room for Divine Presence; no, God is the Radical Other who can act and give Himself all the while the creature stands and acts and thrives. In Him we live and move and have our being, Scripture teaches us, and that is so because God is strongly Unique. Note that this is a reworking of the Doctrine of Transcendence, a point Tanner makes in several remarkable ways in her essays. For Almighty God to transcend everything in heaven and on the earth is not the same thing as God 'being far away,' standing remote and hidden from creatures. No, transcendence, properly understood, is a form of *nearness*, of Presence. Just so, I say, the Bible as unique can stand utterly close to the earthly genres and kinds it does not in truth occupy; it transcends them by standing near to them.

But we can say more still about the common character of Holy Scripture and the Living Lord. When we speak of the Bible as Holy Scripture—its own proper identity—we say simply that we encounter God there. I want

---

14. *ST* 1.1.8, co.

15. A theme developed in several places in her work, but most systematically in Tanner, *Jesus, Humanity, and Trinity: A Brief Systematic Theology* (Minneapolis: Fortress, 2001), ch. 1.

to underscore that verb, encounter. I do not think the Bible's holiness stems from some truth it contains, though to be sure it contains many. Nor do I think its holiness can be anchored to its particular events, histories, and peoples, though to be sure the Bible is a specific book from an elect nation. No, the Bible is Holy, the Holy Scripture of the Old and New Covenants, just because we meet God there. The Bible, in this sense, is a *mode of Divine Presence*. Like the nature of the good that G. E. Moore tells us can only be recognized, acknowledged, not defined or described in any other terms, so the Bible as God's Medium and Means can only be *accepted*, recognized, affirmed, admitted. In truth I believe it is stronger than that still. I think the Lord God Himself must give us the eyes, the ears, the heart to acknowledge His Presence in Holy Writ. This is the inescapable dimension of faith in the establishment of the Bible as foundation of all dogmatics. We do not know God, nor encounter Him, nor worship Him apart from Him; He is the Gracious Opener of our heart and mind to His Reality, His Hidden Majesty. Just this, *mutatis mutandis*, is the Doctrine of Inspiration of Holy Scripture. There is of course a long history of the Doctrine of Inspiration, particularly in the post-Reformation Churches, and it turns, in part, on the distinction between the inspiration of the text and the inspiration of the readers. But it will not surprise you by now to learn that I do not think this framework is the right one to apply here. We need not, indeed I believe cannot, choose between text and reader, nor do we want to cut the Gordian knot by simply affirming both. No, we step behind, beyond, the framework itself to see just what it means to say that we, in God's grace, encounter God in Holy Scripture. Inspiration, rather, is the name we give to the meeting of God in the Bible. Like the Fiery Presence of God in the burning bush, we encounter the Fire who is God in the thornbush, we remove our sandals, we turn aside from our daily path and task, we are ourselves addressed and sent, commanded and commandeered and changed, and the thornbush is not consumed. Note that all these elements come together to form one call narrative—indeed *the call narrative* of all Holy Scripture—as a seamless garment. We do not properly ask in what way God is in the bush, nor what parts of the shrub are bearers of God, or God's Holy Name, nor whether we simply know the Name now, nor discover what kind of event and class a "theophany" is, nor whether we could be drawn aside from our flocks and herds and remain the same, nor do we want to spend much time thinking of the bush itself—just what class and kind and perfection it might exhibit. No, what the encounter by Moses of the Lord God in the thorn-bush narrates is the living, vital *axis* of all Holy Scripture. It is the seamless event that characterized and captures the whole of the Bible: it is the part that is the whole. The One Lord burns there, and the creature remains. That is the miracle of Divine Presence, the miracle of the Bible as Holy Scripture. Because Inspiration just is the encounter with one's Maker and Lord in Holy Scripture; there is no need, no room, in truth, for discrete categories such as Revelation or Inerrancy or Conversion requires. We do not ask about the character of the thornbush that makes it the fit bearer for the Divine Name and Fire, nor do we linger at the bush should the Fiery Presence depart. No, we stand in the Holy Precincts here, and the Mystery who is God captivates us, draws us near, sends us forth, undermines all that once was so, and pours revolution, liberty, into this tired earth. Now, the Bible is this Fiery Thornbush. That is why we meet God there.

Now, notice here that I am not drawing an explicit christological analogy. I do not think that the recent proposals to liken Holy Scripture to the Person of our Lord Christ can in truth advance our cause to honor and properly read the Bible. Of course it is a natural assumption for we Christians to make! I would not want to deny that the very notion of the Word of God raises most properly in our minds the Reality of Jesus Christ, the Word of the Father. And to be sure this parallel allows modern readers of the Bible a doctrinal way to honor the creaturely and frail character of the Prophets, the Apostles, and Evangelists who transcribe the sayings and events and actors within Sacred History. It seems at first blush to dissolve many riddles, for we can conceptually locate a human and a Divine nature within the covers of this one Book, and we can find proper value in the altogether human work of hearing, recording, editing, and passing on the traditions once given to the saints. But I think we have reason to hesitate before this widely admired solution. For one, of course, I would not be drawn to such an analogy because I do not think it captures properly the strong uniqueness of Scripture: it is not like anything else, even the Two Nature Christology of our Lord's Person. But I think we can be bolder still. The Modes of Divine Presence, the manners in which our Lord God manifests Himself are each *strongly unique*. I think we can affirm this even in the face of the time-honored Augustinian maxim that all the works of God *ad extra* are one. This is so, I would hazard to say, because Jesus Christ Himself, the Incarnate Son, is without peer, without rival, without genre and kind to His own Glorious Reality. The Incarnation is simply His own Life, and not another. There is nothing that in truth belongs to this Superabundant Gift, no member in a larger set, no instance of the greater genre. No, Christ is Lord just in this way: that He is Utterly Unique, the Only Begotten Son. His is the Mode of the Incarnation, His the Unique Mode of His own Presence among us. "He comes among us as One Unknown," as Schweitzer wrote in an elegiac conclusion to his *Quest of the Historical Jesus,* and He makes Himself known as Lord; He calls and commands and remakes.[16] There is no one and nothing like Him.

Even so we should say that there is no one and nothing like the Holy Scriptures of the Old and New Testaments. They are a Mode of Divine Presence that is its own, a banner planted in the earth that has no peer or likeness. For this reason, the Bible is read as no other book can be. Theology does not rest upon it, and draw its guidance and life there, because it is traditional to do so, or even that it is the heritage and instruction of the magisterial Reformers to do so, nor that it is the Christians' Sacred Text. No, none of these warrants for Scripture as Sacred Ground of theology is strong enough, radical enough, for the place of the Bible in dogmatics. The Bible as the place where we encounter God stands at the head because it can stand nowhere else. It does not belong to the world as other ordinary creatures do. It does not find its place in the stream of all living things, and stand there or stand out there as a powerful or disturbing exemplar. Rather it is so unlike its seeming kin that it can only stand at the *origin,* the beginning of all theology's ways and works. It is foundational in this strong sense, that even placed *in media res* or at the end it will remain first, sovereign, original. We will find the history of Israel there, the history and words of Prophets and Apostles; we will find as glorious goal of all these, the words and deeds and victory of Jesus Christ; all these will be read and learned and found there. But we turn to this Book of Books, this Holy Fire, not because we learn of these things in its pages, but because we meet God there, the very One who chose and formed and taught the People Israel, and the very One who came among us in the Son, mighty to save. Not in virtue of the content, then, but in virtue of the Divine Presence is the Bible the Unique Ground of all theology, of all Christian prayer and contrition and praise. In just this way is Holy Scripture a mighty sword, an unchained word, a refuge and hiding place, and a lamp unto our feet. There really is no other.

---

16. Schweitzer, *Quest of the Historical Jesus,* trans. William Montgomery (London: Adam and Charles Black, 1910), 403.

CHAPTER 7

CHRISTOCENTRISM AND THE IMMANENT TRINITY: IDENTIFYING THEOLOGY'S PATTERN AND NORM

Darren Sumner

KARL BARTH REMINDS US that it is sometimes necessary for theology to "begin again at the beginning." It is fitting that we return over and again to renew the task of dogmatics, which is churchly witness, by drawing from the wellspring from which the discipline is watered. This entails not only thinking about theological topics, hearing anew the Holy Spirit and the Word of God who are speaking in Scripture, but also about what theology is and how it ought to be practiced as intellectual labor. This is the question of theological method, and as a practice of the Christian church it requires careful attention. What we aim here to establish are not principles that stand outside of the discipline of theology, which must be established first in order for its inquiry to be made. Rather all talk of method—principles of judgment, sources and norms, or the ordering of doctrines—is itself already theological. In this sense, there is no such thing as theological *prolegomena*; to speak about method is already to begin to undertake the work.

The history of Christian thought reveals no shortage of distinct methods. What principles ought one adopt? What are the theologian's sources and norms? How, for example, ought Holy Scripture and the traditions of the church be set in relation? And which doctrine or doctrines are wisely given priority over others, so that the decisions one makes with regard to the center of dogmatics benefits the whole? In this essay I will put two such proposals from the modern period into dialogue. The first belongs to Karl Barth, who is today the figure perhaps most associated with a "Christocentric" method. The second is that of John Webster, who has articulated a theology from the doctrine of the Trinity, in particular one that is ordered to the richness of God's inner life.

I will proceed in three stages. The first is a summary of what it means to call Barth a Christocentric theologian, and the second, a discussion of Webster's principled orientation to the doctrine of God. In both instances I will briefly probe each one's motivations for these programmatic decisions. The third stage is constructive. In place of common but simplistic pictures of dogmatics as founded upon a "starting point" or "center," I will propose a more complex analogy drawn from the sphere of mathematics.[1] This, I think, equips dogmatic theology with more helpful (and realistic) ways of relating Trinity, Christology, and other doctrines vital to Christian confession. Among its many benefits this model enables us to see that the Christocentrism of Barth and the Theocentrism of Webster are not in conflict.

CHRISTOCENTRISM IN KARL BARTH

Karl Barth's radical Christocentrism has been well-documented.[2] Jesus Christ stands at the center of theological reflection not only because of the relative importance of the doctrines of incarnation and atonement to the Christian presentation, and not only because as God-made-flesh he is

---

1. This is an alternative to other analogical models that have been applied to doctrinal expression, such as the musical (Jeremy Begbie), the grammatical (Ludwig Wittgenstein, George Lindbeck), and the narrative or dramatic (Kevin Vanhoozer). I do not make the claim that the mathematical analogy is at all superior to these. In each case, one must judge the sufficiency of a model by several factors—not the least of which is its explanatory capacity, which is my focus here.

2. Recent discussions appear in Marc Cortez, "What Does It Mean to Call Karl Barth a 'Christocentric' Theologian?," *SJT* 60, no. 2 (2007): 127–43; and Bruce L. McCormack, "Why Should Theology Be Christocentric? Christology and Metaphysics in Paul Tillich and Karl Barth," *Wesleyan Theological Journal* 45, no. 1 (2010): 42–80 (esp. 77–80). "Radically Christocentric" belongs to Hans Urs von Balthasar, *The Theology of Karl Barth*, trans. Edward T. Oakes (San Francisco: Communio, 1971), 30. Richard A. Muller's warning not to use the term "Christocentric" too freely and too indiscriminately (especially with respect to thinkers of the sixteenth and seventeenth centuries) is also to be heeded. See Muller, "A Note on 'Christocentrism' and the Imprudent Use of Such Terminology," *WTJ* 68, no. 2 (2006): 253–60. For the purposes of this essay, I will take for granted that the descriptor "Christocentric" does indeed have a definite and positive content, with some deference to Cortez's description of its particularities for Barth's thought.

the locus and mediator of divine revelation to creatures, but also because Jesus himself is the mystery of God—the very content of revelation, the mystery kept hidden for ages past but now made manifest to the people of God (Col 1:25–26).[3]

In its authentic expression, the Christian message does not communicate an idea or concept but declares a name—the name of Jesus Christ. And it binds all things to this name, for all of our concepts—God, human, time, eternity, grace, atonement, *et cetera*—"derive their significance only from the bearer of this name and from His history, and not the reverse."[4] They have no special significance or meaning independent of his name, nor is there anything in the Christian message which floats free from it. This appoints to Christology a certain privilege, and assigns to the theologian a definite responsibility:

> A church dogmatics must, of course, be christologically determined as a whole and in all its parts, as surely as the revealed Word of God, attested by Holy Scripture and proclaimed by the Church, is identical with Jesus Christ. If dogmatics cannot regard itself and cause itself to be regarded as fundamentally Christology, it has assuredly succumbed to some alien sway and is already on the verge of losing its character as church dogmatics.[5]

What is this "alien sway" about which Barth worried? It may be politics or culture, philosophy or academic ambition, or preoccupations with apologetics or historical criticism.[6] In short it is anything that would compete with God's *self*-disclosure, "every (positive or negative) *formulation of a system* which claims to be theological . . . whose *subject*, however, differs fundamentally from the revelation in Jesus Christ and whose *method* therefore differs equally from the exposition of Scripture."[7] Barth had the theology of the nineteenth century in view when he summarized all such efforts

---

3. *CD* I/2, §15, "The Mystery of Revelation," (122–202); cf. IV/1 (211), IV/3 (184–85). See also Hunsinger, *How to Read Karl Barth*, 231.

4. *CD* IV/1 (16).

5. *CD* I/2 (123).

6. Implied here are Barth's various quarrels with his fellow "dialectical" theologians, including Friedrich Gogarten, Emil Brunner, and Rudolf Bultmann. Barth's attitude toward Gogarten late in the 1920s, as conveyed to a group of students in 1964, illustrates the point: "I always had the impression that Gogarten was almost more interested in secularity as a background to the gospel than in the gospel itself. He would never just sit down for once and explain Christian faith itself to us, *without* these eternal side-glances to the 'world' . . . and he got worse as time went on" (Eberhard Busch, *Karl Barth: His Life from Letters and Autobiographical Texts*, trans. John Bowden [London: SCM, 1976], 194).

7. Barth, "No! Answer to Emil Brunner," in *Natural Theology*, trans. Peter Fraenkel (London: Centenary, 1946; repr. Wipf and Stock, 2002), 74–5; emphasis original.

as "natural theology."[8] The churchly character of dogmatics is lost where theology's object and method turn upon the human creature, her needs, and her interests, rather than upon God.

In order to maintain fidelity to God as the object of her inquiry the theologian must uphold this positive orientation to Jesus Christ—not only with respect to the pattern of doctrines and their organization but also as it pertains to her own exercise of faith. This is especially true where the task is "dogmatics," that is, as it takes place "within the sphere of the church and of faith's confession of the gospel."[9] Christocentrism for Barth thus speaks neither to a material principle (in abstracto),[10] nor to the deduction of a system a priori from a single starting point, but concretely to the one who bears this name. He is the one who is lord of the Christian life, a life which includes all aspects of theological contemplation and proclamation (what John Webster summarizes as the exercise of "redeemed intelligence"). To the theologian this is not only a command but a promise, for Christ is not only the content of the Christian message but also the one who by his Spirit is its guarantor. In the theologian's speech, "He Himself is there and at work, He Himself makes Himself to be recognised and acknowledged."[11]

From one volume to the next throughout the *Church Dogmatics*, Barth makes it clear that this living Word must never drift into the periphery. The knowledge of God depends upon Christ as its condition and actuality (*CD* II/1); Jesus is both the electing God and the elect human (II/2); creation is given meaning in the covenant which culminates in Jesus Christ (III/1); true and original humanity is not a category applied to the incarnate one *ab extra* but only discovered in him (III/2); revelation and reconciliation are coterminous concepts which find no expression apart from Christ (IV/1–2).

Even when he addresses the freedom of God—a theme which some

---

8. The modern era is not unique in its vulnerability to this "alien sway," however. Barth believes that the church fathers, medieval scholastics, and especially the age of post-Reformation orthodoxy paved the way for the inrush of natural theology. For their part Schleiermacher and Ritschl each attempted to erect a Christocentric theology against this tidal wave. But by then it was too late, and even these two thinkers retained other interests which worked against their christological focus. See *CD* I/2 (123).

9. John Webster, "The Grand Narrative of Jesus Christ: Barth's Christology," in *Karl Barth: A Future for Postmodern Theology?*, ed. Geoff Thompson and Christiaan Mostert (Hindmarsh: Australian Theological Forum, 2000), 45.

10. *CD* I/2 (872); IV/3 (174ff.). Christocentrism should not be seen as reductionist, then, as if Christianity could be boiled down to core principles or an "essence" (Adolf von Harnack)— whether this is done to conservative orthodox or liberal progressive ends. On this point see Stephen W. Sykes, *The Identity of Christianity: Theologians and the Essence of Christianity from Schleiermacher to Barth* (Minneapolis: Fortress, 1984), 174–208; Sykes, "Barth on the Centre of Theology," in *Karl Barth: Studies of His Theological Method*, ed. Sykes (Oxford: Clarendon, 1979).

11. *CD* IV/1 (17).

interpreters suggest frustrates attempts to prioritize God's divine-human history *ad extra*[12]—Barth is finally preoccupied with the expression of this freedom in the concrete, particular reality of the history of Jesus Christ. All other meanings of divine freedom are finally relativized, as *potentia absoluta*, in the light of what God does. God is perfect in God's own life, in no need of creatures nor of an incarnation.[13] And yet, Barth says, this freedom is exercised and made definite in the election of Jesus Christ. Not only are the immanence of God and the freedom of God known in Jesus, but in him they in fact consist:

> The freedom of God must be recognized as His own freedom and this means—as it consists in God and as God has exercised it. But in God it consists in His Son Jesus Christ, and it is in Him that God has exercised it. In all its possibilities and shapes, it remains the freedom which consists and is exercised in Jesus Christ. If we recognize and magnify it, we cannot come from any other starting-point but Him or move to any other goal.[14]

As the one who is free, God *loves* in his freedom. And so in God's self-commitment to creatures—which is the history of Jesus Christ—God is supremely exercising his freedom. Christology demonstrates that God's freedom and God's loving are not in competition, for God is "the One who loves in the very act of His existence."[15] Therefore, Barth continues, Christology "must always constitute the basis and criterion for the apprehension and interpretation of the freedom of God in His immanence."[16]

These are but a few representative examples of the ways in which Barth's christological concentration plays out in his *Dogmatics*. It serves a variety of practical purposes in his thought, not least of which is a particularism which seeks to avoid the sort of speculation regarding God and God's attributes that had characterized much of Western theology.[17]

---

12. Paul D. Molnar, *Divine Freedom and the Doctrine of the Immanent Trinity: In Dialogue with Karl Barth and Contemporary Theology*, 2nd edition (London: T&T Clark, 2017); George Hunsinger, *Reading Barth with Charity: A Hermeneutical Proposal* (Grand Rapids: Baker Academic, 2015).

13. *CD* II/1 (305): "The freedom to exist which He exercises in His revelation is the same which He has in the depths of His eternal being, and which is proper to Him quite apart from His exercise of it *ad extra*."

14. *CD* II/1 (320). Jesus Christ as the Son of God in flesh is, furthermore, the very basis of God's immanence and absoluteness. See *CD* II/1 (315–21).

15. *CD* II/1 (321).

16. *CD* II/1 (320). Barth concludes, "The freedom of God is the freedom which consists and fulfils itself in His Son Jesus Christ. In Him God has loved Himself from all eternity. In Him He has loved the world" (321).

17. See further Hunsinger, *How to Read Karl Barth*, 32–35; McCormack, "Why Should Theology Be Christocentric?," 79–80.

Finally, we should note that when Barth says "Jesus Christ," he means the God-human and not the Logos *simpliciter* (nor, we should hasten to add, the human Jesus *simpliciter*).[18] This is the one who is the very Son of God, and whose existence as *vere homo* is elected in eternity and actualized in time. With this name, Barth never means to suggest a second person of the Trinity who is independent of his incarnation.[19] Rather it is the divine-human Jesus Christ who is the agent of revelation, election, creation, reconciliation, and redemption.[20] And he is identical with the revealed Word of God, which to Barth suggests that Jesus Christ is not only the place of divine revelation but also its content. *Theo*-logy *is* Christology—just as surely as God is human.

There seems to be little in the way of middle ground between Barth's supporters and his critics when it comes to this matter. The former marvel at Barth's consistent and profound orientation of all doctrinal topics to the person and work of Christ. This principal conviction is so fundamental to Barth's project that, without it, it is difficult to imagine the *Church Dogmatics* attaining the same stature over the past two generations. Without his christological concentration, Barth would not be Barth. His critics, on the other hand, have long decried this method as a "Christomonism," a pejorative suggesting that Barth maintains such a singular focus on Christ that at key moments other necessary conclusions are overwhelmed or crowded out.[21] (Barth replied that while theology ought not lose its focus on Jesus Christ

---

18. Logos *simpliciter* here designates the Word as he exists *asarkos*, apart from the incarnation (and thus not as the divine-human one who bears the name Jesus Christ). On the other side of this, Barth's rejection of a Jesus who is *merely* human explains his suggestion in 1924 that dogmatics and preaching ought to become "somewhat less Christocentric" (Barth, *The Göttingen Dogmatics: Instruction in the Christian Religion*, ed. Hannelotte Reiffen, trans. Geoffrey W. Bromiley [Grand Rapids: Eerdmans, 1991], 91). His target here is the theology of Adolf von Harnack, at the heart of which stood the modern reconstruction of the so-called "historical Jesus." See McCormack, *Karl Barth's Critically Realistic Dialectical Theology*, 453–55.

19. That is, a "Logos *asarkos*." Barth does allow for such a notion of God the Son in systematic theology, which he designates with the Johannine "Logos" (*CD* IV/1, 52–53). But this Logos is not a person who is other than the incarnate Lord, but only a placeholder necessary to the affirmation of divine freedom and of Christ's preexistence.

20. These five roughly correspond to the five volumes Barth projected for the *Church Dogmatics*. On Jesus and the Logos, see further Darren O. Sumner, *Karl Barth and the Incarnation: Christology and the Humility of God* (London: T&T Clark, 2014); Bruce L. McCormack, "Karl Barth's Historicized Christology: Just How 'Chalcedonian' Is It?," in *Orthodox and Modern: Studies in the Theology of Karl Barth* (Grand Rapids: Baker Academic, 2008), 201–33.

21. The charge was leveled by Paul Althaus and popularized by Cornelius Van Til, among others. See Althaus, *Die Christliche Wahrheit*, 7th ed. (Gütersloh: Gütersloher Verlaghaus, 1966), 56ff.; Paul Knitter, "Christomonism in Karl Barth's Evaluation of the Non-Christian Religions," *Neue Zeitschrift für Systematische Theologie und Religionsphilosophie* 13, no. 1 (1971): 99–121; Van Til, *The New Modernism: An Appraisal of the Theology of Barth and Brunner* (London: James Clarke, 1946). For Althaus this "Christomonism" signaled arrogant dismissal of the capacity of other religions to possess any knowledge of God; for Van Til Barth's one-note theological method insidiously corrupted all aspects of Christian teaching—not so much because it was oriented to Christology but because Van Til believed it to be based upon a modernist (and therefore innately falsified) Christology.

and the union of God and humankind in him, theology must avoid any "monism" as inevitably reductive.)[22]

This was far from Webster's own objection, however. Though he was concerned with proper proportionality in dogmatics, Webster also acknowledged the salutary value of Barth's unflinchingly christological concentration: "Barth rarely reduces all other doctrines to derivatives or implicates of Christology," and he "remains convinced that Christology and Trinity are inseparable and mutually implicating, and that teaching about the immanent Trinity is of great Christological import."[23] Barth was enthusiastic in affirming Jesus Christ as the center and condition for theological contemplation, but when talk turned to "Christocentrism" as a program, he was cautious, deliberate, and not reckless. But Webster's own convictions regarding method, procedure, and the place of Christology in systematic theology were rather different. To these we now turn.

JOHN WEBSTER ON TRINITARIAN DOGMATICS

"Systematic theology," Webster says, "has a single but not simple object: God and all things relative to God."[24] This perhaps deceptively simple program is reflected in what Webster takes to be the proper order for dogmatics: the doctrine of God is prior to the economy of God's works, both materially and so also logically, since the being of God in and for himself is the ground of God's works.[25] For although it is possible to conceive of God without creation it is impossible to conceive of creation without God. Indeed, the whole of God's activity in the economy of creation and redemption overflows from the fullness of life that God has in himself.

In the terms provided by medieval scholasticism, theology begins with the inner relations and processions of the Trinitarian persons. And it continues on from there to the missions of Father, Son, and Holy Spirit—what Webster calls the "hinge" between God *in se* and God's works *ad extra*.[26]

---

22. Karl Barth, "A Theological Dialogue," *Theology Today* 19, no. 2 (1962): 171–77. The comments were given in a question and answer session during Barth's visit to Princeton in 1962. There he called Christomonism "an awful catchword" (172).

23. John Webster, "Christology, Theology, Economy: The Place of Christology in Systematic Theology," in *God without Measure: Working Papers in Christian Theology* (London: Bloomsbury T&T Clark, 2016), 1:56.

24. Webster, "Christology, Theology, Economy," 45.

25. John Webster, *"Rector et iudex super omnia,"* in *God without Measure*, 1:161; cf. "Christology, Theology, Economy," 46.

26. John Webster, "Principles of Systematic Theology," in *The Domain of the Word: Scripture and Theological Reason* (London: T&T Clark, 2012), 146.

To speak then of divine perfections (or attributes) is properly to coordinate procession and mission—that is, to describe *this* God who acts in *these* ways.[27] In a very real sense, then, for Webster, talk of the Holy Trinity will comprehend the whole of theological contemplation. This doctrine is not one among others but is foundational, the "ruler and judge" over all other Christian teaching. And it is all-encompassing, he says, so that "to expound the doctrine of the Trinity in its full scope is to expound the entirety of Christian dogmatics."[28] In this sense, "there is only one Christian doctrine, the doctrine of the triune God, because in following that doctrine to its end theology will treat all the topics customarily brought together in a systematic theology."[29]

Although this material order is irreversible, the order of exposition need not follow suit. Webster acknowledges that "it would be quite possible to begin an account of Christian doctrine at any point, provided that proper attention is paid to systematic scope in order to prevent the hypertrophy of one article at the price of the atrophy of another."[30] What matters is not that the order of knowing replicates the order of being but that the former not be allowed to overwhelm the latter (that is, to permit the economy to be determinative of God's essential being). So long as the material order remains intact, the theologian is free to invent or adapt the presentation of doctrine as didactic circumstances require.[31]

This does not mean that all theologies are equally sound in construction, so long as they pay sufficient deference to the Trinity. Webster is also concerned to warn of the inflation and imbalance of certain doctrines, naming Christology and soteriology as often guilty parties.[32] Such disproportion occurs when a given doctrine is assigned more work than it can bear, or when the theologian inserts a gap between the being of God and the works of God such that the latter might be expounded without reference to the former. Attempts to define any other doctrine as *articulus stantis et cadentis ecclesiae*, or to organize dogmatics around it as a central dogma, must be checked in the interests of proportion.[33]

---

27. John Webster, "The Immensity and Ubiquity of God," in *Confessing God: Essays in Christian Dogmatics II* (London: T&T Clark, 2005), 87–92. This stands in contrast to "perfect being" theology, which attempts first to describe the divine attributes in the abstract.

28. Webster, "*Rector et iudex*," 159.

29. Webster, "*Rector et iudex*," 161. Similarly, Barth had suggested that dogmatics and Christian preaching are elaboration upon the statement "God is" (*CD* II/1, 257–58).

30. Webster, "*Rector et iudex*," 161; cf. Barth, "A Theological Dialogue," 173–74.

31. Webster, "Christology, Theology, Economy," 46–47.

32. Webster, "*Rector et iudex*," 162–63.

33. Webster, "Principles," 145.

Theology thus begins with God's inner life and ought to maintain proper proportion in the span of its attention. To aid in this, Webster often invokes the notion of a "distributed doctrine." This is an aspect of Christian teaching which cannot be treated and dispensed with all at once in systematics because its import and effects are spread throughout the whole. The doctrine of the Trinity is first among these, since no other topic can be understood adequately without reference to God's inner and outer works. At various places in his corpus, Webster also identifies as distributed doctrines those of creation (and creation *ex nihilo*) and providence.[34]

Most significant for our present inquiry is that he regards Christology, too, to be a distributed doctrine: "No element in a system of theology is unrelated to Christology: to contemplate any of its parts is to have one's mind drawn irresistibly to the name and figure of Jesus Christ."[35] In this way, Christology is privileged not as a starting point or basis for all other doctrines, but as an integral element of the doctrine of God.[36] Because it considers one of the persons of the Trinity, Christology is treated both immanently and relatively, and so it straddles the two domains of systematic theology (theology and economy) in treating both the eternal Word and his temporal mission. The Son's mission includes his participation in creation and the providential maintenance of the world (Col 1:16–17; Heb 1:1–3) as well as the whole course of salvation—his incarnation, earthly ministry, passion and death, resurrection, ascension, and ongoing intercession at the right hand of the Father.[37] If Webster has anything approaching a "Christocentric" instinct, it is here, situated carefully within the doctrine of God.

What may be said about Webster's likely motivations for outlining this sort of theological method? Positively put, he clearly believes that the priority of the doctrine of God is simply suited to theology's object. But we can also speculate regarding the negative side: What is he driven to avoid? What sorts of "theology" does Webster wish to rule out with this methodology, either as harmful or as simply improper? I believe that, like Barth, his approach is provoked in part by worry over "some alien sway"

34. Webster, "*Non ex aequo*: God's Relation to Creatures," in *God without Measure*, 1:117; Webster, "'Love is also a lover of life': *Creatio ex nihilo* and Creaturely Goodness," in *God without Measure*, 1:99; Webster, "On the Theology of Providence," in *The Providence of God: Deus Habet Consilium*, ed. Francesca Aran Murphy and Philip G. Ziegler (London: T&T Clark, 2009), 159. In a certain sense, "distribution" might also apply to election and anthropology. See "Principles," 146.
35. Webster, "Christology, Theology, Economy," 57; for the language of distribution see p. 47.
36. Ibid., 43. Significantly, he attributes this sort of christological thinking to Barth.
37. Ibid., 52.

which could invade and subvert—causing the theologian to be distracted by concerns, presuppositions, or outcomes which are at best secondary to her task and, at worst, foreign and destructive. This is evident in Webster's 1997 inaugural lecture at the University of Oxford, in which he pled for a "theological theology": theology makes its most fruitful contribution to learning not by conformity to the disengaged reason of the academy but precisely by its nonconformity, a renewed "conflict of the faculties."[38] He means that nonconformity permits the theologian to exercise her redeemed intelligence according to the restrictions and requirements not of the modern professional guild but those of the Word of God—that is, to be dogmatic. Christian theology is distinctive among the sciences not merely because it persistently raises questions of ultimacy for conversation at the bar of reason, but "in its invocation of God as agent in the intellectual practice of theology. In order to give account of its own operations, that is, Christian theology will talk of God and God's actions"[39] and not merely of the phenomena of human perception and imperception.

Without such self-understanding, theology that has assimilated itself to the rules of the modern university and its accepted modes of *Wissenschaft* risks benign indifference or, much worse, an erosion of confidence in its ability to speak truthfully of its subject matter. Understanding systematic theology primarily as a mode of public engagement has the result that, in the end, little tends to be said of God in himself.[40] Theology that has lost its nerve to be "theological" (which Webster thought to be the sort of theology commonly practiced within the halls of the English- and German-speaking academy) is simply not theology at all.

All of this is not unrelated to a second worry, which Barth shared. The specter of historical Jesus studies, and with it an attending reduction of Christology to "Jesuology," has been ever-present to theologians since the nineteenth century. Webster places Christology under the auspice of the doctrine of the Trinity, requiring the divine Son's preexistence and full deity, in order to ward off those naturalistic, overly historicized, and other nontheological accounts of Christ that have pervaded the modern

---

38. John Webster, "Theological Theology," in *Confessing God: Essays in Christian Dogmatics II* (London: T&T Clark, 2005), 11–32, esp. 27–28. In the twenty-first century, certainly theology would take the place of the underdog which Kant had assigned to the department of philosophy under the pressures of Prussian censorship. Webster further articulates what "theological theology" ought to entail in "What Makes Theology Theological?," *Journal of Analytic Theology* 3 (2015): 17–28 (reprinted in *God without Measure*, 1:213–24).

39. Webster, "Theological Theology," 25.

40. Webster, "Principles," 134.

period.[41] Even where they might grant Jesus's divine identity, these accounts concentrate so totally on the history of the Word made flesh that they neglect that history's backward reference to the eternal, triune persons as its antecedent ground.[42] Therefore such accounts, Webster says, have led variously to "an expansion of the domain of the economy, a corresponding contraction of the domain of theology," and heightened expectations of Jesus's person and acts as historical quantities.[43]

It should be said that this is not a rejection of Christocentrism as Barth practiced it. In fact, it aims at a shared target: a distortion of dogmatics by the divergent interests of modern rationalism. The subject of Christology is not isolated historicism (nor is it an entirely subjective religious experience); rather, it is the objective and ongoing *presence* of Christ, his reconciling men and women to God by giving himself to them.[44] In ordering the doctrine of Christ to that of the Trinity, once again Webster's implicit concern is that one does not produce a Christology that is not "theological."

These are high stakes that lie close at hand when Webster argues for a form of Theocentrism. Theology's *principium cognoscendi* reflects the *principium essendi* upon which it rests; the venture of Christian theology fittingly reflects the beatitude of God in himself and the benevolence of God for creatures.[45] Christology too deserves a certain privilege, but by its nature the doctrine of the Trinity is more comprehensive and indeed will include within itself the full reach of Christology. Both Barth and Webster are similarly motivated: Barth grounds theological speech upon Jesus Christ so as to thwart appeals to anthropology, while Webster insists upon theology's divine objectivity and subjectivity in order to loosen the grip of naturalism and provoke the theologian to repentance. If their goals are not dissimilar,

41. See Webster, "Christology, Theology, Economy," 53–54.
42. Ibid., 47.
43. Ibid., 54. Not only are naturalist approaches to Jesus Christ odious to the balance of theology and economy, but attempts to counter such approaches have often produced the same result in a different form. Here Webster cites the Christologies of Isaak Dorner (whose imbalance he says favors the order of knowing) and Albrecht Ritschl (who collapses Christology into soteriology and religious fellowship). He concludes that Karl Barth, however, overcame these things by maintaining a consistent and powerful attention to the economy while yet refusing to allow theology to atrophy (Ibid., 54–57).
44. John Webster, "Prolegomena to Christology: Four Theses," in *Confessing God*, 131–49. Jesus Christ is known by "the movement of his being," and not otherwise (137).
45. Its ontological principle is the Holy Trinity, and its cognitive principles are the Word of God in Holy Scripture and the redeemed intelligence of the saints. See "Principles," 135. This talk of "principles" only conceptualizes what is in truth the history of God's free and gracious intercourse with creatures. Thus, they do not come before or float free from the material of theology, nor (as in Barth's worry about "principles" and "systems") do they create the conditions for the deduction of Christian teaching in abstraction from Holy Scripture.

then perhaps their methods and priorities need not be regarded as at odds. For Barth theology is centered on Christ, and this ever points to the triune God; for Webster theology begins with the Trinity, and this includes all of Christology within it. In what follows I will offer a constructive proposal for reading these two together.

THEOLOGY'S PATTERN AND NORM (A PROPOSAL)

When theologians speak of their methods, of the arrangement of topics in the system of doctrine and which teachings ought to shape the contents of others, it is common to speak either of a "starting point" or a "center." The first of these is linear: it suggests a single point of departure which provides a basis for the next topic, and then each subsequent doctrine down the line until the whole range of the system has been explicated. Doctrine here is regarded as cumulative in nature, even if only implicitly; *order* is crucial, as what is explicated first will have the greatest formative impact. What comes last, by contrast, may be the most comprehensive or summative of the whole.[46] As the work proceeds, its contents grow increasingly full and dynamic because each new topic has a larger accumulation behind it upon which to draw. The analogy of "building" expresses this same idea, with the foundation representing that one article upon which the whole stands or falls (the doctrine of justification for Martin Luther).[47]

The second common form taken by systematic theologies speaks of a center point, a controlling doctrine or theme around which the whole of the material is organized. Other topics may be located closer to or further from the center, with varying proximities to one another but all oriented to that central, controlling doctrine. Encircling this teaching is the circle's circumference, which either suggests the limits of orthodoxy which are not to be crossed (a boundary-set), or a frontier ripe for exploration so long as one moves out from the center taking care not lose her bearings (a center-set). Order is now less decisive than *orientation*, or perhaps direction. From this model arise the many proposals for "Christocentrism," "anthropocentrism," "soteriocentrism," "ecclesiocentrism," and the like. Karl Barth himself draws upon circle imagery in tentative and somewhat unconventional ways,

---

46. Such was Friedrich Schleiermacher's intention with the doctrine of the Trinity, located at the end of *The Christian Faith* not as an appendix to dogmatics but as its conclusion.

47. *Luther's Works (WA)* 40 III, 352, 1–3; Theodore Mahlmann, "Zur Geschichte der Formel 'Articulus stantis et cadentis ecclesiae,'" *Lutherische Theologie und Kirche* 17 (1993): 187–94.

suggesting a theology that begins on the circumference of a circle (the center of which is the Word of God) and is directed outward.[48]

If the linear picture may be described as "one-dimensional" and the geometric as "two-dimensional" might there be other, more fully orbed ways of depicting the relationship between doctrines and the mode of their exposition? Perhaps there is another analogy drawn from mathematics that might provoke dogmatics to the imagination necessary for its task. For the sake of this essay I will bypass my unformed thoughts about what shape theological exposition might take if it were called "three-dimensional" ("exponential," or perhaps "logarithmic"). Certainly, examples from the history of theology can be found.

The model I wish to propose instead is better described as a four-dimensional picture of systematic theology. Fractal geometry is a relative newcomer to the discipline of mathematics, first devised in 1975 and popularized during the 1980s. It has proved immensely useful in numerous disciplines, and can be seen throughout the natural world in both microcosm and macrocosm. In short, fractals are the repetition of a set pattern producing an increasingly complex symmetry, wherein the microcosm replicates the macrocosm perfectly in scale. The most simple example is the Koch curve: beginning with an equilateral triangle, replace the middle third of each line segment with two segments at 60-degree angles. The result is the 12-sided Star of David. Now, repeat the process *ad infinitum*. The result is the Koch snowflake, a shape with a finite area bounded by a line that is infinitely long. The curve is also self-similar, made up of smaller copies of itself.[49] Magnify any segment and you will see the same pattern, replicated in infinitely smaller scale.

---

48. *CD* I/2 (869–70); cf. "A Theological Dialogue," 174. Readers of Barth's *Romans* commentary will also be reminded of his depiction of God's encounter with the world as a tangent on a circle, touching it as only at a single mathematical point ("that is, without touching it")—an illustration he would later repudiate. See Barth, *The Epistle to the Romans*, trans. Edwyn C. Hoskyns (London: Oxford University Press, 1933), 30. On variety in centered models see Cortez, "What Does It Mean," 129.

49. Kenneth Falconer, *Fractals: A Very Short Introduction* (Oxford: Oxford University Press, 2013), 5.

The French-American mathematician Benoit Mandelbrot has demonstrated that fractals occur in many places, not only in mathematics but in nature.[50] Fractals demonstrate a degree of order in chaos and can be used to describe the shape of irregular objects and surfaces that still evidence some pattern, such as snowflakes, cauliflower, coral, ferns, trees, and lightning. They have also been applied to everything from ocean waves to geologic fault lines, and from blood and lung vasculature to chaos theory. Mandelbrot's work points out that "clouds are not spheres, mountains are not cones, coastlines are not circles, and bark is not smooth, nor does lightning travel in a straight line."[51] Generations of mathematicians set aside such shapes as "formless." But this shortsightedness only betrayed Euclidean geometry's inability to describe them with any accuracy. Fractals explain how it is that these natural phenomena, for all their irregularity (or "roughness"), are not purely chaotic but are in fact only complex.

Fractal dimensionality has also been applied to the study of human art, architecture, music, and more. Important to our application is the underlying idea that the repetition of a simple base formula produces extraordinary complexity.[52]

How might we apply this analogously to the organization of systematic theology? Two words of caution are in order. We should be clear that this is only an analogy: my suggestion is not that mathematics directs either the form or the content of dogmatics—that would be a most horrific expression of natural theology—but only that fractals provide a useful depiction of conceptual complexity that may be applied to the organization of doctrines. "Starting point" and "center," like Euclidean geometry, are not sufficiently capable of describing the challenge at hand. Second, we ought to honor Barth's warning to resist systems as the imposition of controlling principles other than the Word of God (especially when those principles are drawn from a sphere outside of dogmatics). To force one's theology into any such pattern—even one as complex and pliable as fractal geometry—is to succumb to the temptation of self-will and so lose dogmatics' necessary orientation to the Word of God. "Systematization," said Barth, "is always the enemy of true theology."[53]

With these cautions at hand let us consider how a fractal model allows us to reconfigure the relationship between Trinity and Christology. According

---

50. Benoit Mandelbrot, *The Fractal Geometry of Nature* (New York: W. H. Freeman, 1982).

51. Ibid., 1.

52. This is seen visually in the now famous "Mandelbrot set," which reiterates the simple formula $z \rightarrow z^2 + c$. What results has been called the most complex of all mathematical objects.

53. Barth, "A Theological Dialogue," 174; cf. *CD* I/2 (883).

to Mandelbrot the most useful fractals involve three crucial things: *chance* (which produces irregularities), *scaling* (the degree of their irregularity is identical at all scales), and *dimension* (shapes grow increasingly complex with each iteration).[54] In a theological application, dimension should reflect the doctrine of the Trinity, the whole that is perceived with increasing complexity as it is reiterated through the topics of God, creation, reconciliation, and redemption. These aspects of presentation will never accumulate to a finished or complete understanding of God, just as the fractal need not conclude with any particular iteration.

Scaling best reflects the proper role of Christology in dogmatics. This is the shape that each iteration takes, the geometric pattern (one arm of the snowflake) that is repeated throughout all doctrinal topics and which remains the same both in macrocosm (Christology proper) and in microcosm (the christological shape of other doctrines). This pattern does not insist upon matters of anthropology or sin or the church, as though they themselves are merely repetitions of Christology proper, or reducible to it. But it does provide that all things—*all* things—are normed by Jesus's person and work.

Mandelbrot's notion of chance is more difficult to apply, but we should avoid the temptation to map it onto either the Holy Spirit and Pneumatology or (*pace* Schleiermacher) the individual's subjective religious experience. In fractal geometry, chance retains a chaotic element: although chaos indicates a certain degree of pattern, it is not wholly predictable or explainable. Perhaps the best place we can take this in our theological analogy is to Barth's dialectical understanding of the Word of God. This Word at the center of dogmatics is invisible, self-positing, and irreducible, so that the theologian in her work cannot presume mastery of it but only bear witness to it. God in Jesus Christ is at once both veiled and unveiled to creaturely eyes. Like the notion of chance, this sort of reasoning unsettles our attempts to control the object of theological inquiry, for God's self-communication is "permanently disorienting."[55] Hence the theologian is called upon to "renounce the attempt to usurp a kind of transcendent vantage point,"[56] to acknowledge her lack of knowing and fall silent in the face of the divine mystery.

---

54. Mandelbrot, *Fractal Geometry*, 1. "Dimension" may also pertain to Mandelbrot's observation that the measurement of irregular phenomenon (such as a coastline) becomes longer the more closely it is measured. As "a geometry of things that have no geometry" fractals better measure the roughness that Euclidean geometry can only approximate. See Mandelbrot, "Fractals and the Art of Roughness," TED Talk, 2010, https://www.ted.com/talks/benoit_mandelbrot_fractals_the_art_of_roughness.
55. John Webster, "Confession and Confessions," in *Nicene Christianity: The Future for a New Ecumenism*, ed. Christopher R. Seitz (Grand Rapids: Brazos, 2001), 122.
56. *CD* I/2 (877).

We may summarize the results of our application in this way: Dogmatics is properly Trinitarian in its *object* and christological in its *pattern* or shape. Per Webster the doctrine of God is seen in the Koch snowflake's finite area, which is the definite whole of the theological enterprise. All matters pertain to God and God's works, *ad intra* and *ad extra*. And, per Barth, the doctrine of Jesus Christ is the snowflake's infinite line, the pattern of which is repeated at all points and in infinite scale. No element of Christian teaching is explained sufficiently without decisive reference to Jesus and the revelation of God in him. These two—Trinity and Christology—are not in conflict with one another, nor do they simply address different subject matters. There is no measurable area without the boundary line (*ordo cognoscendi*), nor does the line's existence fail to produce a discernable shape (*ordo essendi*).

I conclude briefly with two advantages that the fractal model may provide. First, as just stated, the model illustrates that the relationship between certain doctrines in the Christian presentation—I have focused here on Trinity and Christology—is noncompetitive. Linear models suggest an ineluctable privilege to that which comes first and, in some cases, to what comes last as theology's sum and telos. Geometric models also privilege one doctrine as the "center" around which all other topics are oriented. Attempts to complicate this with the image of an ellipsis with two foci are only self-encumbered. Both foci cannot be determinative of the whole; even the theologian cannot serve two masters (Matt 6:24)![57] In practice both models end up reductive to greater or lesser degrees. But the fractal analogy is sufficiently complex to accommodate the multidimensionality of the network of doctrines in systematic theology, including their movement (or iteration), their patterned replication, and their mutual referentiality.

Against the trend of modern theology, the doctrines of Trinity and Christology should be thought together, considered in their organic interrelatedness.[58] But the point at which one enters this system could be anywhere,

---

57. Such is Barth's criticism of the theology of Schleiermacher, which tried to hold the two foci of the divine Logos and the human experience of God (which Schleiermacher identified with the Holy Spirit). The gravitational pull of the latter proved so great, in Barth's judgment, that the former finally collapsed into it and proved unnecessary to the system. See Barth, *Protestant Theology in the Nineteenth Century* (Grand Rapids: Eerdmans, 2002), 443–59. Webster also criticized the image of two equipoised foci in "Perfection and Presence: God With Us, according to the Christian Confession," Kantzer Lectures in Revealed Theology, lecture 1, September 11, 2007, http://henrycenter.tiu.edu/resource/immanuel-gods-presence-with-us/. (My thanks to Michael Allen for calling my attention to this.)

58. A case for grounding this relation christologically is in Robert J. Woźniak, "The Christological Prism: Christology as Methodological Principle," in *The Oxford Handbook of Christology*, ed. Francesca Aran Murphy (Oxford: Oxford University Press, 2015), 519–30.

and so long as these two receive their proper due, the order of one's treatment could vary radically (no two snowflakes being quite the same).

Second, depicting the arrangement of doctrines with a fractal model has at least the potential to render dogmatics more ready for cross-cultural and interdisciplinary uses—two places where "doctrine" and "dogmatics" are often regarded as (usually antiquated) conceptual tools, if they are not avoided altogether. The model accounts for the more practical realities that stem from the fact that Christian dogmatics is neither linear nor geometric in nature. The scale and symmetry of the fractal picture can accommodate not only different doctrinal emphases and orders of treatment but also diverse cultural conditions and applications. It has at least the potential to diffuse tensions between dogmatics and other theologically minded concerns and subdisciplines. It might even display a new friendliness toward other disciplines, such as philosophy or the study of religions, by allowing scholars space to affirm the integrity of their own pursuits with a certain calmness. In practice, then, the model might embolden a more "theological" theology.

CONCLUSIONS

"As a whole," Barth said, "i.e., in the basic statements of a church dogmatics, Christology must either be dominant and perceptible, or else it is not Christology."[59] Either dogmatics will orient itself wholly and at every point to Jesus Christ in his particularity, or it will find itself unable to speak about him effectively. John Webster affirmed this but, rather than ordering all things to Christology, he ordered Christology and all things to the doctrine of God. The proposal I have outlined here attempts to retain Barth's insight while accommodating a multiplicity of starting points and, with Webster, acknowledge that theological speech has the triune life of God as its subject and source. The exercise of Christocentric reasoning does not dilute the importance of the doctrine of the Trinity; in fact it depends upon it.[60] Geoffrey Bromiley's statement that for Barth the centrality of Christ is meant "to point to (and not away from) the centrality of the triune God"[61] here may be affirmed and also reversed: the Christian doctrine of God properly works itself out in a christological form. This is expressive

---

59. *CD* I/2 (123).

60. Cortez suggests helpfully that a "Trinitarian focus" is material to the sort of Christocentrism operative in Barth's theology. See Cortez, "What Does It Mean," 139–41.

61. Geoffrey W. Bromiley, *An Introduction to the Theology of Karl Barth* (Grand Rapids: Eerdmans, 1979), xi.

of the fact that neither the doctrine of the Trinity nor Christology may be explicated without the other.

I wonder, though, if it is Christology that provides the ground and soil for a full accounting of the triunity of God, rather than the other way around (especially given the history of the articulation of these doctrines from the first through the fourth centuries). Webster's ordering of Trinity-then-Christology of course makes a great deal of analytical sense, not least because the person of the Son is *one* of the Trinity and not the totality of the triune God. But it is less obvious from the point of view of the history of dogma, where expressions of God's triune nature largely have followed from affirmations about Jesus Christ. This need not be decisive for anything other than the *ordo cognoscendi*, and probably should not be so; "Is Jesus divine because God is three, or is God three because Jesus too is divine?" is without a doubt the wrong sort of question to ask. But if Barth is right in his critique of classical metaphysics, and particularly of the prioritizing of being over act, the analytical judgments which lead to Trinity-then-Christology at least become less obviously true.[62]

This is meant only as a tentative judgment, a defense of the ongoing relevance not simply of Christocentrism in general but of the specific sort of Christocentrism practiced by Barth—one that is capacious in its extension beyond the more ordinary explanations of preexistence and incarnation. And this judgment is certainly not to dismiss the dogmatic priority of the doctrine of God (as the above proposal makes clear). Trinity and Christology remain equally basic in the methods of theological exposition. Barth reminds us that the theologian cannot proclaim an authentically Christian theology without returning to the living Word of God as its pattern and norm. And Webster reminds us of whom we speak when we do this: the triune God from whom all things are, in whom "we live and move and have our being" (Acts 17:28). Theology is concerned with this God and his works, and an unflinching Christocentrism shows us this God as he truly is.[63]

---

62. Cf. *CD* II/1 (261–63). Space does not permit a full exploration of this here. It may be noted, however, that Webster too believed that the metaphysics of classical "theism" render inconceivable an ontological unity between God and humanity in the incarnation. This is because theism fills out the terms *theos* and *Christos* without reference to one another, leaving the doctrine of incarnation unworkable. See Webster, "Incarnation," in *Word and Church: Essays in Christian Dogmatics* (Edinburgh: T&T Clark, 2001), 129–30.

63. My thanks to Michael Allen for his thoughtful comments on an earlier draft of this essay, and to those who offered feedback during this session of the Los Angeles Theology Conference. I wish to dedicate this essay to the memory of my *Doktorvater*, John Webster.

CHAPTER 8

THE WORD OF GOD AS TRUTHMAKER FOR CHURCH PROCLAMATION: AN ANALYTIC BARTHIAN APPROACH TO THE DOGMATIC TASK

James M. Arcadi

Dogmatics serves Church proclamation.

KARL BARTH[1]

INTRODUCTION

My purpose in this essay is to proffer a constructive proposal in response to the question "what is the dogmatic task?" while keeping an eye on the question "what is dogmatics?" My program is to probe resources in Karl Barth's consideration of the matter in his *Church Dogmatics*, especially his ruminations in I/1. Barth offers a number of ideas on the nature of dogma and the relation this has to the person of Jesus Christ. For Barth, so I will

---

1. *CD* I/1 (83). From G. W. Bromiley and T. F. Torrance, eds. (Peabody, MA: Hendrickson, 2010). All references to the *Church Dogmatics* in this essay are from this edition.

exposit, the Word of God makes the talk about God found in church proclamation true. However, this relation—this truthmaking relation—is often vaguely stated. Thus, I will adjoin this reflection to some considerations of truthmaker theory in an effort to answer the headlining questions. However, let me register a caveat at the outset: this is not an adventure in the exegesis of the Swiss theologian's corpus. What I offer is a constructive proposal that is *Barthian*—as in, Barth-inspired—that may or may not be specifically *Barth's* proposal. That being said, I hope that my analysis and the conceptual tools I bring to the task may along the way illuminate Barth's thought in a manner that is helpful to Barth devotees. In simple terms, the picture I paint holds dogmatics to be a discipline dedicated to making distinctions. Dogmatics analyzes church proclamation to the end of discerning those elements of church proclamation that are made true by the Word of God and thus properly categorized as dogma.[2]

In order to exposit the dogmatic task, I first lay out some definitions and distinctions with respect to key terms in the project. In fact, a bulk of the project is simply getting clear on just what those components to the concept of dogma are. These terms are drawn from Barth's reflection in the *Church Dogmatics*. This is followed in a second part by a presentation of pertinent aspects of truthmaker theory. Along the way, the principles from truthmaker theory are applied to the terms defined in the previous section, the execution of which pushes our understanding of the nature of the dogmatic task to a deeper level. Finally, once these conceptual pieces are in place, I offer some concrete suggestions for how the dogmatic task—as it is here conceived—may be accomplished in the church in the here and now.

TERMINOLOGICAL AND CONCEPTUAL FOUNDATION

Like many before me, my first distinction is that dogmatics is but one component of theology. "Theology" is a wild and wooly term whose wooly-ness we theologians regularly encounter during our first lecture in an intro-course. Many of us gesture toward something like breaking theology down etymologically and calling it the study of God or, more Barthian,

---

2. Note that this is a *Barthian* understanding of the term "dogma." If one held the term dogma to be defined by some authoritative source, like the Roman Catholic teaching magisterium, then one might take issue with the picture sketched here. In this case, I simply invite this person to think of their term "dogma" as "dogma1" and what I offer here as "dogma2," and see if dogma2 is or is not a helpful component to one's theology.

talk about God. But of course talk about God can occur in various and sundry times and places. Barth himself holds that the church talks about God (a) "by its specific action as a fellowship," (b) "in proclamation by preaching," (c) "the administration of the sacraments," (d) "in worship," and (e) "in its internal and external mission," which includes "works of love amongst" (i) "the sick," (ii) "the weak," and (iii) "those in jeopardy."[3] For my purposes I will hold that when talk about God occurs in (b), (c), and (d)—that is, preaching, sacraments, and worship (what I will exposit as the paradigmatic locus)—this talk about God is properly *church proclamation*.

Barth is unfortunately vague about his definition of church proclamation, although he does say that it is "primarily and decisively preaching and the sacraments."[4] However he also goes on to state that "the task but not the reality of proclamation may be reduced and restricted to these two categories of preaching and sacrament."[5] Barth does not give necessary and sufficient conditions for church proclamation. Neither am I going to do so. Rather, I want to point to a paradigmatic locus of talk about God: the Sunday morning worship experience that countless Christians have participated in—and continue to participate in—on a weekly basis across time and place. In this context, instances (b), (c), and (d) are most clearly seen. I think it ought to be remembered that for the vast majority of the faithful, their experience of theology is not through academic texts, or theology conferences, or in the seminary classroom. Rather, for good or for ill, the lion's share of the faithful's theology comes from what they experience on Sunday morning. I do not rule out other related loci for church proclamation, say a Wednesday evening Bible study, or a wedding, or an evensong, or a Billy Graham crusade. These other instances simply highlight the archetypal nature of the Sunday morning experience.

Barth asserts that not all talk in the church's worship, my paradigmatic case, seeks to be church proclamation. He says, "It does not seek to be such when it is talk addressed by man to God,"[6] such as prayers, songs, or confession. Neither, I suppose, would Barth include in church proclamation such instances of talk about God on Sunday morning as when a music minister starts extemporaneously talking about God during a slow song, when the pastor welcomes new attendees telling them that God is pleased they are there, or the "meet and greet" time when the congregation is to say hello

---

3. *CD* I/1 (3).
4. Ibid, 80.
5. Ibid.
6. Ibid, 49.

in the name of the Lord. None of these instances, so far as I can tell, would clearly count as church proclamation in Barth's mind. However, I find this unnecessarily restrictive as a definition of church proclamation. By and large, people—the faithful and unchurched alike—come to the Sunday morning experience expecting God to be the subject of communication. That this communication occurs by way of the sermon, the sacraments (if celebrated), the liturgy (by which I just mean "what goes on in the service"),[7] the architecture, the music, the lighting, the candles, or the video screen is of no consequence. Although the sermon and the sacraments are the principle loci of talk about God, there are a myriad of other elements of the service that speak volumes about the God Christians are purporting to worship. So, for me, I will simply define church proclamation as every aspect of the Sunday morning experience—in its entirety—that communicates about God.[8]

Before moving on from the definition of church proclamation, I offer a brief note on who is doing the proclaiming in this picture that I am sketching and this foreshadows some of my practical application points to come. Although Barth holds that the task of proclamation is only indirectly assigned to the church in general, he avers that the question of dogmatics is "aimed first and directly at those entrusted with the task of proclamation."[9] Yet, it seems to me a simple fact of the matter, that in modern Sunday morning experiences "those entrusted with the task of proclamation" are not just senior pastors or teaching pastors or the like—as Barth likely had in mind. It is not just the person preaching that day or administering the sacraments (if they be administered) who issues church proclamation in the sense I am understanding it. Rather anyone who plays a liturgical role is being entrusted with the task of church proclamation. These leaders may be the music minister and the band, the choirmaster and the choir, the readers of Scripture, or even, in some churches, the videographer, the

---

7. By "liturgy" I just mean the flow of words and actions of the paradigmatic case, the "script" as Nicholas Wolterstorff has recently called it (see his *The God We Worship: An Exploration of Liturgical Theology* [Grand Rapids: Eerdmans, 2015]). This term encompasses all that "goes on" in a service, whether it is done in St. Peter's Basilica or Saddleback Community Church. Many a "nonliturgical" church has a liturgy as strictly worked out as the highest high church.

8. I note that there may be resources within Barth's thought to push against his delimiting of church proclamation to preaching and sacraments for he says, "the prayers and praises of the Church cannot be regarded as of no dogmatic importance at all; the liturgy and the hymnal must be taken seriously from the standpoint that their substance consists of human words and can thus be effective as proclamation perhaps as very distorted proclamation" (81). I am not so sure, however, that liturgy and hymns are any more susceptible to distortion than sermons or the administration of the sacraments.

9. *CD* I/1 (77).

creative team, and the soundboard technician. All who communicate about God in the paradigmatic case are participating in church proclamation and thus are subject to having their communication treated by the dogmatician.

That was church proclamation and who does it. The next key term I want to discuss is the contentious word "dogma." Barth works to describe in *CD* I/1 an older definition of dogma that has been, to his mind, corrupted by the Roman Catholic tradition. Yet, this older tradition is in line with what he wants to say about dogma. Let me offer a smattering of quotations from Barth, which will highlight some Barthian themes that I will appropriate in my own conception of dogma. Barth writes, "The true content which is sought [by Christian talk about God] we shall call dogma"[10]; "Talk about God has true content when it conforms to the being of the Church"[11]; "the dogma which dogmatics investigates is not the truth of revelation, it aims at the truth of revelation"[12]; and again, "Dogma aims at the truth of revelation."[13] We have here a cluster of concepts and terms and their relations to one another: "true content," "truth," "conformity," "aims," etc.

This cluster leads to three important characterizations of the concept of dogma. Dogma, as I offer it, is a term that denotes success, relation, and category. Let me corroborate these characterizations with some Barthian evidence. On success, Barth says, "Dogma is the agreement of Church proclamation with the revelation attested in Holy Scripture."[14] I take "agreement" to be a term of success. On relation, Barth specifically states, "Dogma in the true and original sense as the epitome of all dogmas and dogmatic propositions is a concept of relation."[15] Finally, we can discern two categories in this enterprise: one for those instances when the agreement relation successfully obtains, and one for those instances when it does not. Hence, those instances of church proclamation that successfully bear the appropriate relation are properly categorized as dogma. I will have much more to say about the nature of this relation further on, but first we must pivot to how these preliminary explications of the concepts of church proclamation and dogma lead to a definition of *dogmatics*.

Dogmatics, then, as noted before, is a distinction-making discipline that categorizes the various aspects of church proclamation into dogma

---

10. Ibid., 11.
11. Ibid., 12.
12. Ibid., 267.
13. Ibid., 268.
14. Ibid., 265.
15. Ibid., 268.

and nondogma. "As a theological discipline," Barth headlines, "dogmatics is the scientific self-examination of the Christian Church with respect to the content of its distinctive talk about God."[16] The dogmatician inspects what has been offered in church proclamation to discern when it does or does not bear the appropriate relation. Hence, in light of this, dogmatics is an inherently reactionary discipline. As Barth states, it "follows the talk of the Church,"[17] coming after the fact to differentiate all that is communicated concerning God in the paradigmatic case. Dogmatics is but parasitic on church proclamation. You just cannot do the distinguishing work of dogmatics without the "raw material" of church proclamation to divvy up or differentiate into dogma and nondogma. But the good news is, as long as church proclamation occurs, the dogmatician has a job to do. Like the Lord's mercies, the raw material the dogmatician works with is new every (Sunday) morning. Even though dogmatics is primarily reactionary, I will sketch below a way it can be a proactive servant as well.

That dogma is a success term indicates that it denotes a category of church proclamation that bears an appropriate relation. Clearly we must understand what this relation is, and what the relata are, if we are to know when success occurs and thus what is in the category of dogma. Barth uses a number of terms for this relation, his favorite of which is "agreement" (*Übereinstimmung*). This relation is the "*agreement* of the Church's distinctive talk about God with the being of the Church";[18] "Dogmatics is the critical question about dogma, i.e., about the Word of God in Church proclamation, or concretely, about the *agreement* of the Church proclamation done and to be done by man with the revelation attested in Holy Scripture";[19] "The task of dogmatics is the examination of Church proclamation in respect of its *agreement* with the Word of God";[20] "dogma is Church proclamation that is really in *agreement* with the Word of God."[21] A clearer picture of the relation begins to emerge. On one side of the relation is church proclamation, what I understand as all aspects of the Sunday morning experience that communicate about God. The relation is, in Barthian terms, "agreement." And finally the other side of the relation is "the being of the Church,"[22]

---

16. Ibid., 3.
17. Ibid., 4.
18. Ibid., 4; emphasis added.
19. Ibid., 248; emphasis added.
20. Ibid., 250; emphasis added.
21. Ibid., 268; emphasis added.
22. Ibid., 4.

which, according to Barth, is "identical with Jesus Christ."[23] Thus, finally we can deploy a fuller Barthian definition of dogma: dogma is church proclamation in agreement with Jesus Christ. The task of dogmatics, then, is to distinguish those instances of church proclamation that are actually in agreement with Jesus Christ from those that are not.

Have we come to the end of our analysis? I think not. I think that there are depths of explanation still to be plumbed. For just how are we to understand this agreement relation? And how are we to understand this relation when one *relata* is communication about God and the other *relata* is an entirely different category, a person, Jesus Christ the eternal Word of God? Here is where I think pivoting to truthmaker theory can assist our depth-plumbing.

TRUTH-BEARERS, -MAKERS, -MAKING

Like my Barthian description of dogma, a standard account of truthmaker theory, say Armstrong's,[24] makes a tripartite distinction into two *relata* and a relation in the truthmaking situation: (a) the truthbearer, (b) the truthmaker, and (c) the truthmaking relation. As with anything in philosophy, the natures of these three entities are hotly contested. Instead of just expositing these notions independent of the task at hand, in what follows I will walk through these entities and along the way apply them to the dogmatic context.

The majority opinion among truthmaker theorists is that truthbearers are propositions. I think this is a fine way to go and can easily be adapted for church proclamation, as I am here understanding it. When the preacher ascends to the pulpit and says to the congregation, "Jesus Christ is God and a human being," the preacher utters a sentence that communicates a proposition about Jesus Christ, namely <Jesus Christ is God and a human being>.[25] Countless other propositions are communicated as well by the preacher in the preaching activity. These propositions are the bearers of truth value. Of course, propositions can bear a false truth value as well.[26]

---

23. Ibid., 41. He says again, "Jesus Christ is the being of the Church" (42), where, in light of the previous quotation, I think we ought to understand the "is" in this sentence as the is of identity.

24. The *locus classicus* is D. M. Armstrong, *Truth and Truthmakers* (Cambridge: Cambridge University Press, 2004). I have been helped in my thinking about truthmakers by Gonzalo Rodriguez-Pereyra, "Truthmakers," *Philosophy Compass* 1, no. 2 (2006): 186–200; and Timothy Pawl, "Traditional Christian Theism and Truthmaker Maximalism," *European Journal for Philosophy of Religion* 4, no. 1 (2012): 197–218.

25. I will follow the convention of some philosophers in putting propositions in angle brackets.

26. So perhaps it would be better to conceive of truthbearers as *truth value bearers*, but "truthbearer" is the term in the literature.

A propositionalized instance of church proclamation has a true truth value when it meets the conditions I will sketch below, and when it does so, it is categorized on my Barthian schema as dogma.

But, recall, I want to understand church proclamation as all instances of communication about God during the Sunday morning experience. I stated that I think many of these instances are not limited to the sermon. Rather, there are numerous communications about God that take place in and through countless utterances, actions, and gestures of the worship time. What I think needs to be specified is that while not all communication about God in church proclamation comes in the form of propositions, all communication about God can be propositionalized.[27] When the priest elevates a consecrated piece of bread and the kneeling congregation crosses themselves, with bells ringing and incense wafting, this is not a proposition, yet to the observer these actions communicate a proposition like <The bread of the Eucharist is the body of Jesus Christ>. This proposition would then constitute an instance of the raw data that the dogmatician would categorize into dogma or nondogma.[28]

So (a) the truthbearer in dogma is a propositionalized instance of church proclamation. Within the Barthian dogmatic framework, as we saw above, what makes it such that an instance of church proclamation is dogma is its agreement with or conformity to Jesus Christ. Thus, within the truthmaking explication, the truthmaker is none other than the eternal Word of God, Jesus Christ himself.[29] This fits well with the truthmaker theorists' standard concern to maintain a cross-categorical relation between truthbearers and truthmakers. Typically, whereas truthbearers are propositions, truthmakers are not; they are some other ontological entity. Take the proposition <there is at least one human>. This truthbearer is made true by some nonpropositional entity like Socrates, Plato, or Oliver Crisp. What is helpful about the truthmaking motif for our purposes—in distinction

---

27. I understand that this is a contentious position. For an argument in the neighborhood of what I conceive, see William P. Alston, "Irreducible Metaphors in Theology," *Divine Nature and Human Language: Essays in Philosophical Theology* (Ithaca, NY: Cornell University Press, 1980), 17–38. However, I do not think my picture hinges on this point. If one thought some communication was nonpropositionalizable and one thought, as some truthmaker theorists do, that truthbearers need not be limited to propositions, then the analysis still goes through.

28. If one held this proposition to not agree with the Word of God, then one would categorize this proposition as nondogma.

29. It should be noted that this then cuts off one route of explication of the nature of truthmakers in the contemporary literature, that of the notion that truthmakers are properties. For discussion of other reasons this route is difficult to square with Christian theology, see Timothy Pawl, "Truthmaking and Christian theology," *Proceedings of the American Catholic Philosophical Association* (2016). doi: 10.5840/acpaproc201610548.

from a general correspondence theory of truth—is the manner in which a one-to-one correspondence is not required for truthmaking. That is, a truthbearer can be made true by multiple truthmakers, or inversely, one truthmaker can make true multiple truthbearers. For <there is at least one human> is made true by Socrates, Plato, and Oliver Crisp. But Socrates makes true multiple truthbearers, such as <there is at least one human> or <there is a human named "Socrates">. On the Barthian framework I am sketching, one truthmaker—namely, the Word of God—is the truthmaker for all the true truthbearers of church proclamation.

Within the analysis of dogma and dogmatics, the Barthian conception of (c) the truthmaking relation is one of "agreement" (*Übereinstimmung*). But what could this be? First, we must note that there is no consensus in the truthmaker literature as to just what the truthmaking relation is. Entailment, supervenience, dependence, grounding, or others are all candidate concepts for this relation. These terms attempt to characterize the nature of an *in-virtue-of* necessitation relation between truthbearers and truthmakers. So how is a Barthian-inspired concept of agreement going to do the work of the in-virtue-of relation that links truthbearers and truthmakers?

Actually, I want to hold that question to the side for a moment to first raise a potential worry regarding (b) the truthmaker as Jesus Christ. In addressing that worry, I hope to add some greater clarity to (b) which will allow me to specify what is going on in (c) the truthmaking relation.

A WORRY ABOUT (B)

Timothy Pawl writes, "According to Truthmaker Theory, truthmakers must *necessitate* the truth of the propositions they make true. . . . If David Armstrong is a truthmaker for the truth, *that David Armstrong exists*, then in any world, at any time at which David Armstrong exists, the proposition *that David Armstrong exists* is true."[30] The idea here is that in every possible world where a truthmaker exists, the truthbearers that are made true by that truthmaker are true. According to traditional Christian theism, the eternal Word of God, the second person of the Trinity, exists in all possible worlds.[31] God is a necessary being, and all three members of the Trinity are necessary. There is no possible world in which the Word of God fails to exist. Yet, traditional Christian theism also holds that at least some if

---

30. Pawl, "Traditional Christian Theism and Truthmaker Maximalism," 198. In this section, I largely follow the presentation of a similar worry about truthmaker maximalism raised in by Pawl.

31. And I think this fits with Barth's conception of God. But if it does not, then it is no matter because this is something that I affirm and thus is a worry I have.

not most of the propositions that might constitute an instance of church proclamation are not necessary, they are contingent. This latter notion is a safeguard for divine aseity and the doctrine of creation *ex nihilo* is a means for doing this safeguarding. God was free to create the cosmos or not, the Word was free to become incarnate or not, God was free to appear to Moses on Mt. Sinai or not. Barth is representative of the Christian tradition in holding that all these acts that God did perform are free, gracious, and contingent actions. Thus, a proposition like <God the Father Almighty is the creator of heaven and earth> is a contingent truth. Yet, if this proposition is a truthbearer necessitated by the Word of God, and if the Word is necessary, then the proposition <God the Father Almighty is the creator of heaven and earth> is true in every possible world. But this means that God was not free not to create. And it appears as though we have arrived at a contradiction in combining the notions that at least some of the propositions of dogma are contingent while the truthmaker of dogma is necessary. We could hold that (i) all dogmatic propositions are necessary, (ii) the Word of God is contingent, (iii) the whole Barthian dogmatic picture is hopeless, or we could (iv) modify (b) so as to include an element of contingency. Barth hints in the direction of (iv), and thus I will pursue that route.

". . . TO MAN": THE SECOND-PERSONAL NATURE OF (B)

Although the second person of the Trinity is necessary, the Word's actions are not. This in fact is just what the freedom of the Word consists in, the Word's only contingently doing some things, such as becoming incarnate or speaking and revealing God to humans. This is what I think Barth is focusing on when he describes the Word of God as that in virtue of which church proclamation is true. That is, (b) is not simply the person of Jesus Christ; we need to hold that (b) is more specifically Jesus Christ as and in a free, gracious, contingent act of revelation, reconciliation, and address. Let me offer some textual support to corroborate this claim.

For instance Barth writes that dogmatics "makes the assumption as in and with the Church it believes in Jesus Christ as the revealing and reconciling address of God *to man*."[32] Likewise, he says, "The criterion of past, future, and therefore present Christian utterance is thus the being of the Church, namely, Jesus Christ, God in His gracious revealing and

---

32. *CD* I/1, 12; emphasis added.

reconciling address *to man.*"[33] And further, "We accept and shall continue to accept the incomprehensibility of the fact that the Word of God is spoken *to man.*"[34] For Barth, the situation is not just that the eternal Word of God is the truthmaker for dogma; rather, it is the Word of God *in act*, the Word of God performing the actions of revealing to, of reconciling with, of addressing humans. The truthmaker is the person of the Word plus the accidental or contingent feature of the Word's freely acting. The mixture of a contingent feature categorizes the truthmaker itself as contingent, and thus a truthbearer necessitated by such a truthmaker is also contingent. Which is what we want for the truths of dogma.

Let us take an example. Suppose we think of the proposition <there is an author of this paper>. I am the truthmaker for that truthbearer. But suppose we make this proposition of a more second-personal nature, <I wrote this paper for you>. The truthmaker for this proposition requires an entity, a person—me—plus some free, intentional activity—my performing the act of writing to you. I *simpliciter* am not the truthmaker for the proposition <I wrote this paper for you> in the way I am for the proposition <there is an author of this paper>. Instead, the truthmaker for <I wrote this paper for you> is me plus some accidental, contingent, intentional activity.[35]

A similar analysis, I think, obtains for the Barthian conception of dogma. The truthmaker for dogma is not just the Word of God; it is the Word of God plus the free, contingent, and intentional activity of addressing humans. What is more, on the Barthian scheme, the situation is not even so vague as to hold that the Word is addressing humans in general or an abstract notion of humanity. The situation is much more concrete than that. As the above-quoted selections indicate, Barth holds that the second-personal activity of the Word revealing, reconciling, and addressing humans happens every time there is veridical dogmatic church proclamation. Every time the preacher ascends to the pulpit and speaks forth church proclamation, it is only dogma if the Word of God, the agential person of Jesus Christ, grounds those propositions by a free and discrete act of revelation, reconciliation, and address to those concrete, specific humans gathered together

---

33. Ibid., 4; emphasis added.
34. Ibid., 249; emphasis added.
35. Truth be told, even though I do not know specifically who will read or hear this paper, I certainly have had an audience, a second-personal target, in mind throughout the composition. This includes at least the persons I know will read the paper (Fred Sanders, Oliver Crisp, colleagues I know who will attend LATC), as well as the kind of people I think will attend LATC (based upon my past attendance: professional theologians, pastors, interested laypersons, theology and ministry students).

in the paradigmatic locus. This is a lively, dynamic, new every Sunday morning state of affairs that matches the way the preacher, addressing the congregation's side of the bridge, has to work with a shifting target. Now, I do not think that this at all means that the Word is shifting and changing such that in one congregation the Word will make it true that <Jesus Christ is God and a human> and in the next sermon the Word will make it true that <Jesus Christ is only a human>. Rather these same propositions, given the second-personal restriction, need to be revealed by the Word *to* the congregation newly, freshly, and diversely.

Hence, while the truthmaker for church proclamation includes a necessary component—the Word of God—it also includes a contingent element—the free activity of the Word. This renders dogma contingent as well, and the potential contradiction noted earlier is avoided.

BACK TO (C)

As I have modified (b) slightly to show the truthmaker in the dogmatic situation to be not just Jesus Christ, but Jesus Christ in a free act, now we can reengage with (c), the "agreement" truthmaking relation. Recall that what we are looking for is an understanding of the *in-virtue-of* relation between the propositions in church proclamation and Jesus Christ in free act. Simply put, a dogmatic proposition agrees with Jesus Christ's free act, when Jesus Christ is actually freely acting to communicate that proposition to specific persons at a specific time. A dogma-truthbearer is true in virtue of the Word's free activity of address to the recipients of the dogmatic propositions. This then serves to both ground or link the dogmatic propositions to the Word and preserves the Word's agential freedom. Dogma, then, means the free, revealing, reconciling, addressing act of Jesus Christ directed to specific individual humans. And the dogmatic task is to discern those instances of success or failure, when dogma does or does not obtain.

PRACTICAL APPLICATION

I want to conclude with some comments on a practical application of the foregoing reflections on the nature and task of dogmatics. It would seem very odd indeed to spend a whole paper probing the connection between church proclamation and dogmatics without offering some serious visions about how to go forward in real life. So let me offer two practical suggestions to the practitioners of dogmatics, one hinted at by Barth and one, I think illegitimately, downplayed by him.

PREACHING

I want to probe a reflection here on where the frontline of dogmatics actually is. For it seems to me, if the picture I am painting of the dogmatic task in relation to the overall mission of theology is apt, then the frontline of dogmatics is the pastor's study. The frontline is not in the academy or the seminary, the frontline is not at AAR/SBL, it is not in Durham, North Carolina or Durham, England. No, rather, the frontline of dogmatics is every single Monday through Saturday when pastors across the country and across the globe sit at their desks, open the Bible, and ask themselves, what am I going to say this week?[36] Thus, the first area of practical application is in the realm of preaching. Barth repeatedly incites dogmaticians to ply their craft on the preaching of "to-day and yesterday."[37] I want to suggest that the dogmatician concern herself not just with an abstract notion of the sermon yesterday and today, but more concretely with the sermon last week and next. It is last week's sermon or next week's that is the tangible locus of the dogmatic task, where the activity of distinguishing those propositions that have been or will be communicated into dogma or nondogma based upon their agreement with the Word of God occurs.

Church proclamation builds a bridge from the acting Word of God—the freely revealing, reconciling, and addressing person of Jesus Christ—to the present congregation. The target, the congregation, is always moving because the concerns, interests, deficiencies, and needs of a congregation are, again, like the Lord's mercies, new every (Sunday) morning. Likewise, the manner in which the propositions of dogma are communicated can vary greatly. Similar to the manner in which multiple truthbearers can be made true by one truthmaker, multiple sentences—or acts of communication—can express one and the same proposition. A propositional truthbearer like <God the Father Almighty is the creator of heaven and earth> is intentionally revealed by the Word of God, but the means of communicating that proposition are legion. The preacher can utter, "Our heavenly Father is the source of all that the empirical sciences will ever investigate, and so much more!" Or, "Look at all this stuff around you. Without God, there wouldn't be a single thing here!" Or, "Like a painter before a blank canvas, God creatively painted the picture of the world . . . plus God made the canvas and all the paints." The dogmatician works with the raw data

---

36. For Barth writes, "From the situation of the parson in the pulpit, who not only has to say something somehow, but has to say it in face of the open Bible and supposedly in accordance with the Bible and in exposition of the Bible" (*CD* I/1, 254).

37. Ibid., 268.

of church proclamation, discerns the proposition it attempts to communicate, and then distinguishes this proposition into dogma or nondogma. However, even as I noted that Barth thinks dogmatics "follows the talk of the Church,"[38] as a reactive enterprise, I suggest here that it is better to be a proactive dogmatician than a reactive one.

Those who preach on a regular basis, or even on an irregular basis, know that the majority of time spent "sermonizing" is not the fifteen, twenty, or forty minutes on Sunday morning when the sermon is delivered to the congregation, but the fifteen, twenty, or five hours spent Monday through Saturday (or in the wee hours of Sunday morning) figuring out what to say to the people come Sunday morning. Ideally, the dogmatician has a standing midweek meeting with the preacher where one is able to speak to the issues of the sermon of last week, but more importantly one works with the preacher in preparation for the sermon of next week (or in the weeks to come), distinguishing what in that potential church proclamation is dogma and what is not.

Allow me a brief "sermon" illustration. I have a very good friend who is an associate pastor at a large Baptist church. He preaches a few times a year, and it is common for us to have phone conversations as he prepares for a sermon. We discuss exegesis of the passage he is preaching on, the theology embedded therein, what the needs of the congregation are at the time, and what his sense of the Holy Spirit's leading is for that week. I do not pretend that I am a better exegete than all the commentaries he has access to, nor that I am a better repository of theology than Barth or Aquinas or Calvin, but I am there in real time, in dialogue, and in relationship, assisting him in his work of preparing to speak church proclamation to his people in the here and now. My role, as a sort of dogmatic midwife, is to help him in his sermon give birth to dogma. The Barthian-inspired dogmatician likewise can come alongside the preacher to serve in the task of proclaiming dogma.[39]

LITURGICS

Secondly, I turn to liturgics.[40] The dogmatic task is to help church proclamation to be dogma. Barth rightly pinpoints the primary locus of this talk

---

38. Ibid., 4.

39. For those of us who are a rare species, the preacher and dogmatician, do not think that we get off the hook because somehow, naturally or magically, all our sermons will be automatically *in toto* dogma. Rather we need to look over our own shoulders to engage in the dogmatic task of distinguishing. Or we need to get help from other dogmaticians.

40. Recall that I mean liturgy in a deflationary sense. Simply "the stuff that happens" during the Sunday morning worship experience.

about God in preaching and the administration of the sacraments. I agree with placing preaching and sacraments as primary, but I want us not to underestimate the power that liturgy plays in being church proclamation. Here again, the frontline of the dogmatic task in this sphere is not just the sixty to ninety minutes of the service on Sunday morning. Rather, at this point, depending on the context, the frontline moves out of the preacher's study and into the staff meeting room, or into the worship pastor's study, or into the music minister's head. There are innumerable ways that one talks about God in the countless decisions that go into putting together the Sunday morning worship service. All this communication about God has the potential for being dogma, true truthbearers in mediating the active presence of the person of Jesus Christ, but they also have the potential for being nondogma. I want to commend to dogmaticians to develop the proficiency for being able to distinguish that which is done on Sunday morning outside the sermon as bearing the truth of the Word of God or not. Dogmaticians can then encourage their pastors (or others on the pastoral staff) to work toward the increasing of those elements of the service that bear these truths and decreasing those that do not. Does the use of a fog machine communicate dogma? Does the distortion on the Fender advance propositions that are grounded in God? Does the incense or video bumper or candles or PowerPoint agree with the Word of God? If what I am sketching is apt, dogmaticians cannot simply hand the liturgy over to the musicians or the videographer or the soundboard technician or the sacristan or the verger, well-meaning as they are. No, like the dogmatician serves the preacher in preparation for the sermon, the dogmatician likewise serves the music minister or creative team or worship team in the preparation of the liturgy.

However, let me highlight here that the Barthian model cannot advocate for a calcified conception of liturgy. The congregation is an ever-evolving, ever-moving target for church proclamation. Like the skilled preacher, the skilled liturgist—assisted by the skilled dogmatician—discerns both shores that the bridge of church proclamation spans in order to successfully put the congregation in contact with Jesus Christ the truthmaker. What is attractive, and challenging, about the Barthian motif is that there is not a woodenly rigid answer to any liturgical question. It might very well be that in bridging the worlds of the revelation of Jesus Christ and the context in which that revelation is communicated, fog machines are the perfect church proclamation to do so. In other contexts, if the liturgist wants to use smoke to communicate about Jesus Christ, incense is the apropos means. In either context, the dogmatician assists the liturgist in making this decision based on the active Word of God, not merely pragmatics or convenience or cool-factor.

CONCLUSION

Talk about God occurs all over the place. When that talk about God occurs in the paradigmatic locus of the Sunday morning worship experience, that talk is church proclamation. Although church proclamation occurs primarily in preaching and the administration of the sacraments, it also occurs throughout the liturgy, in word, gesture, and song. When those instances of church proclamation are made true by a free act of address by the Word of God to the congregation, they are categorized as dogma. Thus, the dogmatic task is to distinguish when this does and does not happen. However, rather than being purely reactionary, I implore dogmaticians to take a proactive-servant role in their churches working with preachers and liturgists (of all kinds) to ensure that the church proclamation of next week is indeed dogma.[41]

---

41. I am grateful for helpful comments from the participants of the LA Theology Conference, Oliver D. Crisp, Timothy Pawl, Jordan Wessling, J. T. Turner, David Hunsicker, Jesse Gentile, Jared Powell, and Christopher Woznicki.

CHAPTER 9

DIVINE PERFECTIONS, THEOLOGICAL REASONING, AND THE SHAPE OF DOGMATICS

BRANNON ELLIS AND JOSH MALONE

INTRODUCTION

In the doctrine of the divine perfections, the theologian attempts to answer the question "What is God like?" by carefully elaborating the revealed character of God through the wise use of sanctified reason. God's perfections are neither diverse realities possessed by God nor conceptual labels we place upon him, but distinct characteristics or qualities uniquely naming him. These perfections are proper descriptions of God's simple, triune being, which we know to provide a true and coherent account of the identity of the incomprehensible One on the basis of faith in his trustworthy self-disclosure in scriptural word and deed.

While we seek to describe God according to the ways he has given himself to be known, we must always remember that even our fitting descriptions aren't prescriptions that determine the identity of the self-existent One who remains free even in giving himself. The divine perfections are never attributions in that sense, defining God's being on the basis of human reasoning and therefore speaking of no God at all. Yet this freedom of God is no barrier to theological reason. Even in his aseity, the true God—given in Christ through the Spirit and the Word—is inexpressibly more faithful and consistent and *even more present and palpable*

178

than whatever shadows of him and his ways we may conjure from our own heads and hearts.

In this essay, we take the position that Christian theological reasoning about the divine perfections should be formed entirely by the God who bears these perfections in himself and therefore in his free self-disclosure. We believe a fruitful way of thus disciplining our reasoning is to approach the doctrine of God's perfections in light of two sets of coordinate doctrines: aseity paired with simplicity and Trinity with Christology. Aseity and simplicity *form* our reasoning about God's perfections, in the sense of bracketing the scope and shape of our doctrinal claims, while Trinity and Christology *inform* our reasoning, in the sense of grounding the veracity of those claims, pervasively characterizing their content, and governing their interrelations. As such, we suggest that this approach is useful for speaking not only of God's character but also of his ways, and thus it proves to be fruitful for the whole scope of the dogmatic task.[1]

ASEITY AND SIMPLICITY

To confess God's aseity is to say that he inherently and underivatively possesses the ground and continuance of his being in the inexhaustible riches of the triune life. To confess God's simplicity is to say that he is self-consistent—that every particular aspect or characteristic of the divine nature is entirely true of the triune life. Thus, aseity and simplicity cooperate to continually refocus our reasoning on the living God from whom and to whom are all things, not only as the ultimate bearer of all his perfections but as the unique subject of each and all. This interplay between aseity and simplicity carries the special dogmatic burden of calling us to confess that the Lord, our God, who is a fountain of life (Ps 36:9) and who is faithful to do all he has promised (1 Thess 5:24), is one (Deut 6:4).

It's fitting to begin our theological reasoning about God's perfections with his aseity because everything we're saying is a claim about the One who is *sui generis*, uniquely and incomparably this God without precedent or peer. We can think of aseity as our *terminus a quo*. It should always be our "from where?" in reasoning about the divine perfections, testifying to God's own "from where," his existence *a se*. In this sense, all the divine

---

1. For this essay, we define the dogmatic task as the theologian's calling within the church to render faithful theological judgments about God's character and ways on the basis of his scriptural self-disclosure.

perfections are implicated by or present in God's aseity—not because of logical deduction, but because even when we begin to speak of the "from where?" of his character, he is already fully "there." God is wholly who he is apart from and before our beginning to speak of him.[2] God's aseity calls us to receive what we've been given, placing an emphasis on the sheer *givenness* of God's life in himself and toward us. Our theology is a response to this free and gracious self-giving; beginning with aseity isn't only fitting to the uniqueness of God, therefore, but to the posture of faith.

Likewise, it's fitting to end our theological reasoning with simplicity because everything we will have claimed for the uniquely self-existent God applies *entirely* to the Father, the Son, and the Holy Spirit and should stand in utter consistency with whatever else is true of each person and all together as God. We are true to God when in this way we confess God to be true to himself. Simplicity is the *terminus ad quem* of our theologizing in the sense that it's always our "unto what?" in reasoning about the divine perfections, interrogating every conclusion of our theological reasoning in order to render it fit to approach the living God.

In this way, beginning with aseity is especially appropriate to exercising the gift of faith, and ending with simplicity is fitting to bearing the gracious fruits of faithfulness.[3] We cannot speak in faith without at the same time repenting of the idols of the nations and of our hearts: so alluring one minute and so mundane the next—so unlike God! Likewise, we cannot reason faithfully without walking in the holiness the Spirit supplies. Every assumption, every deduction, every implication stands or falls not on analysis or common sense but ultimately on the sustaining grace of God, a grace that challenges and disciplines our reasoning in the process of setting it apart as holy. So by faith we confess the only true God who is incomprehensible yet gives himself to be known, and through faithfulness we maintain this confession's focus on God himself as its mysterious and merciful coherency.

---

2. This implication of God's perfections in his aseity, therefore, doesn't involve only those that seem conceptually to correlate with aseity, such as immutability or self-sufficiency. See Bavinck, *Reformed Dogmatics*, ed. John Bolt, trans. John Vriend (Grand Rapids: Baker Academic, 2003), 2:152.

3. By beginning with aseity and ending with simplicity, we're not addressing aseity before anything else and then promptly leaving it behind, or ignoring simplicity until there's nothing else left to say. The Spirit who gives faith and enables faithfulness is one, no less so in granting us, with himself, the knowledge of the Father and the Son. In treating aseity as theological reasoning's *terminus a quo* and simplicity as its *terminus ad quem*, both are always in play, but from different perspectives. Theological reasoning is always from faith and unto faithfulness, each always present and necessary, both informing the whole and yet with a discernible order—a whence and whither.

TRINITY AND CHRISTOLOGY

So aseity is the "from where?" It asserts God's exclusivity as uniquely God alone. And simplicity is the "unto what?" It asserts God's consistency as wholly and always exactly who he is in his exclusivity as Lord. But on their own, apart from the actual content of the self-disclosure of the Father in the Son by the Spirit, these bookends and everything between them are as prone to be like "trying to find a black cat in the dark" as any other claim about the characteristics of a God with whom we really have nothing to do. *Qualis sit Deus* again becomes just another curious topic for philosophers and theologians to debate—always searching but never coming to a knowledge of the truth (2 Tim 3:7). In fact, claiming aseity and simplicity for such an unknown God heightens the problem of our ignorance in the face of his utter incomprehensibility.

This is why the other set of coordinate doctrinal claims—Trinity and Christology—is critical. The triune God is the *principium essendi* of the divine perfections, the reality to which—to whom—these descriptions apply.[4] The God who reveals his exclusive name as YHWH emphatically refuses to share that name and its divine glory with any other (Isa 42:8). Yet that name above every name is borne no less gloriously by Jesus (Phil 2:9–10), and together with Jesus, Paul confesses the Spirit to be *kyrios*, the Lord (2 Cor 3:17). The one name into which we're baptized—the one God in which we glory, the God known in all his perfections—that name belongs to the Father, Son, and Spirit (Matt 28:19).

Likewise, Jesus Christ is the *principium cognoscendi* of the revealed knowledge of the perfections, as the one in whom all true revelation of and speech about God cohere, the Icomprehensible incarnate, the *principium essendi* who has made his dwelling among us. Traditionally, Protestants have identified Scripture as the principle of our theological knowledge, and we believe this is also true: Jesus possesses in himself both the self-knowledge of God and the fullness of all creaturely knowledge of God, and he reveals that knowledge unto salvation by his Spirit through the scriptural word of the prophets and apostles.[5] So both the beginning and the end of theological reasoning—which

---

4. On the Reformed orthodox employment of this idea, Richard Muller says, "The identification of God as the *principium essendi* of theology, far from generating a theological system deduced from the doctrine of God, actually produced a theological system in consistent dialogue with the doctrine of God, often to the extent that aspects of the doctrine of God derive from concerns at the heart of other *loci*, notably Christology, soteriology, and eschatology." Muller, *Post-Reformation Reformed Dogmatics* (Grand Rapids: Baker Academic, 2003), 3:33.
5. So Junius argues in his famous *Theologia vera*, one of the foundational prolegomenal works of

is just to say, scriptural reasoning—find their moorings in Jesus. Surely he is the Alpha and Omega of all things, theology not least of all! Jesus is the God who is known and the one who makes God known. The author and perfecter of our faith is the one who first knows and loves his Father in perfect faith and faithfulness, who then conforms us to his own image by giving us his Spirit and word, so that what belongs to Jesus belongs to us in him.

GOD'S (WRATHFUL) LOVE: A TEST CASE

How does this approach look when considering a particular divine perfection? God's love offers a promising example.

God's love flows forth from his triune life, which he freely shares with his creatures, drawing them into the loving fellowship he forever enjoys in himself. Because of his love's inexhaustible source within himself, God can give from his fullness without reserve. In this love, God is not in need of love from us; instead, he gives his creatures life and breath and everything (Acts 17:25), and lovingly draws us into fellowship with himself without losing what he had or gaining what he lacked.

God loves his creatures from this freedom. Although the love he extends to his creatures is both contingent and free, it bears the same character and depth as the love he has in himself because in his simplicity he is wholly who he is in all his actions. Love characterizes God in his consistency and unity, thus it completely describes his manifold perfections. His love is good and holy and just; his goodness, holiness, and justice are loving.

Everything God is, he is as the loving God in the communion of Father, Son, and Spirit. In the created economy, we don't receive a reduced expression—or even a deeply rich manifestation—of God's love for sinners in Christ. In Jesus we experience God's love for sinners with his own two hands. We encounter the God who is love made manifest, the Son expressing the love of his Father in the love of their Spirit, a love that is whole and complete in each and all together. That perfect love is freely shared with us (John 17:23). Since God is indivisible, there's no aspect of him which is against us in the gospel, no moment when our Father regrets adopting us, or no extenuating circumstances where the indwelling Spirit might reconsider his guarantee of our inheritance. The God who is *entirely* for us in Christ is *always* for us in Christ.

---

the era of Protestant orthodoxy. See *A Treatise on True Theology with the Life of Franciscus Junius*, trans. David Noe (Grand Rapids: Reformation Heritage, 2014).

Because God is wholly love, we must affirm that God is also loving toward those who don't embrace his forgiving, transforming, covenant-keeping love in Christ. With the Bible, we need to be careful about *whom* and *how* we say God loves. God is only our Father in the fullest sense if we have become his sons and daughters in his only begotten Son. Nonetheless, the God *who is* love is always himself. God is the same God to those in whom his love finds fruition as he is to those who spurn him (cf. Acts 17:26–27).

God's love is a dangerous thing; sometimes it embraces, and sometimes it exposes. Mark tells us Jesus "loved" the rich young ruler when he uncovered his greed and sent him away sorrowful (Mark 10:21); Jesus says anyone who doesn't hate their own most cherished family members compared to their love for him cannot follow him (Luke 14:26). God loves us whether his loving pursuit induces us to love him back, or whether we twist it into one more motive for rejecting or disdaining him.

It's here that we start to see something of the relation between divine love and wrath. God's wrath doesn't exist apart from his love, but flows from it as a mode of his love toward sin and rebellion. It is love shown forth in the context of active offense. God doesn't need to be wrathful in order to be who he is, yet this conduct is entirely befitting a God who is utterly good, just, and holy in his freedom to display his mercy and his wrath (Rom 9:22). Yet even as God displays his wrath, he isn't ill tempered or out of control—his is a wrathful love. God will not let sinners forever rule themselves and ruin others because that would be the unloving thing to do. As Elie Wiesel famously said, "the opposite of love is not hate, it's indifference."[6] Indeed, God who is perfect in goodness, holiness, and justice as well as love *therefore* exercises wrath against sin, evil, hatred, and injustice because he is always exactly who he is in that context too.

So we see that, as a mode of his love, God's wrath is *a se*, uniquely characterized by his own nature; it's simple, completely consistent with his justice, holiness, goodness, and so on. God's wrath is Trinitarian—it's no more or less an expression of the Father's love as wrath in the face of sin than it is an expression of the Son's wrath as judgment (Rev 19:15) and an expression of the world's conviction by the Spirit according to that judgment (John 16:11). And finally, wrath is christological, to be understood concretely according to God's self-revelation in Christ.

In the cross of the incarnate God, we see the most powerful manifestation

---

6. In an interview with Alvin P. Sanoff, "One Must Not Forget," *U.S. News & World Report* (October 27, 1986), 68.

possible of the Trinity's wrathful love and its exposure and embrace of sinners. Did God *hate* the world by revealing the deepest darkness of the human heart that day? Was it God's *spite* that put our self-centeredness on display at Golgotha before sun, moon, and stars, which all turned in shame at the sight? Of course not, certainly not in the way we think of it. Jesus showed us—and let us show ourselves—who we really are as sinners that day. Was that love? Yes—thunderous and speechless, reckless and wise, burning with all the wrathful passion of the living God yet pitiful in its apparent futility to thwart a fickle mob and a few jaded soldiers. "This is love, not that we have loved God, but that he loved us and sent his Son to be the propitiation for our sins" (1 John 4:10 NASB).

CONFLATING TRINITY AND CHRISTOLOGY

We believe our advocacy of an account of the perfections along these lines carries a deeply classical motive, even as it teases out the theological well-roundedness sometimes only implicit in classical expositions. We're aware, certainly, that not all attempts at doing so are equally successful at remaining classical while contributing something new.

Theology after Barth, on the one hand, has tended to employ a form of Christocentrism to avoid problems that can, and sometimes have, arisen in the most reified forms of classical theology. Some theologians have shown a tendency to conceive of the divine perfections (such as love) apart from their concrete manifestations in the gospel economy. For example, they might conceptualize the divine love between two perfect agents in maximal mutual delight apart from any explicit reference to the pattern of love between Christ and his Father revealed in Scripture. To solve this problem, many have conceived of the dogmatic task through Christ as both the *principium cognoscendi* of theology as well as its direct *principium essendi*. Accordingly, to be Chalcedonian in this sense is to confess the shape of theology to be Christomorphic because the being of God is.[7] Grounding the whole Christ, God and man, in the divine life in this way fully identifies theology and economy—closing the classical analogical interval—in order to guard against theological abstraction.

This instinct of not eliding Jesus at any point in our theological reasoning

---

7. For an example of a post-Barthian approach developed in rejection of reified forms of scholastic theology which overcorrects by intensifying the "Chalcedonian pattern," viewing God's willed, eternal being as Christomorphic, see Bruce McCormack, "Grace and Being," *The Cambridge Companion to Karl Barth* (Cambridge: Cambridge University Press, 2000), 103.

is a good one. However, a potential conflation of theological reasoning (which is Christomorphic) with theology's object (which is now conceived of as Christomorphic) threatens here. And if Trinity and Christology collapse into a single point, we not only lose the real distinctions and interplay between them, but we also lose much of what must be said between aseity and simplicity. Instead, by treating Trinity and Christology as an irreducible pairing of complementary doctrinal claims we can avoid this pinch. We can certainly take up the central constructive insight of Barth—that in Christ the fullness of the one true God really does dwell—and we can add to it the crucial proviso, in *bodily form* (Col 2:9). It is the presence of both these moments that most faithfully trace the Chalcedonian pattern: without confusion, exchange, separation, or division.

NEGLECTING TRINITY AND CHRISTOLOGY

On the other hand, some theologians have pushed back on the modern desire for a more Christomorphic doctrine of God, and we think rightly so in view of the solid Christian consensus that God's free economic activity in no way determines his immanent identity. This more classical approach is really comfortable lingering on aseity and simplicity. But as with anything else, it can be taken too far—the nature of God isn't intrinsically Christomorphic, but the nature of theology is.[8]

Jesus is the one in whom all our dogmatic claims and conclusions about God, the world, and their relations hold together. Jesus isn't all of God, but he is all that God is, and we get all of God in him. Jesus isn't the Father, but he is all the Father is and the only one who reveals him. Jesus isn't the Spirit, but he sends him from the Father, and gives only what is his own. The Spirit who guides into all truth—which must include theology!—does so by bringing us to the Father in his Son, the only God who is at the Father's side and thus the only one who can make him known. Why would this apply any less to knowledge of the one God or his perfections? Jesus is the one in whom these hold together for us, too.

We believe the desire of many contemporary theologians to take up the insight never to leave Jesus behind in our dogmatic reasoning should be strengthened, not weakened, by affirming the sheer Godness of God

---

8. For an example of a theology developed in conscious reaction to divine Christomorphism, which nevertheless goes too far in rejecting a "Chalcedonian pattern" to the "God-world relation," see Sonderegger, *Systematic Theology*, vol. 1 (Minneapolis: Fortress, 2015), xxiii n5.

implicated by robust doctrines of aseity and simplicity. But while aseity and simplicity can frame a fitting theology of God's perfections, they cannot ground it or reveal its substance; rather, Trinity and Christology must be free to do their proper dogmatic work of informing the content and interrelations of our doctrinal claims if these claims are to faithfully describe the true God whose name is Father, Son, and Spirit.

TWO SIGNIFICANT APPLICATIONS FOR THE TASK OF DOGMATICS

It's axiomatic that what happens in theology proper deeply shapes (or should) the remaining theological loci. God does what he does, in the way he does, because he is who he is. As we wrap up, we'd like to highlight two significant applications of the approach we're advocating here.

First, *God's aseity applies no less to his activity than to his identity.* Christian theology has often been tempted to map the doctrine of God onto one or another intellectually or aesthetically or culturally compelling ontology. Think of the psychological analogy, the social analogy, or the analogy of love or of being. All such attempts at *extrapolating* the divine nature and its workings are risky, not least because to some extent we end up speaking of God by speaking about something else in a way that's governed to some degree by our understanding of that other thing. The same temptation arises when we turn to other theological loci.

Reasoning from God's aseity throughout the dogmatic task helps us remember that the character of *this God's* extrinsic activity is just as incomprehensibly unique and scandalously exclusive as he is. Creation, for example, isn't something we can understand or even observe rightly unless we begin to speak of it theologically—from the beginning, *ex nihilo.* Where were we, as God asks Job (38:4)? The world and human beings within it have no category for speaking of what was not before it came to be, except through knowledge of the only One who has always been, the One through whose eternal Word everything came to be (the Word who himself came to be flesh, John 1:1–3, 14).

Or take providence. Providence is simultaneously the most pervasive activity of God and completely undetectable in and of itself. At one and the same time, in the very same acts, God is active in divine wisdom, holiness, and grace, and we're active in all the mixed motives of human beings. And don't forget the countless layers or strands of nonhuman creaturely activity pervading and mediating every human act. Even God's acting is mediated, unapologetically so—indeed, so much so that his typical ways of acting constitute a large part of his hiddenness, veiled behind the rest of creation doing what to us feels alternately arbitrary or inevitable. Yet in all of it God is accomplishing exactly what he has intended from eternity. We could say the same sorts of things about the doctrines of humanity, salvation, and so on. God's aseity grounds the uniqueness of both the Christian gospel and its dogmatic expressions.

The second significant application of our approach we'd like to highlight is that *any conception of a divine perfection that precludes Jesus bearing that perfection is inadequate.* Theological reasoning that puts distance between the character of God and his ways, and the person and work of Jesus, diminishes the hope of the gospel. An aseity that cannot see Jesus as dependent on his teenage mother for bodily sustenance is a philosophical abstraction; an eternal person that cannot become flesh is a conception beneath the true dignity of God. The same goes for a Jesus who cannot suffer while he enjoys beatitude, or cannot uphold all things because he is forsaken, or cannot be wrathful because he bears sin for our sakes.

How much of God do we get in Jesus? One third? More? Less? If we only know a part or aspect or effect of God's character and action in Christ, then is he truly *God himself* with us? How could we ever be confident that we know the "immortal, invisible, God only wise" just because we've taken the word of a rabbi who walked the roads of Palestine and hung on a Roman cross two millennia ago? How can our hope be in God (1 Pet 1:21) if God isn't *in* our hope? If Jesus's heart is out of perfect sync with his Father's heart in any way—indeed, if their heart for us isn't *one*—then our hope is in vain. Christian hope isn't playing the odds or wishing for the best. When the odds were impossible and the worst we could've imagined happened—the Savior of the world crucified, dead, buried, cursed—when the heart of God in Christ stopped beating, *that's* when hope began to come alive for us. Our hope sits ruling at the Father's right hand until he comes in glory, a living hope with a beating heart, which, though once stopped, will never cease again.

CONCLUSION

We submit that consistently employing these two sets of coordinate doctrinal claims—aseity with simplicity and Trinity with Christology—allows theologians to more fully unfold a doctrine of the perfections that is unqualifiedly divine yet centered on the gracious revelation of the triune God in

Christ. This approach should, to the same extent, also assist us in carrying out the entire dogmatic task in deeper faith in and faithfulness to our one Lord. Aseity and simplicity keep us from thinking we can domesticate almighty God merely by describing him in and through our creaturely speech; Trinity and Christology keep us from having nothing worthwhile to say. So in all our theological reasoning, aseity is where we should begin, and simplicity is where we should end, but God in Christ is where we must stand.

CHAPTER 10

DOGMATICS AS ASCETICS

MICHAEL ALLEN

WORSHIP, DISCERNMENT, AND THEOLOGY: CAN DOGMATICS SERVE THESE SANCTIFYING ENDS?

I appeal to you therefore, brothers, by the mercies of God, to present your bodies as a living sacrifice, holy and acceptable to God, which is your spiritual worship. Do not be conformed to this world, but be transformed by the renewal of your mind, that by testing you may discern what is the will of God, what is good and acceptable and perfect.

ROMANS 12:1–2[1]

PAUL'S WELL-KNOWN APPEAL involved a call to "spiritual worship" by way of "living sacrifice" of one's whole self (Rom 12:1). And to that liturgical and spiritual end, he identified a need for "discern[ing] what is the will of God, what is good and acceptable and perfect" (12:2). Worship is not only bodily but also intentional, rational, and reflective. The testing of discernment shapes and sustains the course of self-sacrifice. Paul also warns of a twofold threat to this discerning offering of one's own body: first, warning that we might be "conformed to the world" (12:2) or led astray by cultural malformation, and second, that we might simply remain where we are and as we are or left in our own calcifying darkness. Indeed,

---

1. Unless otherwise noted, English Scripture passages in this chapter are taken from the ESV.

it is crucial to observe that he not only calls for a stiff-arm to be thrown to the whelming flood of cultural pressures but that he then presses away from the spiritual status quo as well: "be transformed by the renewal of your mind" (Rom 12:2). So Paul's call to worshipful discernment must press away undue influence but cannot rest content there; it must also press into the sanctifying, renewing work of God upon our own minds.

Theology must serve spiritual purposes. Theology leads to praise, and theology shapes wise and prudential reasoning.[2] But to those ends, Christian theology first cuts against the cultural grain and cuts across our own sinful selves. The question for us becomes: can dogmatic theology with its focus upon seemingly settled resources be a practice of unsettling our sinful ways? Might this most ecclesiastical of Christian intellectual enterprises be a tool for the "renewing of our minds" or must it inherently privilege the status quo? We do well to note that suspicions have arisen in recent years regarding the supposedly ontotheological, hegemonic, and phallocentric tendencies of systematic theology in contemporary theological discussions.[3]

Perhaps unsurprisingly, another pathway has dominated theological discourse in recent years as a purported means to address this stultifying status quo: "Theology and . . ." Many such pairings have garnered significant attention in recent decades: theology and economics, theology and gender, theology and literature, and perhaps more obviously, theology and politics. Drawing on other realms of thought has been seen as a way of enlivening the doctrinal task, loosening the stultifying grip of old orthodoxies, and fostering a more faithful humanism. The following essay might be thought to offer yet another pairing: theology and ascetics. Perhaps ascetics is simply another conversation partner which can—must!—leaven dogmatics. In such an approach, ascetics would add moral and self-renunciatory facets to a dogmatics which is itself anything but. But I wish to suggest that dogmatics holds a unique place in the intellectual work of the Christian church. It is not superior work. In many ways, it is subservient to other tasks. For instance, the discernment and worship

2. For helpful guidance in this regard, see especially Vanhoozer, *The Drama of Doctrine: A Canonical-Linguistic Account of Christian Theology* (Louisville: Westminster John Knox, 2005); Daniel J. Treier, *Virtue and the Voice of God: Toward Theology as Wisdom* (Grand Rapids: Eerdmans, 2006); Michael Horton, *The Christian Faith: A Systematic Theology for Pilgrims on the Way* (Grand Rapids: Zondervan Academic, 2011), 13–34; Vanhoozer, *Faith Speaking Understanding; Performing the Drama of Doctrine* (Louisville: Westminster John Knox, 2014); Kevin J. Vanhoozer and Daniel J. Treier, *Theology and the Mirror of Scripture: A Mere Evangelical Account,* Studies in Christian Doctrine and Scripture (Downers Grove, IL: IVP Academic, 2015), 131–57.
3. Sarah Coakley, *God, Sexuality, and the Self: An Essay 'On the Trinity'* (Cambridge: Cambridge University Press, 2013), 42.

that Paul attests, as of penultimate and ultimate significance in Romans 12:1–2, and its practitioners, as officers of the church, serve to equip the saints for the work of ministry (Eph 4:11–12). Worship and witness are the first order activities of Christian language, but the wisdom won by being wrestled to the ground with God's truth serves as an instrument and means of intellectual discipleship without which we dare not journey.[4] Construed as a tool of discipleship, then, Christian dogmatics plays a unique role in the rhythms of Christian sanctification and, by God's grace, does so with its own disciplinary integrity.

To offer something approximating an argument for this claim, I will begin by considering what likely seems to be the most companionable approach to an ascetical theological method today, namely, the *théologie totale* articulated by Sarah Coakley in her systematic theology. I will then compare Coakley's account of desire and knowledge with the way in which the late John Webster articulated the "holiness of theology." In so doing, I will seek to show that Webster sustained the spiritual and even ascetical intuitions so powerfully articulated by Coakley, though he did so by pressing beyond mere systematic theology to the task of Christian dogmatics. I will progress further still in concluding the essay with some principles for envisioning Christian dogmatics as a practice of intellectual asceticism and discipleship.[5]

THEOLOGY, DESIRE, ASCETICISM: SARAH COAKLEY ON *THÉOLOGIE TOTALE*

Purgation and desire go together, at least that is the wager of Sarah Coakley, who has previously argued so poignantly that power and submission are

---

4. Language of intellectual discipleship has been helpfully unpacked in Fergus Kerr, "Tradition and Reason: Two Uses of Reason, Critical and Contemplative," *IJST* 6, no. 1 (2004): 37–49; Frederick Christian Bauerschmidt, *Thomas Aquinas: Faith, Reason, and Following Christ*, Christian Theology in Context (Oxford: Oxford University Press, 2013), 36, 81, 140. Some parallel approaches in medieval literature are thoughtfully analyzed by Peter M. Candler Jr., *Theology, Rhetoric, Manuduction, Or Reading Scripture Together on the Path to God*, Radical Traditions (Grand Rapids: Eerdmans, 2006), with regard to the use of the language of *ductus*, *skopos*, and an *itinerarium*, though his theological account fails to press on to offer much covenantal or christological specificity in its broadly participationist metaphysics and also offers a severely mangled reading of early Protestant theology and the development of *sola Scriptura* (esp. 13–16); similarly inclined, though overly focused on categories of embodiment, is Nathan Jennings, *Theology as Ascetic Act: Disciplining Christian Discourse* (New York: Lang, 2010).

5. I hope thus to extend the arguments offered years ago in J. I. Packer, "An Introduction to Systematic Spirituality," in *Serving the People of God: Collected Shorter Writings on The Church, Evangelism, the Charismatic Movement, and Christian Living*, Collected Shorter Writings of J. I. Packer 2 (Vancouver: Regent College Publishing, 1998), 305–16.

necessary bedfellows.[6] In the much acclaimed first installment of her systematic theology, *God, Sexuality, and the Self*, Coakley argues that "theology involves not merely the metaphysical task of adumbrating a vision of God, the world, and humanity, but simultaneously the epistemological task of cleansing, reordering, and redirecting the apparatuses of one's own thinking, desiring, and seeing."[7] Theology does address metaphysics, with the divine and the creaturely realm coming in for assessment together, sure enough, but such ontological talk simultaneously concerns purifying the mind, the heart, and the eyes.

Theology, then, is "fundamentally purgative of idolatry."[8] This purifying is no small matter, for Coakley attends to three looming threats, each of which are oftentimes presumed to render systematic theology invalid. First, ontotheology supposedly flattens the categories of the divine and the creaturely in a totalizing and thus blatantly idolatrous fashion.[9] Second, hegemony lurks as a threat whereby the powers and principalities can bend discourse and shape its very questions to prop up their own interests, suggesting that the system, as it were, determines what is systematic, even in theology.[10] Third, a specific feminist concern about the more subtle hegemony of male dominance—what might be called theology's phallocentric form—has so permeated the Western tradition, at least, as to inscribe a male imaginary into the confessions and expositions of theology.[11] These three threats are actually one in manifold form: "Each presumes that the systematician idolatrously desires mastery: a complete understanding of God, a regnant position in society, or a domination of the gendered 'other'; and each presumes that the same systematician will thereby abuse his knowledge, his power, or his 'male' mode of thinking, for purposes of intellectual, social, or sexual dominance."[12]

Theology cannot be severed from contemplation, if such threats without and within are to be exposed and defeated by grace. "The very act of contemplation—repeated, lived, embodied, suffered—is an act that, by grace, and over time, inculcates mental patterns of 'un-mastery,' welcomes the dark realm of the unconscious, opens up a radical attention to

---

6. See Sarah Coakley, *Powers and Submissions: Spirituality, Philosophy, and Gender*, CCT (Oxford: Blackwell, 2002), esp. ch. 2.

7. Coakley, *God, Sexuality, and the Self*, 20.

8. Ibid., 20.

9. Ibid., 44–47.

10. Ibid., 47–49.

11. Ibid., 49–50.

12. Ibid., 51.

the 'other,' and instigates an acute awareness of the messy entanglement of sexual desires and desire for God."[13] Contemplation proves crucial here, for Coakley inverts one maxim of Freud, arguing instead that "desire is more fundamental than sex," while affirming another such principle of his, namely, that sublimation of such desires is essential.[14] Theology "comes, that is, with the urge, the fundamental desire, to seek God's 'face,' and yet to have that seeking constantly checked, corrected, and purged."[15] Those urges are not merely false judgments but, indeed, urges or desires: "To speak theologically: unredeemed desire is at the root of each of these challenges to the systematic task."[16] And such needed checks and balances take the form of systematic concern: "Wherever one desires to start has implications for the whole, and the parts must fit together."[17] They not only fit together but form one in that manner, for "the contemplative task, which rightly sustains systematics, is itself a progressive modulator and refiner of human desire: in its naked longing for God, it lays out all its other desires . . . and places them, over time, into the crucibles of divine desire."[18]

Contemplation cannot be myopic, then, but must be drawn upward and out to consider not only God and certain divine things of spiritual prestige. No, such would be to set the gaze upon the easily ossified. Coakley calls for a *théologie totale* which "makes the bold claim that the more systematic one's intentions, the more necessary the exploration of such dark and neglected corners" as those found in the nooks and crannies of the Scriptures, the etchings of the catacombs, and the prayer-life of charismatic sects. And so the scope and sequence of her first volume—an "essay 'on the Trinity'"—moves from two chapters which offer a programmatic and methodological entryway to the multivolume project toward a sequence of chapters on "praying the Trinity" in patristic texts on desire (ch. 3), on fieldwork investigations of English congregations in the charismatic world (ch. 4), on iconographic representations of the triune God (ch. 5), and then two final chapters addressing her own account of patristic Trinitarianism (ch. 6) and the interplay of desire, Trinity, and apophaticism (ch. 7).

The title of her volume—*God, Sexuality, and the Self*—is not mere hodgepodge. She really does articulate a rather cogent, seamless garment wherein

---

13. Ibid., 43.
14. Ibid., 7–8.
15. Ibid., 45.
16. Ibid., 51–52.
17. Ibid., 41.
18. Ibid., 52.

an account of the Trinity and an understanding of desire (in God and in humanity) coalesce. She sublimates gender breakdowns or dichotomies, for example, in the triune account of God, avoiding a common move (by supposed conservatives or purported liberals) to pattern social practice on the triune life.[19] Rather, "twoness [of gender], one might say, is divinely ambushed by threeness [of triune reflexivity]."[20] And this third, the Holy Spirit, is thus determinative, for the Holy Spirit is the "inherent reflexivity in the divine."[21] The Trinitarian account shares much with recent revisions regarding doctrinal history. She disputes the dominant East/West dichotomy of the late nineteenth and twentieth centuries.[22] She opposes the proposals of so-called doctrinal critics, expounding the ascetical, exegetical, and simultaneously apophatic accounts of triunity found in Nyssa and others.[23] She even defends the traditional naming of the triune God as Father, Son, and Holy Spirit over against largely feminist concern about its gendered connotations.[24]

Yet she also turns Trinitarianism somewhat on its head. Coakley operates with a strict dichotomy of her own, opposing what she calls an "incorporative" or "reflexive" model of the Trinity over against the "linear" schema. The linear model, so focused on processions and missions, finds its fullest expression in the Gospel according to John and bears within it the tendency toward an orthodoxy that may subordinate the Spirit, the other, the dark margins that alone can purge us.[25] A "prayer-based" and "Spirit-leading" approach will take up an incorporative or reflexive view of the Trinity, drawn primarily from Romans 8. Origen holds both views,[26] and writings of Nyssa and others (especially in oft overlooked texts) gesture toward this more enfolding approach, wherein the hope for our desire being retooled and recast comes from our being caught up in the divine life through the reflexively incorporative mission of the divine Spirit. Not only are we caught up, but she speaks of a "divine force" to overthrow our divine desire. We do contemplate the divine, so real agency is espoused

---

19. Ibid., 270–271. She points out further that we may imitate the incarnate Son (in as much as he is human) though not the triune Godhead as such (ibid., 309).

20. Ibid., 58.

21. Ibid., 56.

22. Ibid., 269–70.

23. See, e.g., ibid., 105–11. Hans Boersma has raised significant questions regarding the viability of her employment of Nyssa in this regard (see *Embodiment and Virtue in Gregory of Nyssa: An Anagogical Account*, OECS [New York: Oxford University Press, 2012]).

24. Ibid., 324–27.

25. Ibid., 101 (esp. n1), 105, 111n12.

26. Ibid., 140n42.

of the human practicing such intellectual and erotic purgation. Yet divine agency of a particularly intrusive sort is affirmed herein as necessary due to an affirmation of an Augustinian doctrine of sin.[27]

Coakley rightly treats mind and will together, although one will have to wait for her second and third volumes to see if her desire-tilted anthropology and Trinitarian schematic are balanced by a needed intellectualism rooted in the Logos of God. Even now, her blending of spirituality and theology can be perceived clearly and appreciated. Further, her commitment to a robust doctrine of sin and a concomitant account of divine agency in transforming, even purifying human selves and longings calls for profound gratitude. How rare to have someone, cognizant of the dangers of power and self-delusion alike, speak of the shape of submission or of asceticism in the midst of being enfolded or incorporated into the divine life.[28] We do well to explore, then, if a commitment not to systematic theology simply, much less to *théologie totale*, but to Christian dogmatics can also offer an account of intellectual asceticism and a spiritual vision of doctrine as a chastening instrument in the purgative work of God's sanctifying presence.

"The Holiness of Theology": John Webster on the Eschatological Sanctification of Reason

In a lecture given in the late 1990s at the University of Otago, a theologian addressed the "culture of theology" and in so doing called for "attentive, ascetic reading" of Holy Scripture and the classics of the Christian tradition.[29] The language occurs amidst discussion of what he calls the "rhetoric of effacement," itself a correlate to "Christian eschatological culture" wherein "attention dispossesses us of our expectations; it involves self-renunciation, so that the gospel itself may speak of its own presence and vitality." The language sounds ascetical: effacement, self-renunciation, dispossession, attentiveness unto the eschatological. In years when theology had been dogged by so-called doctrinal criticism and was beginning to be shaped by the emboldened claims of Radical Orthodoxy, such calls sounded a markedly different note. Several years later, John Webster took up those

---

27. Ibid., 299; see also 6.
28. Further analysis is owed to Sarah Coakley, *The New Asceticism: Sexuality, Gender, and the Quest for God* (London: Bloomsbury, 2015).
29. John Webster, "Texts: Scripture, Reading, and the Rhetoric of Theology," *Stimulus* 6, no. 4 (November 1998): 14 (10–16).

concerns again in the first chapter of his book *Holiness*, an essay entitled "The Holiness of Theology."[30] That essay's very existence is telling, in as much as Webster addressed the holiness of God, of the church, and of the Christian in later chapters only after first characterizing the very task of intellectual reflection in a certain way by attentively noting the holiness of theology.

What demanded sustained attention in this quest to practice theology in a holy posture? Like Coakley, Webster attended to the ever-present threat of idolatry in its mental or intellectual form. Thinking about the divine is not inherently good unless one thinks about the true God in a faithful way. As this is not the only option in the religious market or even in the dark recesses of our hearts, "we need to make sure that we are thinking about the true God, and not about some God of our own invention."[31] Webster was drawing on specifically Reformed resources, such as Calvin's keen eye toward idolatry, in offering such a theological stiff-arm to undue speculation or underdisciplined theological exuberance.[32] Webster introduced this book, of which "The Holiness of Theology" serves as the introductory essay, as a "Trinitarian dogmatics of holiness."[33] It, thus, provides a helpful point by which we might assess how a specifically dogmatic theology may or may not flow from and further fund a pursuit of intellectual asceticism. We must assess in what ways Webster's project moved with and diverges from that of Coakley. A sketch of his approach sets the stage, then, for such comparison.

He offered a thesis: "A Christian theology of holiness is an exercise of holy reason; it has its context and its content in the revelatory presence of the Holy Trinity which is set forth in Holy Scripture; it is a venture undertaken in prayerful dependence upon the Holy Spirit; it is an exercise in the fellowship of the saints, serving the confession of the holy people of God; it is a work in which holiness is perfected in the fear of God; and its end is the sanctifying of God's holy name."[34]

A number of elements therein deserve expansion. First, this theological enterprise—the *very act of considering* what it means to be holy—is itself "an exercise of holy reason," for "like all other aspects of human life, reason is a field of God's sanctifying work."[35] Contrary to the idealized view of

---

30. John Webster, *Holiness* (Grand Rapids: Eerdmans, 2003).
31. Ibid., 9.
32. *Inst.* 1.11.8.
33. Webster, "Holiness of Theology," in *Holiness*, 1.
34. Ibid., 9–10.
35. Ibid., 10.

knowledge and understanding in the Enlightenment era and as entrenched in modern rationalism, thinking is affected by sin and, thus, must be sanctified by God. Dogmatics begins with the recognition, gleaned not from feminist or postcolonialist theory but from Holy Scripture itself, that our minds are darkened and that we are wise only in our own eyes (e.g., 1 Cor 2:14; Isa 5:21; Prov 3:7). But dogmatics affirms that God does not leave us to our sinful selves; God sanctifies or sets apart our reason, and dogmatics is an instrument or tool in that divine work (Rom 12:1–2). The first rule of such thinking laid out by Webster noted the significance of this move: "Theological thinking *about* holiness is itself an exercise *of* holiness. Theology is an aspect of the sanctification of reason, that is, of the process in which reason is put to death and made alive by the terrifying and merciful presence of the holy God."[36]

Second, this theological enterprise—the *very act of considering* what it means to be holy—"has its context and content in the revelatory presence of the Holy Trinity."[37] That God reveals himself provides the context for theology's possibility; not only that, but God's revelation of himself is the very content of theology's consideration. In other words, theology is a "positive science" which thinks after (*nachdenken*) that which God has revealed, working "both from and towards" the given. So "holy reason is not a *poetic* but a *receptive* enterprise; indeed, in Christian theology, poetics is tantamount to idolatry."[38]

Webster labors at just this point, for it is in his diagnosis and prescription against idolatry that his project differs from so much of the contemporary scene: "Theology is nothing other than an attempt to repeat the name which God gives to himself as he manifests himself with sovereign mercy, 'I am the Lord, your Holy One' (Isa. 43.15)."[39] Two attending claims follow by necessity: first, theology is not religious phenomenology or, specifically in this case, the *very act of considering* what it means to be holy does not focus upon a human experience of the "tremendous mystery" (as in Rudolf Otto) or the numinous; second, theology attends to Holy Scripture as its norm and limit.[40] We might ask why that negation and that affirmation are so central. In so doing, we can see that Webster locates intellectual self-renunciation in a more densely defined context, it seems, than does Coakley.

---

36. Ibid., 8.
37. Ibid., 12.
38. Ibid., 16.
39. Ibid., 16–17.
40. Ibid., 18–19, 19–21.

Idolatry is not something that we bat off with our own two hands, as if we were the last line of defense. We do not defeat the gods, whether of the world or of our own imagining. Like Coakley's affirmation of divine agency here, Webster speaks of God's encountering us and refusing to be mastered.

> Because God is majestic and therefore to be feared before all things, to encounter him is to be encountered by that which we can never master, which can never become an object, an idea or pattern of words or experience that we can retrieve and inspect at will. . . . Reason can only be holy if it resists its own capacity for idolatry, its natural drift towards the profaning of God's name by making common currency of the things of God. A holy theology, therefore, will be properly mistrustful of its own command of its subject-matter; modest; aware that much of what it says and thinks is dust.[41]

And Webster also offers an ecclesial location for this intellectual chastening; he speaks of theology as *"an exercise in the fellowship of the saints, serving the confession of the holy people of God."*[42]

Precisely here, Webster's ecclesiology and concomitant methodology diverge from Coakley. Coakley attends to the "dark corners" of the church, turning not to Trinitarian treatises much less the creeds and confessions of the church, but to indirect attestation in individual writings on virginity and asceticism, to assessment of icons, and to fieldwork in a smattering of British charismatic communities. This *théologie totale* values breadth and catholicity, but it is questionable to what extent apostolicity proves to be an animating principle. Dogmatic theology, however, fixes first upon the apostolic writings and their prophetic precursors as the norm and limit to theological reflection and then upon the ecclesiastical rules which function as a guide for rightly dividing the word. It does so precisely because these texts are the embassies of divine self-revelation, taken up and sent out by the Risen Lord Jesus himself.[43]

So we have a divergence between extensive and intensive postures, conversational or dogmatic theology. Admittedly, Webster noted, "a good deal of contemporary systematic or dogmatic theology tends . . . to be

---

41. Ibid., 28.

42. Webster, "Holiness of Theology," 10.

43. For a mature exposition of Holy Scripture as apostolic embassy in God's divine economy, see John Webster, "The Domain of the Word," in *The Domain of the Word: Scripture and Theological Reason* (London: T&T Clark, 2012), 3–31.

conversational or comparativist in approach. 'Conversational' theologies . . . construct Christian theology by drawing on a wide range of cultural, philosophical and religious sources to build up an account of the Christian faith through elaborating the associations and interrogations which occur as Christianity talks to others."[44] Coakley's volume draws primarily on resources from the Christian faith, whether icons or fieldwork, exegesis or patristic *ressourcement*. Compared to, say, the various iterations of the Workgroup on Constructive Theology, her *God, Sexuality, and the Self* may well appear remarkably antiquarian and ecclesiastical in tone, resources, and claims.[45] Yet it is similarly driven in many ways by questions, concerns, animating principles from other fields, not least feminist and gender studies. Even in her inversion of some of these fields, Coakley has privileged their concerns and questions in constructing her theology. If ever there was an example of extensive theology, this *théologie totale* must be it.

How did Webster describe his dogmatic approach? "By contrast, the kind of theology attempted here is less sanguine about the prospects for such exchanges. It more naturally thinks of its host culture, not as Athens, but as Babylon. It is acutely conscious of the menace of wickedness in the life of the mind."[46] Initially, Webster may sound like Coakley, but the divergence comes quickly thereafter. "And it is intensive before it is extensive. That is, its work is focused upon a quite restricted range of texts (the biblical canon) as they have been read and struggled with in the complex though unified reality which we call the tradition of the Church."[47] He admits, of course, that such may seem stultifying. "Such an understanding of theology enjoys rather little contemporary prestige, and is commonly judged to be naïve, assertive, authoritarian, above all, closed."[48] But it is worth noting that his claim runs just the opposite way. "Yet although it is intensive in this way, it is not stable or settled. The persistence with which it returns to its singular

---

44. Webster, "Holiness of Theology," 4.

45. See, e.g., Peter Hodgson and Robert King, eds., *Christian Theology: An Introduction to Its Traditions and Tasks* (Minneapolis: Fortress, 1982); Rebecca Chopp and Mark L. Taylor, eds., *Reconstructing Christian Theology* (Minneapolis: Fortress, 1994); and Serene Jones and Paul Lakeland, eds., *Constructive Theology: A Contemporary Approach to Classical Themes* (Minneapolis: Fortress, 2005). David Ford has written of the widespread significance of "conversational theology" in modern British systematics in "Theological Wisdom, British Style," *Christian Century* 117 (2000): 388–91. For critique, see John Webster, "David F. Ford: *Self and Salvation*," *SJT* 54, no. 4 (2001): 548–59; and response in David F. Ford, "Salvation and the Nature of Theology: A Response to John Webster's Review of *Self and Salvation: Being Transformed*," *SJT* 54, no. 4 (2001): 560–75. One longer attempt to broker this disagreement may be found in Michael Allen, "Divine Transcendence and the Reading of Scripture," *Scottish Bulletin of Evangelical Theology* 26, no. 1 (2008): 32–56.

46. Webster, "Holiness of Theology," 4–5.

47. Ibid., 5.

48. Ibid., 4.

theme is an attempt to face the reality of the gospel as a permanent source of unsettlement, discomfiture and renewal of vocation."[49] And he locates this rattling of the intellectual sabers within the action of the very present God: "The intensity of this kind of theology is not the internally-directed energy of an achieved, separated world of ideas, but that of a way of thinking which might be called eschatological—always, that is, emerging from its own dissolution and reconstitution by the presence of the holy God."[50]

So Webster's Reformed approach to catholic doctrine shares a self-renunciatory and purgative facet with Coakley's project. The two projects also share a common commitment to an Augustinian hamartiology and its necessary overcoming by the gracious missions of Son and Spirit. Webster's approach fixes more concretely upon scriptural authority and hearing the Word of God, whereas Coakley's approach ranges widely to "dark corners" and disciplinary conversation partners as ways of jarring the spiritual status quo of Christian intellectual life. That principled difference is ultimately rooted in a different notion, it seems, of the character of God and the consequent covenantal shape of ordered life with God for those human creatures who participate by grace in the full life that is his alone by nature. Might we even say that Webster's approach offers a divinely provided and ordered means of ongoing ascetical discipline, by means of the Reformed Scripture principle, which is only somewhat contingently matched by Coakley's dependence upon intellectual scavenging for unsettlement? Might it be the case that dogmatics actually offers a sustained and structured approach to intellectual asceticism that outpaces the desires of even a *théologie totale*? We do well to attend to some principles for such a path forward by way of conclusion.

ASCETICAL DOGMATICS: REFORMED CATHOLIC THESES FOR A SPIRITUAL THEOLOGY

Dogmatics serves discipleship, governing the intellectual life (as with the bodily and relational facets of human existence) by the Word of God. Frequently, contemporary theologians have estimated dogmatics impotent to such ends and have felt the need to enlist other disciplines as ancillaries, handmaids, or, perhaps at times, tutors to school dogmatics in its ethical responsibilities. So we do well to conclude with some principled theses for

49. Ibid., 5.
50. Ibid.

how such a dogmatics might undertake its labors, aware that it must remain earnest at all times lest it drift from a posture of faith into an arrogance of sight and of closure. Four concerns deserve our consideration: the Trinitarian matrix of ascetical dogmatics, the perfection of God and its formative shape in giving birth to the Reformed Scripture principle, the relationship of contemplation and radically anti-speculative theology, and the difference between intensive and extensive (or interdisciplinary) theology.

First, an ascetical dogmatics must be grounded in the biblical Trinitarianism of the catholic creeds if it is to be a protocol of God's grace, flowing from his own triune perfection and unto self-displacing and renewing discipline, rather than from a posture of self-mastery, accenting our autonomous intellectual projects. Here we need not deny what is affirmed by Coakley, though we must walk back some of her suggested negations and contextualize her account to make it serviceable. Remember that she has argued in favor of an incorporative approach to the Trinity rooted in Romans 8 over against the linear structure, which she deems to be founded in Johannine Trinitarianism and developed later in the official creedal texts of the fourth century. Again, such claims are not an analytic commentary on implicit judgments but are her own explicit statements regarding what is to be affirmed, what must be denied, and where they are both rooted in Scripture and tradition. She does note that "distinction between the two models is not necessarily absolute," but she speaks only of the negative potentiality of the linear model.[51] Why does she go this route? The incorporative model draws us into the very life of God through prayerful incorporation of the human self and their desire into the triune movement, specifically through the reflexive posture of the Spirit. The linear model involves a hierarchical approach that invariably minimizes the Spirit's role of return unto Father and Son.

A classical account of the Trinity might affirm the incorporative work of the Trinity and might show its eternal roots by locating it amidst the so-called linear model which Coakley denies. Indeed, the linear model shows that the missions of Son and Spirit are rooted in God's own life (*theologia*) and not merely express some economic reality (*oikonomia*).[52] That the Spirit flows forth or proceeds eternally from the Father and [through] the Son (*filioque*) serves to root the spiritual ascent of humans ultimately

---

51. Coakley, *God, Sexuality, and the Self*, 111.
52. See esp. Scott R. Swain, "Divine Trinity," in *Christian Dogmatics: Reformed Theology for the Church Catholic*, ed. Michael Allen and Scott R. Swain (Grand Rapids: Baker Academic, 2016), 103–5.

and eternally in God's own being and action, willed from all eternity. Such claims do not undermine the economic reality of spiritual incorporation—far from it—for their purpose is to characterize and specify such ascent as truly willed by the one true God according to triune order befitting and expressive of God's eternal character.[53] Still further, Matthew Levering helpfully reminds us that incorporation cannot be an undifferentiated experience. As he says, "The emphasis on the order of origin—on the Father begetting the Son and the Father (and Son) spirating the Spirit—enhances the incorporative model by showing us that our unexpected entrance into the divine life means not pure relationality but an ordered relationality."[54] Incorporation occurs through the Son by the Spirit; even Coakley's preferred passage in Romans 8 manifests a precise concern to offer what can be deemed prepositional theology, and these distinct prepositional monikers mark out a specific order (taxis) to the divine economy and its attendant spiritual implications for human incorporative ascent.

Why is this pertinent here? Why are such matters of triune being and action pertinent to a discussion of dogmatics as ascetics? Why do they in any way relate to the question of whether dogmatics can sustain a self-renunciatory pattern of intellectual discipleship? Trinitarian order helps displace the self-directed approach to God in one's own manner.[55] God defines the terms of approach. Just as the God of Israel sketches the contours of holiness by which priests might enter his presence in the book of Leviticus, so the Trinitarian logic of the Gospel according to John and of Romans 8 provides a paradigm fully of God's design for covenant life with him. Union and communion with God occur by our desire, but only secondarily, for God has first desired or elected life with us. Further, this incorporative ascent occurs only by his design and as revealed in his own triune self-disclosure. The transcendentals might be pursued in various modes; the idol might be approached willy-nilly; the triune God, however, brokers only one pathway into his presence. Much more could and should be said here regarding displacement via dogmatic discipline—for instance,

53. John Webster, "'It Was the Will of the Lord to Bruise Him': Soteriology and the Doctrine of God," in God without Measure: Working Papers in Christian Theology (London: Bloomsbury T&T Clark, 2016), 1:143–58.

54. Matthew Levering, Engaging the Doctrine of the Holy Spirit: Love and Gift in the Trinity and the Church (Grand Rapids: Baker Academic, 2016), 37–38 (see 36–40 for wider reflection upon Coakley's proposal); see also Christopher Holmes, The Holy Spirit, New Studies in Dogmatics (Grand Rapids: Zondervan Academic, 2015), 33–42 for critique of a "Spirit-leading approach."

55. Similarly, ascetical implications are drawn out of Irenaeus's focus on the divine economy by John Behr, Asceticism and Anthropology in Irenaeus and Clement, OECS (Oxford: Oxford University Press, 2000), ch. 1.

to take up Otto Hermann Pesch's terms, that a dogmatic theology will not sacrifice existential concern in its pursuit of sapiential ends, but will pursue existential discipline and grace precisely in and by the discipline of a decentering vision that Pesch terms sapiential.[56]

By enabling wisdom (*sapientia*), reduction (*reductio*) of one's presenting concerns to theological *principia* serves not only intellectual but ascetic or self-displacing ends.[57] Augustine of Hippo infamously taught that we may enjoy (*frui*) God and must use (*uti*) all other things and then nuanced his distinction, in a positive rhetorical way, to help us sketch what it means to love God for his own good and to love all else for God's own sake, thus avoiding idolatry.[58] In other words, in loving other persons or goods, we must love them in such a way that we still love God and that our fulfillment of the second facet of the great love commandment does not negate the ever-looming command of its first facet. To honor this distinction demands resolute discernment. Henry Chadwick observed, "In 'correct use' there is an implication of reflective detachment, whereas by contrast what is enjoyed is all-absorbing."[59] That use of other goods is not merely detachment from them, but reflectively or intentionally (even if subconsciously) suggests the need for intellectual formation. Formation in tracing all things back to God helps one discern what is itself divine and worthy of enjoyment in and of itself and, by contrast, what deserves love only for its use unto love of God. Dogmatics, then, reduces all things unto God that we might know when and how to love rightly. In Paul's terms, "the renewal of your mind" leads to moral discernment of that which is "good and acceptable and perfect" (Rom 12:2).

Second, the perfection of God serves a fundamental role not only in

---

56. For the distinction between sapiential and existential theology, see Otto Hermann Pesch, *Theologie der Rechtfertigung bei Martin Luther und Thomas von Aquin: Versuch eines systematischtheologischen dialogs* (Mainz: Matthias Grünewald Verlag, 1967), 918–48; Pesch, "Existential and Sapiential Theology—The Theological Confrontation between Luther and Thomas Aquinas," in Jared Wicks, ed. *Catholic Scholars Dialogue with Luther* (Chicago: Loyola University Press, 1970), 61–81.

57. On *reductio* in dogmatics, see not only Bonaventure, *Itinerarium Mentis in Deum*, Works of St. Bonaventure, ed. Philotheus Boehner, trans. Zachary Hayes (St. Bonaventure, NY: Franciscan Institute, 2002); but also Herman Bavinck, *Reformed Dogmatics*, ed. John Bolt, trans. John Vriend (Grand Rapids: Baker Academic; 2003), 2:29: "All the doctrines in dogmatics . . . are but the explication of the one central dogma of the knowledge of God. All things are considered in light of God, subsumed under him, traced back to him as the starting point."

58. See Augustine, *De vera religione*, 12.24, and *De doctrina christiana*, 1.3–40.

59. Henry Chadwick, "Frui-uti," *AugLex* (Basel/Stuttgart: Schwabe, 1986); see also especially William Riordan O'Connor, "The *Uti/Frui* Distinction in Augustine's Ethics," *Augustinian Studies* 14 (1983): 45–62; Oliver O'Donovan, "*Usus* and *Fruitio* in Augustine, *De doctrina christiana* I," *Journal of Theological Studies* 33 (1982): 361–397; Gerald Boersma, *Augustine's Early Theology of Image: A Study in the Development of Pro-Nicene Theology*, Oxford Studies in Historical Theology (New York: Oxford University Press, 2016), 240–42.

identifying God but in rooting the ordered form of God's sanctification of human reason and demonstrating that we are disciplined by direction unto the very means of our intellectual-spiritual discipline in Holy Scripture, as our only final authority in his fatherly hands. In other words, the doctrine of God is not only a doctrine of God but of God's works, which include the way in which God puts to death and makes alive human reason. The Reformed Scripture principle serves a pivotal role here in Webster's own theology that is unmatched by the prolegomenal materials marshaled by Coakley, and this shapes the eschatological and ascetical vigor of the two accounts.[60] Whereas she turns to "dark corners," he calls for a focus upon the light of the written Word.[61] Verbal descriptions of theology, then, must note the way in which it follows always responsively to God's revelation: "theology as holy reason finds its completion in such acknowledgment and indication."[62] Verbs matter, and we must observe that "acknowledgment" and "indication" are not akin to the far more active verbs of contemporary intellectual culture, especially in its activistic register. Yet these verbs season the language of Zion, of a people who have been illumined from outside and led from on high through the murky and dangerous wilderness. The people of God are decentered by the life-giving agency of the God who takes center stage.

A deeper point ought not be missed either, namely, that the Reformed Scripture principle flows from a radicalizing of the catholic doctrine of divine perfection as applied to our intellectual provision. Christians have for centuries attested God as the perfect one, fully sufficient in and of himself. The Reformed tradition has not augmented or supplemented of those claims; rather, it consistently applies God's triune fullness to the whole of theology. Indeed, Herman Bavinck argued beautifully that the varied distinctives of Reformed theology can, each in their own way, be related or traced back to a fundamental radicalizing of divine fullness, which he terms its "root principle."[63] Note that Bavinck is not arguing for a so-called "central dogma" from which we might somehow logically deduce attendant doctrinal claims.

---

60. For assessment of the shape and development of Webster's own theological principles, and the place of the Reformed Scripture principle therein, see Michael Allen, "Toward Theological Theology: Tracing the Methodological Principles of John Webster," *Themelios* 41, no. 2 (2016): 217–37 (esp. 225–226 n45 on his bibliology). For his most thorough, mature accounts of this terrain, see "Biblical Reasoning" and "Principles of Systematic Theology," in *The Domain of the Word: Scripture and Theological Reason* (London: T& TClark, 2012), 115–49.

61. Nathan Eubank has shown that Nyssa's *Life of Moses* moves from the moment of darkness to that of the tabernacle, such that it does not end with sheer apophaticism ("Ineffably Effable: The Pinnacle of Mystical Ascent in Gregory of Nyssa's *De vita Moysis*," *IJST* 16 [2014]: 25–41).

62. Ibid., 29.

63. Herman Bavinck, "The Future of Calvinism," *The Presbyterian & Reformed Review* (1894), available at http://scdc.library.ptsem.edu/mets/mets.aspx?src=BR1894517&div=1.

The nineteenth-century typologies that suggested a Reformed rooting of all dogma in predestination, perhaps over against a Lutheran rooting in justification by faith alone, mangle not only the architectural shape of Reformed dogmatics but also the varied seams connecting one piece to another. Yet Bavinck is right to note that an unstinting perception of God's fullness, his perfection, what might be termed his self-sufficiency and immensity, has shaped the way in which the many works of God are viewed. Each of them flows from and manifests the God who has all within himself; none, therefore, marks out a terrain wherein God is completed, augmented, supplemented, corrected, or even approached from without.

A doctrine of divine perfection has been matched, of course, by an attendant participatory construal of creaturely reality and of human moral agency. Some Reformed theologians—not least John Webster—have been leery of the language of participation. Their concern, as stated pointedly at times by Webster, was that participation is easily heard in ways that elide the profound distinction between created and uncreated being.[64] Over against participation, then, language of covenant fellowship was often suggested as a means of affirming a dogmatics of divine perfection that did not cease to be truly ethical and to give real legitimacy to human moral responsibility. Affirming Webster's worry without necessarily following his terminological hesitancy, I think we can appreciate how creaturely being participates in the perfect God's life and how that participatory fellowship is ordered according to the biblical categories of covenant.[65] Webster and the Reformed tradition make a much bigger deal of divine perfection—and its other related divine attributes—than does Coakley, in whose volume they receive no focused attention. And a corollary, I believe, is a similar focus upon participatory rest being covenantally ordered and, as structured by God's lead, as shaped authoritatively by scriptural guidance.[66] We have seen

---

64. See, e.g., John Webster, "Perfection and Participation," in Thomas Joseph White, ed. *The Analogy of Being: Invention of the Antichrist or the Wisdom of God?* (Grand Rapids: Eerdmans, 2011), 379–94. In more recent works, especially some as yet unpublished essays on creation and providence, Webster had tilted toward a more assertive use of categories that parallel or involve participatory language.

65. Such approaches are not foreign to the early Reformed tradition, on which see J. Todd Billings, *Calvin, Participation, and the Gift: The Activity of Believers in Union with Christ*, Changing Paradigms in Historical and Systematic Theology (Oxford: Oxford University Press, 2007); more recent expansion may be found in Michael Allen, *Justification and the Gospel; Understanding the Contexts and the Controversies* (Grand Rapids: Baker Academic, 2013), chs. 1–2.

66. I have tried to sketch these connections between the doctrine of God, the doctrine of the covenant, and the doctrine of Holy Scripture in Michael Allen, "Knowledge of God," in *Christian Dogmatics*, 7–29; see also Scott R. Swain, *Trinity, Revelation, and Reading: A Theological Introduction to Scripture and Its Interpretation* (London: T&T Clark, 2012), chs. 1–2.

then two principles regarding how the doctrine of God shapes the principles of an ascetical dogmatics, corresponding to the Trinitarian order and the perfect character of the God of the gospel. We must now turn briefly to two corresponding anthropological principles, pertaining to the ends and the manner of such a dogmatics.

Third, an ascetical dogmatics walks the careful line of pursuing contemplative ends while maintaining a radically antispeculative posture. Metaphysics serve contemplation, even as exegesis shapes metaphysics.[67] We must clarify, therefore, the two ways in which theology can be speculative, only one of which is salutary. Katherine Sonderegger has helped greatly in this regard.[68] Early in the first volume of her systematics, we encounter the claim that "metaphysical claims about Oneness and idolatry go together."[69] One might think that this would prompt a protocol of specification for the sake of avoiding idolatry, commending a theology with strict contours and sharp edges so as to avoid veering into paganism. Without detracting from edges and specifications, Sonderegger points to a more startling reality: the call to honor the divine mystery. "Divine mystery is not a sign of our failure in knowledge, but rather our success. It is because we know truly and properly—because we obey the axiomatic First Commandment—that we can know God as mystery. His metaphysical predicate of Oneness, when known, yields mystery."[70] Elsewhere the point is repeatedly pressed home that mystery is an intellectual achievement flowing from divine presence, not a limit owing to divine absence.[71]

Radically antispeculative theology rooted in exegesis of the scriptural testimony of the triune economy generates the focal point of such contemplation of the divine mystery. Mystery does not equal abstraction in the sense of nonspecificity. Mystery relates to the supersaturated shape of the divine self-revelation in the full scope and sequence of biblical attestation. Contemplative theology attends to the "whole counsel of God" (Acts 20:27), tracing or reducing all topics back to their end in God without

---

67. For more on the contemplative ends of theology, see Matthew Levering, *Scripture and Metaphysics: Aquinas and the Renewal of Trinitarian Theology*, CCT (Oxford: Blackwell, 2004), 23–46; Karen Kilby, "Aquinas, the Trinity, and the Limits of Understanding," *IJST* 7, no. 4 (2005): 414–27, seeks to reorient theology in a grammatical and apophatic fashion. Her concerns are significant, though they need not be juxtaposed with Thomas's contemplative commitments (which are fundamentally purgative).

68. My reflections here are drawn from http://zondervanacademic.com/blog/common-places-engaging-with-kate-sonderegger-the-one-and-the-many/.

69. Sonderegger, *Systematic Theology* (Minneapolis: Fortress, 2015), 1:19.

70. Ibid., 1:24.

71. Ibid., 1:40, 42, 50, 87, 460.

becoming speculative in any unloosed manner but remaining tethered to the canonical form of spiritual presentation. With Bavinck, we can attest, "Mystery is the lifeblood of dogmatics. . . . In truth, the knowledge that God has revealed of himself in nature and Scripture far surpasses human imagination and understanding. In that sense it is all mystery with which the science of dogmatics is concerned, for it does not deal with finite creatures, but from beginning to end looks past all creatures and focuses on the eternal and infinite One himself."[72]

Fourth, dogmatics fixes its eyes intently upon a very limited set of resources, providing a lens whereby Christians might then engage other intellectual sources. Dogmatics is not an interdisciplinary activity in the sense of connecting Christian theological analysis with that of other fields. Such work is not illegitimate; intellectual conversation proves essential on many fronts, for Christ is Lord of all, and his children are called both to learn of him from his book of nature as well as his apostolic emissaries (Ps 19) and to seek the welfare and benefit of spheres beyond the churchly (Jer 29:5–7).

Sarah Coakley's project may seem resolutely theological, in that its presenting problems (all in the realm of sex, gender, and self) are resourced by averting attention toward church fathers, biblical exegesis, and congregational fieldwork. But it is worth noting the kind of attention given here. Kevin Hector has commented that "the idea here, again, is that theologians are constantly tempted to self-deception, bias, partiality, and so forth, and that they can effectively resist such temptations only on the basis of a sort of principled interdisciplinarity, the aim of which is to force oneself to remain open to other points of view, to loosen the grip of one's prejudices and presumptions, and, in sum, to make it more difficult for one to see objects as corresponding to one's desire-inflected preconceptions of them."[73] One can perhaps appreciate the method by considering the two facets of "sanctity of mind" in Thomas Aquinas that are highlighted in Bauerschmidt's apt study: "Thomas's particular sanctity of mind combined both intellectual openness and unswerving evangelical purpose. Thomas believed in following arguments where they led, but he also believed that truthful arguments could never lead us away from Christ."[74] Coakley's project does not seek to shirk Christ, of course, though it is arguable that her first volume's focus

---

72. Bavinck, *Reformed Dogmatics*, 2:29.
73. Kevin W. Hector, "Trinity, Ascesis, and Culture: Contextualizing Coakley's *God, Sexuality, and the Self*," *Mod. Theo.* 30, no. 4 (2014): 564.
74. Bauerschmidt, *Thomas Aquinas: Faith, Reason, and Following Christ*, 36.

on intellectual openness, both to many extracanonical discourses as well as to a strand of canonical reasoning found in Romans 8, leads to a loss of that evangelical purpose (exemplified so by her shirking of the witness of Johannine Trinitarianism). Here we surely have Christ with extension, but I fear we may also have only a Christ without absolutes.[75]

Again, in the realm of interdisciplinary attempts to stave off self-satisfaction in the status quo, Trinitarian matters are not far from the surface. Eugene Rogers asks, "Is the Christology to be all eschatological, all in what the Spirit will work, and not historical, in what the Spirit has already conceived? Perhaps Coakley will say that only after we train our eyes to see Christ in our neighbor are we really able to see Christ anew in Jesus."[76] Coakley has responded that the delay of a proper Christology is intentional, and that "my main interest in vol. 1 is deliberately to destabilize any complacent sense that we can get our hands around 'Jesus' without prior pneumatological displacement."[77]

One element here is that her interdisciplinary effort to hear the Spirit in various discourses raises the question of targets and of breadth. Has she listened in the right places? And has she listened widely enough?[78] Truthfully, I am not sure how such questions could ever be satisfied given her protocol. But a more fundamental question raised by Rogers haunts more profoundly: can we really expect to hear the Christ of Scripture only after hearing the Spirit in his world? Is this not exactly the reverse of what Calvin taught regarding the need for a scriptural set of lenses through which we might glean how the whole world serves as a theater of God's glory?[79] Why would we expect and structure our theological approach to "pneumatological displacement" around nontheological theories or disciplines? Why the focus on "dark corners" and distant lands rather than illumined hallways and the churchly homestead? A more densely developed Christology and pneumatology would provide resources for a more intensive focus, I think,

---

75. See Sarah Coakley, *Christ Without Absolutes: A Study of the Christology of Ernst Troeltsch* (Oxford: Oxford University Press, 1988).

76. Eugene F. Rogers Jr., "Prayer, Christoformity, and the Author: New Sites of Discussion for Theology," *Mod. Theo.* 30, no. 4 (2014), 558.

77. Sarah Coakley, "Response to Reviewers of *God, Sexuality, and the Self*," *Mod. Theo.* 30, no. 4 (2014), 592.

78. Mary Catherine Hilkert has asked "how a different location for pastoral fieldwork or qualitative social research might have affected some of her theological conclusions" ("Desire, Gender, and God-Talk: Sarah Coakley's Feminist Contemplative Theology," *Mod. Theo.* 30, no. 4 [2014]: 580). Similarly, Katherine Sonderegger has stated that a grateful reading of this volume with its many forays is nonetheless left demanding, grasping, desiring more ("Review Article: *God, Sexuality, and the Self*," *IJST* 18, no. 1 [2016]: 98).

79. *Inst.* 1.6.

upon Holy Scripture and, subserviently, upon the church's attention to that revelation in her witness and wisdom, from which we can then turn to assess the illumination thrown on all the world as God's own theater (as suggested by Calvin's favored image).

In sum, I hope that this sketch of the terrain and these brief theses help suggest that the seemingly establishmentarian might just be the most eschatological, for dogmatics serves within the triune economy, by God's mortifying and vivifying grace, to discipline our minds and hearts. Not burning down the house, in a fit of vibrant revolt, but finding the fire of the tabernacle to light our very minds unto holiness. Dogmatics does so precisely by decentering our own presenting questions and assumptions, reducing all data and questions unto the triune God. Such intellectual discipline, however, demands a careful walk toward contemplative wisdom rooted in a radically antispeculative approach to biblical reasoning. While dogmatics shapes and forms one to engage in interdisciplinary reasoning and extensive conversation, the discipline itself fixes its sights upon a certain set of divinely gifted resources and angles of inquiry.

CHAPTER 11

WHY SHOULD PROTESTANTS RETRIEVE PATRISTIC AND MEDIEVAL THEOLOGY?

GAVIN ORTLUND

NEARLY A DECADE AGO JOHN WEBSTER drew attention to the rising influence of "theologies of retrieval," describing them as too diverse to constitute an official movement or school.[1] If retrieval practices have only grown more diverse since that time, they are nonetheless so pervasive throughout contemporary theology that it is difficult not to conceptualize them as a kind of movement.[2] Like the turn toward theological interpretation in biblical theology, the turn toward retrieval in systematic and historical theology lacks official boundaries and resists precise definition. It is better understood as a set of shared loyalties or instincts in theological method—an overall attitude guided by the conviction that premodern resources are not an obstacle in the age of progress, but a well in the age of thirst.

Of course, in one sense theological retrieval is nothing new. A posture of reception and transmission is a basic part of Christian identity, and the

---

1. John Webster, "Theologies of Retrieval," in *The Oxford Handbook of Systematic Theology*, ed. John Webster, Kathryn Tanner, and Iain Torrance (Oxford: Oxford University Press, 2007), 584.
2. The first book-length treatment of theological retrieval as a contemporary "movement" appeared recently by David Buschart and Kent Eilers, *Theology as Retrieval: Receiving the Past, Renewing the Church* (Downers Grove, IL: IVP Academic, 2015).

church has always drawn from her past to meet the challenges of her present.[3] Nonetheless, retrieval has come to have a more specific and deliberate use in the late modern West, where the individualism and freedom from authority that characterizes the secularizing culture have compelled the church to look for new sources of inspiration and synthesis. It is this cultural context, perhaps, that explains why retrieval movements are springing up in so many different traditions—from the *ressourcement* theology or *la nouvelle théologie* of Henri De Lubac and other French Roman Catholic theologians to the Radical Orthodoxy of John Milbank (Anglican), the paleo-orthodoxy of Thomas Oden (Methodist), the ecumenical labors of Donald Bloesch (UCC) or Robert Jenson (mainline Lutheran), the ancient-future movement of Robert Webber (also Anglican), and so forth.[4]

Alongside these various Catholic, Anglican, and mainline Protestant movements, retrieval is on the rise in evangelicalism. In 2015, two book-length treatments of theological retrieval came out from evangelical authors, published by evangelical presses and covered with blurbs from evangelical theologians.[5] At the same time, there remains considerable ambivalence in many Protestant circles, particularly evangelical Protestant circles in the United States, about the retrieval of patristic and medieval theology. This ambivalence often manifests itself, at both popular and technical levels, in sheer neglect: one wonders how many evangelical pastors or divinity students could say a single solitary thing about, say, the tenth century; or the seventh. Cardinal John Henry Newman complained in the nineteenth century that England's "popular religion scarcely recognizes the fact of the twelve long ages which lie between the Councils of Nicaea and Trent."[6] If Newman's conclusion that "to be deep in history is to cease to be a Protestant" did not strictly follow, its overall sentiment is difficult to dismiss—particularly because underneath the antihistorical bent of popular

---

3. Of course, different Christian traditions disagree regarding what the reception and transmission of history should look like, and such differences are among the chief causes of division within Christendom. For an overview of some of the differences within and between Protestant, Anglican, and Roman Catholic views on Scripture and tradition, with a special focus on Albert Outler's recent employment of the "Wesleyan Quadrilateral," see Edith M. Humphrey, *Scripture and Tradition: What the Bible Really Says* (Grand Rapids: Baker Academic, 2013), 9–17.

4. Michael Allen and Scott R. Swain, *Reformed Catholicity: The Promise of Retrieval for Theology and Biblical Interpretation* (Grand Rapids: Baker Academic, 2015), 4–12 offer a list of twelve different contemporary movements in the church characterized by retrieval.

5. Buschart and Kent Eilers, *Theology as Retrieval*, provide on overview and guide to retrieval, focusing on six different "typologies" of what it looks like in practice; Swain and Allen, *Reformed Catholicity*, offer a "manifesto" for a specifically Reformed account of retrieval.

6. John Henry Newman, *An Essay on the Development of Christian Doctrine*, 6th ed. (Notre Dame, IN: University of Notre Dame Press, 1989), 8.

Protestantism lie deeper patterns of historical interpretation that have often marked even the most eloquent expressions of the Protestant faith. One thinks, for instance, of the recurring identification of the antichrist with the papacy, a view that finds its way into the *Westminster Confession of Faith*.[7] Or in more recent times, Protestant interpretations of church history are often shaped by the old Enlightenment caricature of the medieval era as a "Dark Age" of superstition and ignorance,[8] and by the Anabaptist view of a "great apostasy" or "great fall" in the early church.[9] On the whole, Protestants today often regard the Christianity of Caedmon and Charlemagne as more different than similar to the Christianity of John Bunyan and Billy Graham.

In what follows, I suggest that the affirmation of a robust Protestantism need not prohibit, but should rather encourage, an appropriation of the wisdom of the early and medieval church.[10] First, I probe different understandings of what it means to be Protestant by examining B. B. Warfield's retrieval of Augustine, contrasting his approach with the retrieval practices of the Reformers. Second, I suggest four ways that patristic and medieval theology can resource contemporary Protestant theology, each with a metaphor and then an example or case study. Finally, I discuss three early particular medieval theologians/texts that may be especially helpful for modern Protestants to retrieve.

---

7. *The Westminster Confession of Faith* 15.6 (Glasgow: Free Presbyterian, 1966), 109–10.

8. This characterization of medieval intellectual life is ironic in light of the fact that the modern university is essentially a twelfth century invention, deriving from the great monastic schools of the eleventh century that in turn grew out of the tenth century cathedral schools spawned by the Carolingian Renaissance. For a recent defense of medieval Christianity against its usual caricatures, and a call for evangelical Christians to humbly engage this aspect of our heritage, see Chris R. Armstrong, *Medieval Wisdom for Modern Christians: Finding Authentic Faith in a Forgotten Age with C. S. Lewis* (Grand Rapids: Brazos, 2016).

9. The "fall of the church" paradigm, usually seen as coinciding with Constantine's conversion or sometimes setting in as early as the second century, has been a classical tenet of Anabaptist theology and are carried on by many free-church and Baptist theologians into the present day—e.g., Malcolm B. Yarnell III, *The Formation of Christian Doctrine* (Nashville: B&H, 2007), 150–65, esp. 157–58. Yarnell rejects the notion of the invisible church as articulated by Herman Bavinck (54–56); he believes that classical ecclesiology, including its Reformed and evangelical expressions (e.g., that of John Webster) must be rejected (xiv, 62–67); and he expresses concerns about other Baptist calls for ecumenicity, such as those of Timothy George (71). For a helpful critique of the notion of the fall of the church, see D. H. Williams, *Retrieving the Tradition and Renewing Evangelicalism: A Primer for Suspicious Protestants* (Grand Rapids: Eerdmans, 1999), 103–72. For a briefer overview and critique, see Bryan M. Litfin, *Getting to Know the Church Fathers: An Evangelical Introduction*, 2nd ed. (Grand Rapids: Baker Academic, 2016), 13–16.

10. For a broader case that theological endeavor is well served by listening to the Christian tradition, see Stephen R. Holmes, *Listening to the Past: The Place of Tradition in Theology* (Grand Rapids: Baker Academic, 2002), 5–36, who argues that theology must engage tradition because of our historical locatedness as temporal creatures, and because of our status as members in the larger community of saints, past and present. On this latter point, cf. also Swain and Allen, *Reformed Catholicity*, 17–47.

RETRIEVING THE LEAVENED BREAD OUT OF THE UNLEAVENED: WARFIELD ON AUGUSTINE

Some of the eccentricities of modern Protestant interpretation of patristic and medieval theology can be observed in B.B. Warfield's appropriation of Augustine's theology.[11] Warfield argued that the doctrine of *grace* is Augustine's greatest legacy and the truest center of his thought. He located Augustine's significance as being the first of the church fathers to give adequate expression to "evangelical religion"—that is, the religion of faith, as opposed to the religion of works.[12] For Warfield, "a new Christian piety dates from [Augustine]," as well as "a new theology corresponding to this new type of piety," such that Augustine may be termed the author of grace as well as the father of evangelicalism.[13]

Warfield was not, however, blind to the aspects of Augustine's theology that seem to stand at odds with this interpretation: his complex sacramentology, complete with doctrines of baptismal regeneration, a sacrificial understanding of Mass, and an *ex opere operato* understanding of sacramental efficacy; his hierarchical ecclesiology, complete an affirmation of the papacy, the magisterium of the church, and an understanding of the visible church as God's kingdom on earth; and his doctrines of saintly intercession, purgatory, penance, merits, and the perpetual virginity of Mary. With these aspects of his theology in mind, Warfield called Augustine "the founder of Roman Catholicism" who "called into being a new type of Christianity" in which the church is the center of religious feeling.[14]

Ascribing to the same person the titles "father of evangelicalism" and "founder of Roman Catholicism" conjures up a sense of ambivalence that may usefully describe Warfield's broader attitude toward the whole of medieval Christianity stemming from Augustine. Indeed, he suggested, "the problem which Augustine bequeathed to the Church for solution, the Church required a thousand years to solve."[15] Warfield describes these two sides of Augustine's thought—his "evangelical" doctrine of grace and his Roman Catholic ecclesiology—as "two children . . . struggling in the womb of his mind." But for Warfield, Augustine's doctrine of grace

11. Benjamin Breckinridge Warfield, *Calvin and Augustine*, ed. Samuel G. Craig (Philadelphia: P&R, 1956).
12. Ibid., 319–20.
13. Ibid., 320–21.
14. Ibid., 313.
15. Ibid., 322.

is the "child of his heart."[16] Thus in Warfield's interpretation, the *real* Augustine is the desperate and prayerful Augustine of the *Confessions*, the anti-Pelagian Augustine who prays, "command what you will, and give what you command."[17] In his doctrine of the church, by contrast, we get the vestiges of Cyprian and Tertullian, taken on thoughtlessly by Augustine, that gradually diminish throughout his life. In Warfield's metaphor, the leaven of Augustine's doctrine of grace was working through the dough of his doctrine of the church, but "death intervened before all the elements of his thinking were completely leavened."[18] Had Augustine only lived longer, he would have handed down "a thoroughly worked out system of evangelical theology" rather than the contradictions that rended the church for a millennium.[19] These perceived tensions in Augustine became Warfield's rubric for engaging the medieval church as a whole, as evident in his definition of the Reformation as "the triumph of Augustine's doctrine of grace over Augustine's doctrine of the Church."[20]

Warfield's interpretation of Augustine poses challenges. One wonders, for instance, whether Augustine was quite so decidedly on his way toward becoming a proto-Protestant, had he only lived a little longer. But underneath these interpretational matters lies a more basic methodological issue regarding how we do retrieval as Protestants. In Warfield's method of retrieval, Augustine's theology get sifted through the grid of the Reformation, such that the good in Augustine's theological legacy is distinguished from the bad by its sixteenth-century consequence. Warfield's approach could give the impression that a modern Protestant's primary theological community only includes the last five hundred years of Protestant history, and then from this community one makes a secondary, tentative step into the previous fifteen hundred years of church history. To construct a metaphor, Protestant theology is the castle in which we safely live; patristic and medieval theology is a dark forest surrounding the castle into which we may occasionally venture.

Of course, there is nothing wrong with Warfield reading church history as a Protestant, with Protestant convictions intact under an overall commitment to *sola Scriptura*. But affirming Protestant distinctives is not the same as using them as a filter, and a principial *sola Scriptura* can easily slide

---

16. Ibid.
17. Ibid.
18. Ibid., 321.
19. Ibid., 322.
20. Ibid., 383.

into a practical *sola reformatione*. Approaching the early church indirectly, through the intermediate link of Reformation theology, poses the danger of failing to appreciate patristic and medieval theology on its own terms and in its own context, and thus of hindering our ability to learn from it. After all, there are many doctrines that the Reformers held in continuity with the early and medieval church, but did not engage since they were not in dispute in the sixteenth century. There are many other doctrines that the Reformers affirmed with the early and medieval church, but did so with less eloquence or detail. And there are still other doctrines where the Reformers' approach was different from that of earlier generations, and yet we may not be convinced that their efforts are the final word on the matter. In Warfield's account, it never seems to come into view where Protestant theology might be profitably stretched or challenged by Augustine. A figure so sharply divided against himself (indeed, in Warfield's account, an entire millennium so sharply divided against itself) needs to be disentangled more than heard.

But there are good reasons for favoring a more inclusive approach in which all two thousand years of church history function as our most basic theological community, and Scripture alone stands above it as our authoritative norm. Indeed, the practice of the Reformers suggests that such an approach is not only more practically beneficial but actually more rigorously Protestant. As severe as the Reformers' criticisms of medieval Roman Catholicism could be, they always distinguished themselves from the Anabaptists, making clear that their intention was to reform, not re-create, the true church of God. To this end they not only regularly retrieved the theology of the early church, but in fact cast their entire reform effort in terms of its retrieval.

John Calvin, for instance, in his prefatory letter to King Francis in the *Institutes*, defended the Reformation cause against the charge of novelty by grounding the Protestant claim to antiquity in "the right of recovery" (*postliminii iure*)—a technical legal term referring to the recovery of lost property or privilege.[21] Rather than overthrowing tradition, Calvin compiled an extensive list of issues—ranging from eating meat during Lent to transubstantiation to ministerial celibacy—on which church fathers stood with the Reformers and against their Roman Catholic opponents.[22]

---

21. John Calvin, "Prefatory Address to King Francis," in *Inst.*, vol. 1, p. 16. As the editor notes, *postliminium* literally means "behind the threshold," i.e., safe, and refers to the recovery of property or privilege so as to be secured.

22. Calvin, "Prefatory Address to King Francis," 19–23.

Elsewhere, in his dispute with Cardinal Sadolet, Calvin again aligned the Protestant cause with that of the early church, claiming against his Roman Catholic opponents: "our agreement with antiquity is far greater than yours, but all that we have attempted has been to renew the ancient form of the church . . . [that existed] in the age of Chrysostom, and Basil, among the Greeks, and of Cyprian, Ambrose, and Augustine, among the Latins."[23] With the other magisterial Reformers, Calvin affirmed the ecumenical creeds and councils, stating that words like *ousia* and *hypostasis* were necessary to confront heresy. In the section on the Trinity in his draft of the French Confession, he wrote, "we receive what was determined by the ancient councils, and we hate all sects and heresies which were rejected by the holy doctors from the time of St. Hilary and Athanasius until St. Ambrose and Cyril."[24]

Martin Luther also affirmed the Apostles' Creed as well as the Chalcedonian and Nicene formulations, and defended the use of technical Trinitarian terminology employed by the church fathers (like *homoousios*) against Martin Bucer who protested that we must use strictly biblical language.[25] In his *On the Councils and the Church*, Luther argued that "the decrees of the genuine councils must remain in force permanently, just as they have always been in force." Luther insisted that *sola Scriptura* entailed the subordination of tradition and creed under Scripture, but not, as it often misconstrued today, any diminution of their proper role.[26] Thus, Luther declared, "we do not reject everything that is under the dominion of the Pope. For in that event we should also reject the Christian church. Much Christian good is to be found in the Papacy and from there it descended to us."[27] Later Lutherans followed in this view, placing the Apostles', Nicene, and Athanasian Creeds at the front of the *Book of Concord* (as Anglicans would with the *Thirty-Nine Articles*).[28] The *Augsburg Confession*, the primary

23. John Calvin, "Reply to Sadolet," as quoted in Robert Letham, *The Holy Trinity: In Scripture, History, Theology, and Worship* (Phillipsburg, NJ: P&R, 2004), 266.

24. As quoted in Letham, *The Holy Trinity*, 266.

25. At the same time, Luther drew a sharp distinction between the church fathers and the apostolic writings—perhaps not always altogether fairly. Jaroslav Pelikan, in *The Vindication of Tradition* (New Haven, CT: Yale University Press, 1984), 9–10, for instance, questions Luther's view that Tertullian was the first significant Christian writer after the apostles, which made it possible to distinguish between Scripture and tradition on *chronological* grounds.

26. Keith A. Mathison, *The Shape of Sola Scriptura* (Moscow, ID: Canon, 2001), 237–53, offers a critique of modern misunderstandings of *sola Scriptura* as out of alignment with the original intent of this doctrine in the context of the Reformation.

27. As quoted in Timothy George, *Theology of the Reformers* (Nashville: B&H, 1988), 81.

28. See the discussion in Carl L. Beckwith, "The Reformers and the Nicene Faith: An Assumed Catholicity," in *Evangelicals and Nicene Faith: Reclaiming the Apostolic Witness*, ed. Timothy George (Grand Rapids: Baker Academic, 2011), 65–70.

Lutheran confession and arguably the most important sixteenth-century Protestant confession, concludes by affirming the continuity of Lutheran doctrine with the true church: "nothing has been received among us, in doctrine or practice, that is contrary to scripture *or to the church catholic.*"[29]

Even from this brief survey, it is clear that there are some significant differences between the early Protestant views of church history represented by Calvin and Luther and those modern Protestant views represented by Warfield. Warfield saw the early church, most basically, as a fall to be recovered from. He could even claim that "to pass from the latest apostolic writings to the earliest compositions of uninspired Christian pens is to fall through such a giddy height that it is no wonder if we rise dazed and almost unable to determine our whereabouts."[30] Luther and Calvin, by contrast, saw the early church as a resource to be utilized, and spoke of the goal of the Reformation as its retrieval.

Granted, the Reformers were often cooler in their attitude toward medieval theology than patristic. Here we must neither downplay the Reformers' critiques of medieval Christianity nor fail to appreciate their nuance. If we wonder, for instance, exactly what Calvin means when in his prefatory letter to King Francis he refers to Protestant doctrine as "laid long unknown and buried,"[31] we get some clue later in the *Institutes* when he refers to the church of Gregory I's day (at the turn of the seventh century) as "well-nigh collapsed" since it "had deteriorated much from its ancient purity."[32] Later he appears to regard the agreement between Pepin the Short and Pope Zachary in 751 as marking a new era of papal temporal power.[33] That Calvin regarded the papacy as falling further into apostasy and corruption from that point is clear from his assertion that the institution was in his own day "a hundred times more corrupt than it was it was in the times of Gregory and Bernard, though even then it greatly displeased those holy men."[34] One might plausibly conclude that Calvin saw the church as progressively degenerating throughout the medieval era. At the same time, Calvin staunchly denied that this degeneration ever resulted in death. In the context of developing his doctrine of the invisible church, Calvin rejected the possibility that the church "has been lifeless for some time,"

---

29. Quoted in Beckwith, "The Reformers and the Nicene Faith," 67–68, italics added.
30. As quoted in Allen and Swain, *Reformed Catholicity*, 1–3.
31. Calvin, "Prefatory Address to King Francis," 16.
32. *Inst.* 4.4.3 (1071).
33. *Inst.* 4.7.17 (1136).
34. *Inst.* 4.7.22 (1141).

and affirmed from Matthew 28:20 that Christ preserves and defends the true church in every generation: "the church of Christ has lived and will live so long as Christ reigns at the right hand of the Father. It is sustained by his hand; defended by his protection; and is kept safe through his power."[35] It is therefore not surprising to find how much energy Calvin spends in the *Institutes* retrieving medieval theology. There is no major medieval theologian ignored, and he especially appreciates Gregory the Great, Peter Lombard, and Thomas Aquinas.

Luther also, for all his anti-Rome rhetoric, always affirmed the preservation of the true church amidst seasons of corruption. Writing in the 1530s, he declared:

> Today we still call the Church of Rome holy and all its sees holy, even
> though they have been undermined and their ministers are ungodly. . . .
> It is still the church. Although the city of Rome is worse than Sodom
> and Gomorrah, nevertheless there remains in it Baptism, the Sacrament,
> the voice and text of the Gospel, the Sacred Scriptures, the ministries,
> the name of Christ, and the name of God. . . . Therefore the Church of
> Rome is holy.[36]

Later Protestants would affirm and develop this doctrine of the preservation of the church, invoking the notion of a remnant ecclesiology. Francis Turretin, for example, in responding to the charge that the Reformed church did not exist before Luther and Zwingli, not only affirmed the true church's persistence in various separatist movements from Rome, both in the East and West—he then supplemented this claim by insisting that "our church was in the papacy itself, inasmuch as God always preserved in the midst of Babylon a remnant for himself according to the election of grace."[37] The best of the later Protestant tradition continued to retrieve both patristic and medieval theology. The Puritan theologian John Owen, for instance, drew heavily from the logic, technical language, and metaphysical tradition of medieval theology, particularly that of Thomas Aquinas.[38] Carl Trueman

---

35. Calvin, "Prefatory Address to King Francis," 24.

36. Quoted in Beckwith, "The Reformers and the Nicene Faith," 63–64.

37. Turretin, *Institutes of Elenctic Theology*, ed. James T. Denniston, trans. George Musgrave Giger (Phillipsburg, NJ: P&R, 1992), 18.10.15 (3:61). Calvin appealed to the notion of a remnant to make the same argument, drawing a comparison between the subsistence of the church amidst seasons of corruption and God's preservation of seven thousand among his people that had not bowed the knee to Baal in the time of Elijah in 1 Kgs 19:18 (Calvin, "Prefatory Address to King Francis," 25).

38. As observed by Carl R. Trueman, *John Owen: Reformed Catholic, Renaissance Man*, Great Theologians (Burlington, VT: Ashgate, 2007), 21, who notes that "the quest for historical precedent in Reformed Protestantism, so important to a church keen to allay any suspicions that it was

notes that Thomas influenced Owen on topics such as divine knowledge, divine providence, divine simplicity, election, and sin, and that from the earliest times in his career Owen drew upon Thomistic trajectories of thought (particularly as developed in the subsequent Dominican tradition) for polemical purposes in his arguments against Jesuits, Arminians, and Socinians.[39] While Owen certainly does not engage Thomas uncritically, he shows a penetrating grasp and respectful utilization of his theology.

On the whole, the attitude toward patristic and medieval theology modeled by the Reformers, and later Protestants like Owen, is far more careful and generous than that entailed by Warfield's metaphor of extracting leavened bread from the unleavened. The Reformers affirmed the preservation of the church in every generation; they drew widely from the wisdom of earlier generations; and they summed up their own goal as returning to the purity of the early church. The last thing in the world they intended was a wholesale rejection of the thirteen centuries separating John the apostle from John Wycliffe. As D. H. Williams put it, the mission of the Reformers was to point "not to themselves as the begetters of a new 'protestantism' but to the establishment of a proper catholicism—anti-Roman perhaps but not anti-catholic."[40]

But to say that Protestants can retrieve patristic and medieval theology is not yet to establish that they should. What makes such an endeavor, not merely permissible, but valuable?

HOW PATRISTIC AND MEDIEVAL THEOLOGY CAN RESOURCE CONTEMPORARY PROTESTANTS

It is difficult to quantify exactly what benefits retrieval can hold, and they may vary widely from one situation to the next. Nonetheless, we might draw attention to four ways that patristic and medieval theology is particularly well-positioned to interact with modern Protestant theology, without precluding other additional benefits as well. First, patristic and medieval theology can help bulk up contemporary Protestant theology in areas where it is historically weak or underdeveloped. A fitting metaphor for this benefit of retrieval might be a student attending a school, or a child

---

introducing novelties of any kind, was not restricted to a canon of authors who wrote before the sixth century, even though such early authors might in general be given slightly more weight than those writing after the great period of Trinitarian and Christological creedal formulation and the dramatic rise to papal power."

39. Trueman, *John Owen*, 23.
40. D. H. Williams, *Evangelicals and Tradition: The Formative Influence of the Early Church*, Evangelical *Ressourcement*, Ancient Sources for the Church's Future (Grand Rapids: Baker Academic, 2005), 120.

learning to talk by listening. This benefit of retrieval stems from the fact that each era of church history faces different theological controversies, and it is usually in the context of controversy that doctrinal precision tends to develop, often along with a shared technical vocabulary. Thus one need not regard church tradition as infallible or comprehensive to recognize that each generation of the church has a unique contribution to offer all the others.[41] In the case of our patristic and medieval forbearers, there are many doctrinal battles over which they agonized and even shed blood, doctrines that we rarely think about today.

One example would be the doctrine of angels. The medieval era represents perhaps the richest period of reflection on angelology in the history of the church. Whereas modern Protestants generally have little use for angels beyond an interest, particularly in certain charismatic circles, in angels' supernatural involvement in our lives, medieval theologians found great consequence in questions concerning the creation of angels, the nature of angels, the fall of angels, the role of angels in redemption, and the relation of angels to material creation. Many a page of Thomas Aquinas's *Summa Theologica* is spent establishing that angels inhabit this universe as part of God's creation along with material bodies, that they have a stewardship role over other material created bodies, that two angels cannot occupy the exact same place at the same time, that one angel cannot occupy two places at the same time, that the movement of an angel from one place in God's creation to another is not instantaneous but requires a duration of time, that angels are capable of assuming a physical body, and other views such as these.[42] These were not idle, "ivory tower" questions for him, as they are often cast today, but they were integrally related to deeper theological matters concerning the nature of God's creation and the relation of the spiritual and physical realms. Modern Protestants may develop more theologically satisfying ways of thinking about created realities like space and time and matter—particularly this side of Einstein—by cultivating curiosity for these questions that drove medieval angelology.

This educational benefit is in some ways the most basic of theological retrieval, but it should not for that reason be considered the most valuable one. Almost invariably, theological retrieval serves a more catalytic role of deepening our sensitivities to theological concerns that we do not already

---

41. For an eloquent expression of the benefit of reading from different historical eras, see C. S. Lewis, "On the Reading of Old Books," in St. Athanasius, *On the Incarnation*, ed. and trans. a religious of C.S.M.V., PPS 3 (Crestwood, NY: St. Vladimir's Seminary Press, 1977).

42. *ST* 1.50–64 (259–324).

feel, and cultivating theological values that we do not already possess. To construct a metaphor, visiting the Sistine Chapel does more than conceptually advance your knowledge of Michaelango's view of final judgment, just as visiting the Grand Canyon does more than provide you information about the history of the Colorado River. There are sensibilities and emotions that are shaped by the whole experience. So also patristic and medieval theology can bolster the theological values and inclinations we lack if we work narrowly within Reformation and modern theology alongside the Bible.

An example of this kind of retrieval can be found within the doctrine of God, and particularly those areas within theology proper that are intrinsic to the divine essence, such as divine simplicity and divine impassibility. Despite being fairly consistent throughout all of church history, East and West, these doctrines are increasingly ignored or rejected within modern Protestantism. More than that, modern theologians and philosophers tend to critique these doctrines for reasons that all too often did not even come into view in their premodern articulations. How do we account for this discrepancy? Retrieving the doctrine of God in its patristic and medieval context helps explain these differing instincts by calling attention to the deeper ontological differences at stake, and thereby helps sensitize us to the values that drove ancient formulations of these doctrines.

With respect to divine simplicity, the influence of Plotinus and (later) Pseudo-Dionysius can be detected in the church's habitual instinct to reason that if God is the cause of being then God must be logically prior to being.[43] Thus, in the West, Boethius called the divine essence "beyond being" and "super-substantial,"[44] and in the East, John of Damascus referred to God as "the super-essential-essence, the Godhead that is more than God, the beginning that is above beginning."[45] While early and medieval theologians rejected the equivocal relationship between Creator and creation that Muslim and Jewish philosophers would come to employ,[46] they equally resisted a univocal relationship in which God and the world are ultimately

---

43. Some of the material that follows is loosely related to Gavin Ortlund, "Divine Simplicity in Historical Perspective: Resourcing a Contemporary Discussion," *IJST* 16, no. 4 (2014): 436–53.

44. Boethius, *De Consolatione Philosophiae, Opuscula Theologica*, ed. Claudio Moreschini, Bibliotheca Teubneriana (Munich/Leipzig: K. G. Saur, 2000), 183–84: "Substance in (God) is not really substantial but beyond substance (*ultra substantiam*)" (my translation). This language is not unique to Boethius. Thomas Aquinas later in the Western tradition would also call God *ultra substantiam*.

45. John of Damascus, *On the Orthodox Faith*, in *Hilary of Poitiers, John of Damascus*, ed. Philip Schaff and Henry Wace, NPNF² 9 (1899; repr. Peabody: Hendrickson, 2012]), 1.12 (p. 14).

46. Maimonides, *The Guide for the Perplexed*, trans. Shlomo Pines (Chicago: University of Chicago Press, 1963), 130–31, for example, explicitly affirmed an equivocal view of the Creator–creation relation and argued that God has no relation to that which is non-God. He therefore claimed that the closest one can come to intellectually cognizing God is picturing whiteness (163).

on the same scale of being (as often assumed in some contemporary critiques of divine simplicity). Aquinas made it presuppositional in *Summa Theologica* that God and creation belong to different ontological frameworks, since God is the author of all being: "God is not related to creatures as though belonging to a different *genus*, but as transcending every *genus*, and as the principle of all *genera*."[47] One might summarize the consequence of the early church's preference of an analogical correlation of God and creation over a univocal one like this: where modern theology often regards God as subsisting within a larger structure of reality, classical theology regarded reality itself as subsisting within the being of God.

Because patristic and medieval theologians had a high view of God's transcendence over the world, they emphasized divine hiddenness and mysteriousness and, thus, were careful in applying the language and logic of created beings to God. Augustine, for instance, warns in *De Trinitate*, "whatever is said of a nature, unchangeable, invisible and having life absolutely and sufficient to itself, must not be measured after the custom of things visible, and changeable, and mortal, or not self-sufficient."[48] While they believed true knowledge of God could be obtained, and (contrary to Maimonides) that God does not have essential attributes, they placed enormous emphasis on divine incomprehensibility, almost as a controlling influence in their doctrine of God. Basil, for instance, warns his readers against applying "arithmetic" to the divine essence, calling God "the Unapproachable One" who is "beyond numbers," and commending the Hebrew practice of abstaining from mentioning God's name out of reverence for it.[49] Gregory of Nazianzus stipulated that in doing theology, "our starting-point must be the fact that God cannot be named," also commending the Hebrew practice of using special symbols to venerate the divine name.[50] So also Anselm, in his *Proslogion*, uses the motif of "inaccessible light" as his running image for God, continually begging God for cleansing and illumination until he finally arrives upon divine simplicity as the answer to the question, "what shall my heart understand you to be?"[51]

47. *ST* 1.4.3, ad. 2 (23).

48. Augustine, *On the Holy Trinity*, in *Augustine: On the Holy Trinity, Doctrinal Treatises, Moral Treatises*, ed. Philip Schaff, NPNF¹ 3 ([1887; repr. Peabody: Hendrickson 2012]), 87.

49. Basil the Great, *On the Holy Spirit*, trans. David Anderson (Crestwood, NY: St. Vladimir's Seminary Press, 1980), 18.44 (71).

50. Gregory of Nazianzus, *On God and Christ: The Five Theological Orations and Two Letters to Cleodinus*, PPS 23 (Crestwood, NY: St. Vladimir's Seminary Press, 2002), 107.

51. Anselm, *Proslogion*, in *Anselm: Basic Writings*, ed. Thomas Williams (Indianapolis: Hackett, 2007), 18 (p. 91).

Reading these accounts of divine simplicity pulls us into a larger context of concerns than are typically present in contemporary treatments of this doctrine. Even if we ultimately end up rejecting a doctrine like divine simplicity, engaging its treatment in patristic and medieval theology can deepen our appreciation of the values that have typically undergirded it and, by drawing attention to the deeper ontological issues involved in its formulation, help us understand why it has made sense to those who affirmed it.

A third example of how the retrieval of patristic and medieval theology can resource contemporary Protestant theology is reframing modern debates by providing a premodern perspective. Specifically, because it operates in a premodern context without a "liberal versus conservative" spectrum as such, pre-Reformation theology can help redirect us away from some of the limiting features that tend to characterize polarized contexts. If our previous metaphors have been going to school and going on a holiday, our metaphor for this kind of retrieval is going to see a counselor to get an outside perspective on your family history. Just as a counselor gives you a perspective on yourself that you might not otherwise have, so contact with the broader Christian tradition can be an illuming influence that exposes modern eccentricities in different directions: both a ninteenth century liberal and a twentieth century fundamentalist would find their theological method seriously challenged if they could travel back in a time machine to, say, the ninth century.

An example of this kind of retrieval would be Augustine of Hippo's doctrine of creation. It is often claimed that the twenty-four-hour-day view is the unbroken consensus of the church until nineteenth century and that "nonliteral" readings come up at that point simply as accommodations to modern evolutionary theory.[52] But Augustine reveals that there have always been those who interpreted Genesis 1 differently, for reasons having nothing to do with evidence for an older earth and older universe, but rather because of details in the text itself.

In his early allegorical work against the Manichees, Augustine treated the days of creation as predictions of the redemptive-historical future,[53] and

---

52. E.g., J. Ligon Duncan III and David W. Hall, "The 24-Hour View," in *The Genesis Debate: Three Views on the Days of Creation*, ed. David G. Hagopian (Mission Viejo, CA: Crux, 2001), 22.

53. *De Genesis Contra Manichaeos* 1.23.35–41, CSEL 91, 104–111. For quotations of Augustine's commentaries on Genesis, I have generally used Edmund Hill's translation in Saint Augustine, *On Genesis*, ed. John E. Rotelle, The Works of Saint Augustine 1.13 (Hyde Park, NY: New City, 2002); for the *Confessions*, those of R. S. Pine-Coffin in Saint Augustine, *Confessions* (New York: Penguin, 1961); for *The City of God*, those of Marcus Dods in Saint Augustine, *The City of God* (New York: Modern Library, 2000); but always in consultation with the critical edition of Augustine's Latin text

then as various stages of the Christian life.[54] His later "literal" reading of Genesis was not intended to exclude allegorical meaning in the text but to relate it to the historical past. Here Augustine maintains that while ordinary twenty-four-hour days may "represent" the original creation days in some respects, "we must be in no doubt that they are not at all like them, but very, very different."[55] Augustine held that the details of Genesis 1 are not intended to convey its timing or sequence at all, since God created all things simultaneously.[56] God's act of creation is depicted in terms of a human workweek, in Augustine's view, as a literary device for the sake of those who cannot understand the notion of simultaneous creation in order to lead them progressively to the understanding of the work of creation.[57] In other words, for Augustine, the portrayal of God's creative work in seven days is an accommodation to human finitude. Augustine held this view not because of abstract philosophical principles but because of various features in the text—particularly the nature of the light in the first three days before the creation of the luminaries on day four, the difficulty of God resting on the seventh day, and the timing of the creation of angels in relation to Genesis 1.[58]

Augustine does regard Genesis 1–3 as having genuine historical reference, distinguishing its genre from Song of Solomon and likening it rather to the book of Kings.[59] He affirms a historical Adam and an Eden that is a real geographical environment, leaving only the caveat that "if the bodily things mentioned here could not in any way at all be taken in a bodily sense that accorded with truth, what other course would we have but to understand them as spoken figuratively, rather than impiously to find fault with holy scripture?"[60] Augustine criticizes the stubborn insistence on

---

in CSEL (Vienna: Tempsk, 1894–1900), and in a few cases providing my own translation where a more literal rendering is helpful to draw out the relevant meaning. All citations of Augustine are as follows: volume and part, CSEL, page number (my translation).

54. *De Genesis Contra Manichaeos* 1.24.43, CSEL 91, 112–14.

55. *De Genesi ad litteram* 4.27.44, CCEL 28:1, 126.

56. E.g., *De Genesi ad litteram* 4.33.52, CCEL 28:1, 133; 5.6.19, CCEL 28:1, 159.

57. *De Genesi ad litteram* 4.33.52, CCEL 28:1, 133.

58. *De Civitate Dei* 11.7, 11.8, 11.9, respectively, CCEL 40:1, 521–25. Andrew J. Brown ("The Relevance of Augustine's View of Creation Re-evaluated" in *Perspectives on Science and Christian Faith* 57, no. 2 [2005]: 136) organizes Augustine's reasons for supposing that the creation week was not an ordinary week into three categories: First, *rationally*, he struggled to accept the notions of "day" and "night" in days 1–3. Second, *exegetically*, he gave priority to Sir 18:1 in the Old Latin version (which reads: "he who remains for eternity created all things at once"). Related to this, he wrestled with how Ps 32:9 and Gen 2:4ff. raise the problem of sequence and vegetation growing. Third, *theologically*, he felt that God did not need sequence of time, and that God's resting must be metaphorical.

59. *De Genesi ad litteram* 8.1.2, CCEL 28:1, 229. Cf. Greene-McCreight, *Ad Litteram*, 62.

60. *De Genesi ad litteram* 8.1.4, CCEL 28:1, 232.

taking textual details figuratively when it is possible to understand them historically.[61] At the same time, Augustine's use of the term "historical" is qualified by his emphasis on the fact that the act of creation is an utterly unique and unrepeatable event beyond our current knowledge, experience, and language.[62]

Augustine was not the first to approach the text in this way; earlier "nonliteral" readings can be found, for instance, in Clement of Alexandria, Origen, Didymus the Blind, and Athanasius.[63] But it was Augustine's view, particularly as qualified later by Gregory the Great, and propagated by both Isidore of Seville and Bede, that had the greatest influence in the subsequent Western church.[64] In fact, Augustine's view was so significant for the medieval discussion that Anselm in the eleventh century could refer to the doctrine of instantaneous creation as the "prevailing opinion" of his day.[65] Thus both Augustine and the tradition of interpretation that followed in his influence should caution us against supposing that twenty-four-hour interpretations are universal throughout premodern Christianity.

A fourth and final example of the benefit of patristic and medieval retrieval is that it opens avenues of agreement and synthesis between seemingly conflicting theological options. This method of retrieval is similar to the previous one. Likewise, it applies past doctrine specifically to current theological disagreements. But this benefit has a more aggressive purpose: here the counselor is not merely providing perspective but is actively seeking to reconcile two parties. A metaphor for this benefit might be that of a guide, showing the way out of a dead end or gridlock in which one appears otherwise hopelessly lost. An example of this kind of retrieval would be the attempt to bring about rapprochement between various competing models of the atonement in contemporary theology by exploring how they worked in harmony in patristic and medieval thought.

Contemporary discussion of the doctrine of the atonement is often organized around the rejection or defense of various species of "objective"

---

61. *De Genesi ad litteram* 8.1.1–4, CCEL 28:1, 229–232.

62. *De Genesi ad litteram* 8.1.3, CCEL 28:1, 230; cf. also *De Genesi ad litteram* 4.27.44, CCEL 28:1, 126.

63. See Andrew J. Brown, *The Days of Creation: A History of Christian Interpretation of Genesis 1:1–2:3*, History of Biblical Interpretation Series 4 (Dorset, UK: Deo, 2014), 26–31. Origen, in fact, advocated a "figurative" interpretation of not only Gen 1, but various details of the Gen 2 narrative as well, even claiming that such an interpretation was unavoidable to all thoughtful interpreters (see Origen, *On First Principles* 4.3.1, trans. G.W. Butterworth [New York: Harper & Row, 1966], 288–89).

64. Gregory synthesized Augustine's views with a broader notion of sequence, applying instantaneous creation to the initial creation of things in their substance but allowing sequence for the creation of their particular final forms. See Brown, *The Days of Creation*, 57–59, 62–64, 102.

65. Anselm, *Cur Deus Homo*, in *Anselm: Basic Writings*, 1.18 (270).

models of the atonement (especially those involving an affirmation of penal substitution). There is a particular turn in the literature toward an Irenaean/Athanasian *recapitulation* model of the atonement as an alternative to Anselmian *satisfaction* models, which are regarded as violent, juridical, and focused on the cross at the expense of Christ's life and resurrection.[66] But in reading Irenaeus and Athanasius themselves, one finds statements about Christ's crucifixion that sound very Anselmian; and in reading Anselm himself, one finds statements about Christ's birth that sounds very Eastern. Reading these theologians in their own context may help us conceptualize an atonement theology in a recapitulatory account of the incarnation and a satisfaction account of his death might be better taken to complement one another, rather than be set at odds with one another.

For example, while the emphasis of Irenaeus's *Adversus Haereses* is on Christ's entire recapitulatory life as spreading divine immortality to humanity and thus restoring human nature, within this schema Christ's death plays a critical role, as does the motif of substitution that corresponds to it. For instance, one piece of the larger Adam-Christ typology that runs throughout the book is Irenaeus's correlation of the Tree of the Knowledge of Good and Evil with Christ's cross. In this context he can makes statements like the following: "the Lord thus has redeemed us through His own blood, giving His soul for our souls, and His flesh for our flesh, and has also poured out the Spirit of the Father for the union and communion of God and man."[67] In his *On the Apostolic Teaching*, Irenaeus offers an extended engagement with Isaiah 53, emphasizing the necessity of Christ's scourges and physical tortures for his accomplishment of our salvation.[68] Reflecting specifically on Isaiah 53:8, Irenaeus affirms that Christ's death on the cross

---

66. Though much contemporary treatment of the atonement sets an Irenaean recapitulation and a traditional Protestant account of penal substitution at odds with one another, an exception is found in Hans Boersma, *Violence, Hospitality, and the Cross: Reappropriating the Atonement Tradition* (Grand Rapids: Baker Academic, 2006), who combines the Irenaean notion of recapitulation with the other traditional "models," including penal substitution (though he faults the "juridicizing, individualizing, and de-historicizing" tendencies that have often marred this doctrine).

67. *Adversus Haereses* 5.1.1 (527). English translation from A. Cleveland Cox in *The Apostolic Fathers, Justin Martyr, Irenaeus*, ed. Alexander Roberts and James Donaldson, ANF 1 (1885; repr. Peabody: Hendrickson, 2012), 315–567. I have engaged at points with the critical edition of William Wigan Harvey's Latin and Greek texts in *Sancti Irenaei, episcopi Lugdunensis, Libros quinque adversus haereses* (American Theological Library Association Historical Monographs Collection, Series 1; 1857); and I have also consulted with the translation of key passages provided in Robert M. Grant, *Irenaeus of Lyons*, The Early Church Fathers (New York: Routledge, 1997).

68. Irenaeus, *On the Apostolic Preaching* 2.3.68, 84. This work was discovered in the early twentieth century in Armenian translation. I use here the translation of John Beher in St. Irenaeus of Lyons, *On the Apostolic Preaching*, trans. John Behr, PPS 17 (Crestwood, NY: St. Vladimir's Seminary Press, 1997).

was vicarious for believers even though it signals the final condemnation of unbelievers: "the judgment has been taken from the believers in Him, and they are no longer under it."[69]

Athanasius also affirms Christ's substitutionary death as a harmonious part of the doctrine of recapitulation. For example, chapter 4 of *De Incarnatione* focuses more explicitly on Christ's death:

> But beyond all this, there was a debt owing which needs be paid; for, as I said before, all men were due to die. Here, then, is the second reason why the Word dwelt among us, namely that having proved His Godhead by His works, He might offer the sacrifice (θυσιαν) on behalf of all, surrendering his own temple to death in place of all, to settle man's account with death and free him from the primal transgression (αρχαιας παραβασεως).[70]

The substitutionary language used here with reference to Christ's death ("on behalf of all" and "in place of all") combined with the legal language and imagery used to interpret that act of substitution ("debt owing which needs be paid" and "to settle man's account") suggest something like a satisfaction account of atonement. Athanasius uses sacrificial and substitutionary language throughout *De Incarnatione* to refer to the act of Christ's crucifixion—he calls it an "offering" and "sacrifice" to the Father, as well as a "substitute" and an "exchange" and an "equivalent" (i.e., of the death of his "brethren"),[71] such that "in His death all might die."[72] Later, affirming from Galatians 3:13 that Christ had to "become a curse for us," he calls Christ's death our "ransom."[73] At the same time, when Athanasius speaks of Christ taking our punishment, his emphasis is on the penalty of *death*, and less on Christ bearing specifically the penalties of guilt and/or punishment.[74]

---

69. Irenaeus, *On the Apostolic Preaching* 2.3.69 (85).

70. Athanasius, *De Incarnatione* 4.20 (49); hereafter *DI*. Cf. Robert Pierce Casey, *The* De Incarnatione *of Athanasius: The Short Recension*, part 2 (Philadelphia: University of Pennsylvania Press, 1946), 30.

71. *DI* 2.9 (35).

72. *DI* 2.8 (34). The Greek text at this point is rich with terminology from the biblical sacrificial system, such as θυμα and ιερεον. Cf. Casey, *The* De Incarnatione *of Athanasius: The Short Recension*, 13.

73. *DI* 4.25 (55).

74. Steve Jeffrey, Michael Ovey, and Andrew Sach (*Pierced for Our Transgressions: Rediscovering the Glory of the Atonement* [Wheaton, IL: Crossway, 2007]) probably go too far from the evidence they marshal in concluding that "penal substitution is thus *central* to Athanasius's thought" (173, italics mine). Nonetheless, they are right to affirm its presence in his writings—in addition to their engagement with *De Incarnatione*, for instance, they cite his comment from John 3:17 in his *Against the Arians*: "Formerly the world, as guilty, was under the judgment from the Law; but now the Word has taken on Himself the judgment, and having suffered in the body for all, has bestowed salvation to all" (quoted on p. 169).

Furthermore, Anselm's *Cur Deus Homo* has a remarkably similar account of the recapitulatory role of Christ's incarnate birth as is found in Irenaeus's *Adversus Haereses*. Anselm declares that the union between divine and human forged at the incarnation fundamentally altered human nature: "There was [not] any degradation of God in his Incarnation; rather, we believe that human nature was exalted."[75] For Anselm, when Christ assumed a sinless human being from the sinful mass at the incarnation, "God restored human nature more wonderfully than he first established it."[76] Moreover, like Irenaeus, Anselm defines this restoration of human nature in terms of an Adam-Christ typology, such that Christ's obedient life brought about the immortality that was originally lost through Adam's disobedience: "it was fitting that just as death entered the human race through the disobedience of a human being, so too life should be restored by the obedience of a human being."[77] Thus, for Anselm, as for Irenaeus, the doctrine of atonement is drawn from the doctrine of creation. Anselm holds that the incarnation accomplished what would have happened if Adam and Eve had not sinned, namely, the completion and transformation of human nature into incorruptibility. And it is in *this* context that satisfaction themes are introduced in the middle and later sections of the book. He argues, for example, that a "perfect recompense for sin" was required, not satisfy some arbitrary legal demand, but rather in order that God "complete what he began in human nature."[78] Here and elsewhere, recompense for sin complements the larger theme of the restoration of human nature to the blessed immortality for which it was originally designed. Thus satisfaction serves recapitulation; forgiveness serves flourishing: "remission of sins is necessary for human beings if they are to attain happiness."[79] As the Eastern Orthodox theologian David Bentley Hart puts it, "In the end Anselm merely restates the oldest patristic model of atonement of all: recapitulation."[80]

Our survey of these theologians demonstrates the possibility of a doctrine of atonement that can hold an affirmation of Christ's life as recapitulating human nature together with an affirmation of Christ's death as satisfying divine honor or wrath. There is no obvious conceptual incompatibility

---

75. *Cur Deus Homo* 1.8 (253).
76. *Cur Deus Homo* 2.16 (309).
77. *Cur Deus Homo* 1.3 (248).
78. *Cur Deus Homo* 2.4 (291).
79. *Cur Deus Homo* 1.10 (261).
80. David Bentley Hard, *The Beauty of the Infinite: The Aesthetics of Christian Truth* (Grand Rapids: Eerdmans, 2003), 360–72, esp. 371.

between recapitulation and satisfaction. In fact, they may even be seen as mutually explanatory. As Hans Boersma notes, for example, recapitulation is a formal concept, while the traditional atonement models (including penal substitution) are material concepts—recapitulation tells the broader aim of Christ's atonement, but not how he actually brings it about.[81] Furthermore, both recapitulation and satisfaction can be logically integrated under the broader rubric of *substitution*: Christ both sums up our humanity, and bears our sins, via the mechanism of self-substitution.

THREE CASE STUDIES OF PATRISTIC AND MEDIEVAL RETRIEVAL

Finally, having provided some reflections on why Protestants should retrieve patristic and medieval theology and some of the benefits that may arise from such an endeavor, we conclude by identifying three early medieval texts/figures that may be particularly profitable for modern Protestants to retrieve. These three figures stand out not only because modern Protestants tend to neglect them, but also because they were hugely influential in previous generations of the church. In other words, modern Protestants are eccentric within the church catholic for *not* retrieving them.

The first example is Boethius's *The Consolation of Philosophy*. Written in the early sixth century while Boethius was in prison awaiting execution, *The Consolation* became arguably the single most translated and most influential text outside the Bible from the medieval into the modern era, so much so that in the twentieth century C. S. Lewis could declare, "until about two hundred years ago it would, I think, have been hard to find an educated man in any European country who did not love it."[82] And yet today Boethius is often regarded as an unoriginal thinker whose main contribution was to transmit Aristotle to the medieval era.[83] Moreover, when *The Consolation* is engaged, it is often seen as a strictly philosophical work with little theological content, since throughout the book Boethius dialogues

---

81. Boersma, *Violence, Hospitality, and the Cross*, 112.

82. C. S. Lewis, *The Discarded Image: An Introduction to Medieval and Renaissance Literature* (Cambridge: Cambridge University Press, 1964), 75. Boethius's work was translated by figures as diverse as King Alfred in the ninth century (into Old English), Geoffrey Chaucer in the fourteenth century (into Middle English), and Queen Elizabeth I in the sixteenth century (into Early Modern English). For further discussion of Boethius's influence, see Margaret Gibson, ed., *Boethius: His Life, Thought, and Influence* (Oxford: Basil Blackwell, 1981).

83. I document this view and offer some reasons to reject this view in Gavin Ortlund, "Explorations in a Theological Metaphor: Boethius, Calvin, and Torrance on the Creator/creation Distinction," *Mod. Theo.* 33, no. 2 (2017): 3–4. doi 10.1111.

with "Lady Philosophy," and there are relatively few explicit references to God.[84] But Boethius was in fact an innovative theologian in his own right, and for him, as for much patristic and medieval theology, philosophy functioned as a handmaiden to, not a replacement of, theology.[85] For modern Protestants Boethius may be a particularly helpful figure for sharpening their doctrine of God, particularly with respect to the Creator-creation distinction, divine simplicity, divine foreknowledge, and the relation of eternity and time. Boethius also affirms a doctrine of human happiness that may counterbalance the more austere outlook that often characterizes the Puritan strand of the Protestant tradition.[86] Furthermore, because of its profoundly formative role upon the medieval church, *The Consolation* may function for modern Protestants as a helpful introduction to that whole era. As Lewis put it, "To acquire a taste for [*The Consolation*] is almost to become naturalised in the Middle Ages."[87]

A second example is Gregory the Great's *The Book of Pastoral Rule*. An important pope at the turn of the seventh century, Gregory was a capable administrator whose reforms and initiatives marked the church for centuries. But Gregory regarded himself as primarily a religious leader, and his greatest influence was arguably upon the church's liturgy, monastic organization, and theology. Like Boethius, his influence was particularly felt by the medieval church, and he was respected by the Reformers as well.[88] Chris Armstrong claims no Western father was read more by the medieval church, suggesting that "if Augustine of Hippo was the father of

---

84. Lady Philosophy and God should not be pitted against one another in *The Consolation*, however—at several points in the book she explicitly acknowledges her limitations and directs Boethius to God (e.g., Boethius, *The Consolation of Philosophy*, trans. David Slavitt [Cambridge, MA: Harvard University Press, 2008], 4.6 [139]). Her presence indicates not the absence of God, but the presence of such a high view of God that he cannot be dialogued with directly, in the way Boethius wants to do.

85. On the innovative approach to theology modeled in Boethius's *Opuscula Sacra*, see John Marenbon, *Boethius*, Great Medieval Thinkers (Oxford: Oxford University Press, 2003), 4–6; John Marenbon, "Introduction: Reading Boethius Whole," in *The Cambridge Companion to Boethius*, ed. John Marenbon (Cambridge: Cambridge University Press, 2009), 1–2. On Boethius's subsequent theological influence, see Edmund Reiss, *Boethius*, Twayne's World Authors Series 672 (Boston, MA: Twayne, 1982), 160–61.

86. On this point, cf. Armstrong, *Medieval Wisdom for Modern Christians*, 168–9.

87. Lewis, *The Discarded Image*, 75.

88. Gregory is recognized as a saint by the Anglican church and many Lutheran churches, and as we have noted above, Calvin regarded him as a "holy man"—in the *Institutes* he notes with appreciation on several occasions Gregory's opposition to any bishop claiming "universal" jurisdiction. E.g., *Inst.* 4.7.22 (1141). It is frequently claimed that Calvin called Gregory the "last good Pope," but I have not been able to find any proper documentation of where this occurs—it is generally cited without page number from book 4 of the *Institutes*, ed. by F.L. Cross (New York: Oxford University Press, n.d.).

medieval theology, then Gregory was the father of medieval spirituality."[89] But Gregory was also a profound theologian who himself appropriated and extended much of Augustine's thought.[90] Moreover, in Gregory's capacity as papal representative to the Byzantine emperor, he lived in a Latin district of Constantinople for almost seven years, and thus his theology was uniquely shaped by, and interactive with, the theology of the Eastern church. As George Demacopoulos notes, after reading *The Book of Pastoral Rule*, the Byzantine emperor Maurice ordered that the book be translated and disseminated to every bishop in his empire.[91] Gregory is the only Latin father whose works were translated into Greek within his own lifetime.

The *Book of Pastoral Rule* argues that pastoral ministry requires a delicate balance of inner and outer qualities—theory and practice, contemplation and activity, a holy detachment from the affairs of the world and a practical skill at engaging those affairs. This dual focus reflected Gregory's own life, in which he had been drawn into various administrative and leadership roles despite his constant desire for the contemplative life. As a result, Gregory's *Rule* has a particularly practical thrust. Comparable works of pastoral theology in the Protestant tradition tend to focus on qualifications for pastoral ministry, and godliness in ministry (one thinks of Baxter's *The Reformed Pastor*, for instance, or Spurgeon's *Lectures to My Students*). While these are emphases of Gregory's also (parts 1 and 2 of his book, respectively), the greater portion of Gregory's text concerns practical matters—its treatment of how a pastor should teach different kinds of people differently in part 3, the lengthiest section of the book, is particularly full of wisdom, and Protestants may find this book supplementing the emphases of their typical literature on pastoral theology, particularly as it is generally neglected among modern Protestants.

A final example is John of Damascus's various writings on the iconoclast controversy. Living in the East in the eighth century, John follows and sums up early Eastern theology, especially that of the Cappadocian fathers, such that Andrew Louth calls him the "pre-eminent representative of the

89. Armstrong, *Medieval Wisdom for Modern Christians*, 146.

90. Gregory is sometimes seen as most basically a transmitter (like Boethius), but his utilization of Augustine's theology did not exclude his own innovations. For a brief overview of some areas in which Gregory left his own stamp on the Augustinian legacy that would shape medieval theology and spirituality, see Justo A. González, *The Story of Christianity*, vol. 1, *The Early Church to the Dawn of the Reformation* (San Francisco: HarperSanFrancisco, 1984), 246–48.

91. George E. Demacopoulos, "Introduction," in St. Gregory the Great, *The Book of Pastoral Rule*, PPS 34 (Crestwood, NY: St. Vladimir's Seminary, 2007), 10. As Demacopoulos notes, this rubs against the common notion that Gregory is fundamentally a transmitter of Augustine.

Byzantine theological tradition."[92] Yet John has frequently been isolated from the Western theological tradition. Apart from a few references in florilegia, he was basically unknown in the West until his *Exact Exposition of the Orthodox Faith* was translated into Latin in the twelfth century, which was then heavily utilized by Peter Lombard and Thomas Aquinas. Its subsequent influence was such that Peter Toon characterizes it as "important in the creation of Western medieval theology."[93] Nonetheless, John's broader writings on the iconoclast controversy, arguably his greatest theological legacy, remained largely unknown, and the later Protestant iconoclasm (particularly in the tradition following Calvin's vigorous denunciation of icons) have only further removed John from Protestant consciousness.

Retrieving John's theology thus brings modern Protestants into contact with a whole stream of Christendom that is all too often completely lost to us.[94] The sheer size and diversity of this slice of Christendom begs for retrieval, and John's writings on the iconoclast controversy are perhaps the most sensible entry point into it, since it was this dispute that dominated the Eastern church in the eighth and first half of the ninth centuries. John's defense of the use of icons against the charge of idolatry was grounded principally in the doctrine of the incarnation, emphasizing that Christ's flesh was not a mere garment but was truly united to incorruptible divinity even while it retained its fleshly status.[95] Moreover, John maintained that all human thought about the divine is inherently pictorial. As a result, rejecting the use of images did not simply threaten one particular devotional practice, but confused the whole task of theology.[96]

As a result of this controversy, the Eastern church was compelled to

---

92. Andrew Louth, *St. John Damascene: Tradition and Originality in Byzantine Theology* (Oxford: Oxford University Press, 2002), 16.

93. Peter Toon, "John of Damascus," in *The New International Dictionary of the Christian Church*, ed. J. D. Douglas (Grand Rapids: Zondervan, 1974), 542.

94. We tend to think of early Eastern Christianity as uniformly Greek, but in reality the ancient Eastern church consisted of a conglomeration of Greek, Syriac, Coptic, Ethiopic, Georgian, and Armenian churches, as well as an emerging Arab Christianity existing under the domination of Islam, and various Slavic churches starting in the ninth century. During the High Middle Ages, Constantinople, the seat of the Byzantine Empire, was the greatest city in Europe. Within her history lies more than a millennium of rich theological reflection, in addition to important political and ecclesiastical developments, such as missionary efforts to India and China. For a helpful introduction to Eastern Christianity during its development away from the Western church, see Andrew Louth, *Greek East and Latin West: The Church AD 681–1071*, The Church in History 3 (Crestwood, NY: St. Vladimir's Seminary Press, 2007).

95. E.g., John of Damascus, *Three Treatises on the Divine Images*, trans. Andrew Louth, PPS 24 (Crestwood, NY: St. Vladimir's Seminary Press, 2003), 22: "I venerate together with the King and God the purple robe of his body, not as a garment, nor as a fourth person (God forbid!), but as called to be and to have become unchangeably equal to God."

96. Cf. Louth, *Greek East and Latin West*, 51–54.

develop a rich theology of art and a high view of the material world, grounded in theological reflection about the nature of the incarnation. For evangelicals, who often have a very shallow view of the arts, and who tend to pit the spiritual and the physical against one another, John's writings may prompt deeper reflection on what our status as embodied creatures entails for the nature of theology.

Scripture Index

Scripture Index

SUBJECT INDEX

Abraham, 119
absolute, identifying the, 33
abstraction and Paul, 96, 98–105
Adam and Eve, 228
affections, 24
Anabaptist theology, 212
analytics, 31–32, 36
angels, doctrine of, 220
Anglican movements, 211
anthropocentrism, 155
anthropology, 27
antiquity, 216
Apostles' Creed, 216
apostolicity, 198
Arminians, 219
art, theology of, 233
asceticism, approach to, 200
ascetics, dogmatics as, 189–209
aseity, and simplicity, 179–80, 186–88
Athanasian, Creed, 216
atonement, the, 30, 35, 71, 145, 225
    models of, 226
Augsburg Confession, 216
Augustine, theology of, 213–16
authority
    biblical, 40, 136
    doctrinal, 76
    freedom from, 211
    scriptural, 200
baptism, 218
Barthian theology, 96–98
beauty of Christian teaching, 51
Bible, the, 50, 132, 134–37, 141–42.
        See also Scripture; Word
    interpretation of, 139

sources of, 77
translating, 109
biblical studies, 106
biblical theology, 52, 53, 68, 102
Book of Concord, 216
Caedmon, 212
"canon sense," 120, 126
catholic creeds, 201. *See also* creeds
catholic faith, 108
Catholic movements, 211. *See also*
    Roman Catholism
celibacy, 215
center, further from the, 155
Chalcedonian pattern, 185
Charlemagne, 212
Christ. *See* Jesus Christ; Son
Christian identity, 82–83
Christocentrism
    in Karl Barth, 145–50, 184
    and the Trinity, 144–62
Christology, 146, 158, 184–85, 208
    and the Trinity, 153–54, 159, 161,
    181–82
Christomonism, 149
church history, 217
church proclamation, 162–77
church, the, 42, 47, 50, 68, 76, 140,
    145, 146, 166, 171, 196, 199,
    212, 214, 218, 220, 229
classical theology, 184
code, 125
communion, 47
conduct, 125
confessions, 27, 50
conformity, 166, 169

239

AUTHOR INDEX

Author Index